ORGANIZATION ⟷ COMMUNICATION

EMERGING PERSPECTIVES III

Lee Thayer, Editor

Ablex Publishing Corporation
Norwood, New Jersey

Printed in the United States of America

Organization<—>communication.

   (People, communication, organization)
   Vol. 4 edited by Lee Thayer and George A. Barnett
   Includes bibliographies and indexes.
   1. Organization. 2. Communication in organizations.
I. Thayer, Lee II. Barnett, George A. III. Series.
HD31.0727 1986302.3'5   85-6159

ISBN 0-89391-274-3 (v. 1)
ISBN 0-89391-425-8 (v. 2)
ISBN 0-89391-995-0 (v. 4)

Ablex Publishing Corporation
355 Chestnut Street
Norwood, New Jersey 07648

Contents

**Part IV—The Internal Environment (Culture, Ecology)
and Some of Its Implications**

Publisher's Note

The Publisher would like to apologize to the editor and contributors for the delay in the production of this volume. Although the original manuscript was received some time ago, the present chapters are entirely updated and current.

The Contributors

Lorin Blewett is a Visiting Lecturer at the University of Illinois at Urbana-Champaign where she is completing a dissertation on the social identity and discursive practices of white anti-racists. Her research interests include conflict within organizations and conflict across social boundaries of race, class, and gender.

James L. Everett (Ph.D., University of Colorado) is Assistant Professor of Communication at the University of Hartford. His research focuses on integrating research and theory in organizational ecology. His most recent work extends the model of cultural ecology presented in this volume to an analysis of the evolution of culture in organizational populations.

Cameron M. Ford is Assistant Professor of Management at Rutgers, the State University of New Jersey. His primary research concerns the study of creativity in managerial decision making. Additional interests deal with organizational innovation and with the role of unconscious information processing and emotion in organizational settings.

Dennis A. Gioia is Associate Professor of Organizational Behavior in the College of Business at the Pennsylvania State University. His research and writing focus mainly on the nature of complex cognitive processes in organizations and the ways that such processes affect organizational sensemaking, communication, influence, and change. He is co-editor of *The Thinking Organization* (1986).

Geoffrey Gurd (M.A. in Media Studies, Concordia University; Ph.D. in Communication, Université de Montréal) is an organizational consultant and researcher in Ottowa, Canada. Prior to that, he taught in the Department of Communication at Duquesne University, Pittsburgh, PA, USA. Before entering the academia he worked primarily in the arts and in the health care field in three different Canadian Provinces as well as at the Canadian Workplace Automation Research Centre in Montreal. His research interests are presently focused on the relationship between organization theories and new information technologies, and employees' identity-work.

Peter M. Kellett (Ph.D., Southern Illinois University at Carbondale) is Assistant Professor of Communication at the University of North Carolina–Greensboro. His research interests include the interpretive study of organizational change processes, and the dialogic management of organizational change.

Iain L. Mangham is Professor of Management Development at the University of Bath, England. He is co-author of *Organizations as Theatre: A Social Psychology of Dramatic Appearances* (Blackwell, 1987) and has written several papers on the dramaturgical perspective on social and organizational life. He is currently studying aspects of rhetoric and character.

Elizabeth A. More (Ph.D., University of New South Wales) is Professor of Management and Deputy Director of the Graduate School of Management at Macquarie University (Australia). She is co-author of *Managing Corporate Communication; Managing Organisational Communication;* and Cooperative *Corporate Strategies in Australia's Telecommunications Sector—The Nature of Strategic Alliances;* and Associate Editor of the *Journal of the Australian and New Zealand Academy of Management..* She has published widely in the area of organization studies and communications technology and policy.

Pamela Shockley-Zalabak (Ph.D., University of Colorado), is Professor of Communication and Special Assistant to the Chancellor at the University of Colorado, Colorado Springs. Her research interests include organizational communication and culture and communication processes in team-based structures located in the U.S. and Europe. She also specializes in large-scale change efforts in Fortune 100 Companies.

Kenwyn K. Smith (Ph.D., Yale University) teaches organizational psychology at the University of Pennsylvania in the School of Social Work, and the Wharton Business School.

Frederick Steier (Ph.D., University of Pennsylvania) is Associate Professor of Engineering Management, and Director of the Center for Cybernetic Studies in Complex Systems, at Old Dominion University. The former President of the American Society for Cybernetics, his research interests include systemic and constructionist approaches to inquiry and change in organizations.

Randall K. Stutman is Associate Professor and Director of Applied Communication in the Department of Communication Science at Temple University in Philadelphia. His current research examines social influence and conflict processes in organizations. He is the author of two books on communication theory and maintains an active consulting practice in applied communication.

James R. Taylor is Professor of Communication at the University of Montreal. He is the author of two recent books: *Rethinking the Theory of Organizational Communication: How to Read an Organization* (Ablex, 1993) and *The Vulnerable Fortress*(University of Toronto Press, 1993). His research interests include the development of a discourse theory of organization and the implications of new technologies in organizational contexts.

Lee Thayer is a retired university professor and a very active consultant to CEOs worldwide at the leading edge of making high-performance or "great" organizations.

Introduction to the Series

The main engine of Western civilization, as we know it, is at once the most indispensable and the least celebrated. It is not money, nor technology, nor even number. It is not science as such, nor ideology as such, nor even "industrialization" or "development" as such. Yet no aspect of Western civilization, as we know it, would be possible without it.

It is *organization*. Or better, perhaps the *idea* of organization.

All human civilization, as we know it, hinges upon some sort of "arrangement" between two or more people as to what role each will play in the pursuit of the larger good. The idea of kinship as central to all human civilization—as argued by Lévi-Strauss—is one example. A love relationship is another. Every business and every institution and every voluntary human enterprise is another. As the popular American song has it, "You do the cookin' honey/I'll pay the rent." Feminists or modernists may argue against *this* sort of arrangement; but they simply want to organize things in some *other* way.

Manifestiations of a given society's *ideas* of and about organization are so ubiquitous as to go unnoticed. Every society believes its way of organizing itself is "natural" or "God-given" or at least "right." To the members of every culture, the arrangements that exist for carrying out human enterprises in *other* cultures—from the domestic to the spiritual—may seem odd, or even bizarre. The main pretext for war, at least as we know it, has been that those odd and alien arrangements for doing things in other cultures were seen as a threat.

Human existence, as we know it, and the life of any society, as we know it, would be impossible without *some* idea as to how every human enterprise that involves two or more people is to be *organized*. Every mind emerges in the way it is trained to organize its grasp and its "understanding" of the world. We cannot exist apart from *some* way of organizing ourselves and the world in which we live.

Yet we know precious little about where our ideas about organizing ourselves and our world come from. We know still less, it would seem, about the *efficacy* of one way of organizing ourselves and our world vs. another (witness the never-ending quest, in our age, for the "best" or the ultimate way of organizing or managing a business enterprise, or of organizing the relationship between male and female). And we know still less, perhaps, about the long-range (or even the short-range) human *consequences* of this way or that way of organizing ourselves and the world in which we live—economically, politically, spiritually. The Navajo said, "Let it be done in beauty." Western man says, "Let it be done rationally." The consequences, even for our physical environment, are radically different.

We know so little about such matters of such great consequence to us, it may be, because any attempt to understand how we organize ourselves and our worlds is at the same time an attempt to understand how we understand. Trying to understand such things as make us human may be, as Alan Watts once suggested, a little like trying to bite one's own teeth.

But the ultimate "frontier" is not space. It is the way we come to be human, and all of the human artifacts we create and utilize to endow us with whatever humanity we may realize in our sojourn on earth. Of these, none is more central to our lives than the ways we have come to organize ourselves—whether for an affair or a space mission. It is those taken-for-granted arrangements between and among people engaged in one or another human enterprise that enable our lives and the life of our society. To understand them is to understand ourselves better. And to understand ourselves better is the only ground upon which we can stand to make better the conditions of our lives, now and for generations following, for us and for all of the peoples of the world.

To speak of organization is to speak of communication. The two may be more than merely coterminous. They may perhaps be two aspects of the same thing.

For if what another says is to have any meaning at all, one must have *some* sense of the nature of the human enterprise in which one is engaged with the other. And one must have *some* sense of the role one plays in that enterprise as that role relates to the role of the other. To "understand" what is going on and to participate in it in some way, one must already have understood how it is organized—whether it is a game, a conversation, a trip across town, or a board meeting. It is *that* understanding, that sense one has of how things are organized and how one fits into them, that makes human communication possible. And conversely. Wherever and whenever there has been evidence of the one, there has been evidence of the other. Paradoxically, to the Western mind, each is the precondition of the other. Each is interdependent with the other.

And thus the sense of the title of this book series: PEOPLE, COMMU-NICATION, ORGANIZATION. Together, they comprise the enabling *system*, the inescapable *system*, which undergirds all human enterprise. As components of that system which undergirds *all* human enterprise, they are inextricably intertwined. To understand one is to understand the other. To be concerned about one necessarily invokes the other. Ulti-mately, we cannot understand people without taking into account how they communicate and the nature of the human organizations they get themselves into. We cannot understand human communication without taking into account the organized structures within which it occurs, and the nature of the people who assume or induce those social arrange-ments. And our understanding of human organization and of organiza-tional life is going to be no better than our understanding of how people make each other, and how they are made, in communication. For it is *in* communication that we energize and give sense to the structures and the conditions of everyday life, those of human existence and of organiza-tional life.

We *say* the structures and arrangements of our world into existence. And we have our lives, both within and without organizations, in the consequences of our saying-so. If there be defects or shortcomings, it is not to our enterprises and institutions to which we must look. If the arrangements by which we conduct the work and play of the world are not as we would have them, then we must look to the origin of those arrangements. We must look to the way in which we recreate them mo-ment to moment, day to day, in what we say of them and think of them. They come into existence and evolve as they do because we *mind* them as we do. It is only as we come to mind them differently that "they" change. If one's marriage is not all that one had hoped; if one's business enter-prise does not return all that it was expected to return; if the legal or other institutions of this society are not functioning as they "should"— then we must look to our ways of minding them—to *how* we understand them and speak of them.

Such social arrangements as bring us together in twos or eights or thousands are not born of necessity. They are born of human imagina-tion—of *how* we can and do speak of the world, and of how we take it into account.

PEOPLE, COMMUNICATION, ORGANIZATION, each enables and constrains the other. How? What are the consequences of enabling ourselves in one way rather than another? Of minding the world one way rather than another? Of organizing ourselves one way rather than another? Of creating and practicing our humanity *in* communication in one form of organization rather than another? Of creating and practicing our humanity *in* organizations that constrain our ways of saying and seeing the world in one way rather than another? Of believing that any one is independent of the other?

This, then, is the charter for this series of books: To address the way we organize ourselves and our enterprises and our institutions as a result of the way we communicate with one another. And to address the way we communicate with one another as a result of how we have organized ourselves and our enterprises and our institutions. And what the human consequences are, or may be.

In doing so, we will want to speak to the thoughtful "practitioner" as much as to the grounded "philosopher," to the practical as much as to the abstract, to the layman as much as to the expert. For there is nothing esoteric about the subject; no one's life falls outside of the intellectual concerns which will guide us here. In this arena of life, unless all gain in understanding, no one does. That is in the nature of what we join here to think about and explore.

Lee Thayer
Series Editor

Introduction to Volume III

More and more is being said and written, it would seem, about "organizational communication."

If academic products — ideas and "theories" and such — suffer the same fate as do other new products in our economy, then something like 8 out of every 10 new "ideas" will fail. A "failed" idea is presumably one that made no difference — one that had no "market," one that appeared but was ignored, one that had no longevity, no immortality.

Editors of academic journals and books may function a bit like Sherlock Holmes: trying to sort out of the myriad offerings those 2 out of 10 books or essays that might have some "success," and the one that Bingo! might be a "bestseller." Wasn't it Oscar Wilde who said, "There is only one thing worse than being talked about — and that's *not* being talked about"?

Scholars invest tremendous amounts of time and effort in research and development of their ideas or "findings." They want to be "talked about." Some will be — most won't.

So, with the mortality rate of most proprietary new academic ideas or "theories," one might ask: Why do they (we) persist? "Truths" have a market — or something that functions quite like a "market." New ideas, new concepts, new "truths" are brought to market relentlessly, and in great and expanding quantities. One competes with an ever-increasing number of alternative "truths": ideas, approaches, paradigms, terms, arguments.

So which one wins the kind of following that would guarantee some immortality — of being "talked about" beyond one's own circle of sycophants, devotees, and disciples? The one that "should"? And how would we know that?

In the marketplace of goods, junk foods may even outsell fruits and vegetables. If the average expenditure in the supermarket for vegetables is less than $2.00 a week, all those arguments about what we *should* be eating are not the ones that are winning. Can it be any less so in the marketplace of ideas? We may assume that the "right" idea or the "true" idea will win out somehow? Do we, however, have any evidence from history that this is the case? We know that the "wrong" idea is sometimes the one that takes root and drives the "right" idea out. Hitler's immortality comes to mind, but it happens in science, economics, religion, education, and child rearing as well. Our hegemonic "truths" — and that's what they are — seem to be as fashionable as anything else about we who claim to be "modern," for to be modern has seemed to mean, almost by definition if not by practice, that ideas and "truths" have to be marketed. The ones that win the largest market share are those that become hegemonic and, once hegemonic, resist the emergence of new ideas — of "new and improved" "truths."

The dilemma is as ubiquitous as it is profound. In a traditional or tribal society, the truths of the tribe transcended all of its members. In a modern (or perhaps even a postmodern) society, truths are voted on by all of its members. Our belief in democracy and democratization has perhaps made it seem obvious that truths are best sorted out in the marketplace, with no agency like a priesthood to stand in judgment of what is and what is not "true." That raises one side of the dilemma, which is, as Geoffrey Vickers put it, "But who is to control the controllers?"

The other side of the dilemma is just as sticky. Since there is at least no historical evidence to suggest that people in large numbers will do the "right" thing, we might ask, "But who is to judge the judgers?" Where did we get the notion that freedom of speech amounts to the same thing as the righteous path of the "true" and the "good"?

What makes the dilemma ubiquitous is that it is just as relevant to the running of an organization as it is to family life or the life of a society. Just because a person accedes to the presidency of a corporation does not make him or her thereby infallible. Almost as many businesses fail as are started each year, presumably because the person in charge believed something to be "true" that turned out not to be. As the 19th-century humorist Artemus Ward put it, "It ain't what we know that gets us into trouble. It's what we know that just ain't so!"

On the other hand, just giving everybody a vote doesn't guarantee a significant rise in the intelligence or even the prudence of the decisions made in an organization.

What makes the dilemma profound is that there is no way, in a civilization like our own, to escape it. What several of the authors address in this volume, either directly or indirectly, is just this point: Who is to have the prerogative of telling whom *what* in our organizations? What is intriguing is that the question is just as pertinent to the system in which the authors create and peddle their products as it is in the organizations they wish to study and understand.

Our claim to be in search of "the truth" notwithstanding, every scholar is a bit like an entrepreneur, and every new idea or perspective on the world that interests us is a bit like a fledgling enterprise. Each challenges our cherished and comfortable truths. Perhaps we cannot therefore fully welcome their challenges to our now-privileged positions in the scheme of things. But we have some obligation — given the irresolvable dilemma characterized above —

to give them a sympathetic hearing. We may disagree, but we do so only from positions of power. As scholars, we are either peddling our own perspectives on the same old things, or else we are looking for a perspective to commit ourselves to. We would encounter stalemates in the marketplace of ideas, as we would be in the marketplace of goods, without the apparently irresistible urge that certain of us have to strike out in new directions, to champion a different way of looking at things, to challenge the status quo. Our economy would fail without entrepreneurs—so would the intellectual marketplace.

We can't know in advance which ones are going to succeed, so we can't afford to judge them from our own perspectives. After all, people who subject themselves to the probability of failure must believe they are on the right track. What we have here is somewhat like a trade show: Here are some new ideas, or some new twists on some old ideas; here are some assessments of the continued market potential for some old ideas; here is some new wine in old bottles, some old wine in new bottles, and, if we're really lucky, here is some new wine in some new bottles. And why should we consider what is here? There is one provocative reason, and that is that every vintage wine was once new. In the making of ideas that hold us in their thrall, as in the making of preferred wines, that is a step that cannot be skipped.

The authors in this volume raise an unusual number of questions from an unusual range of platforms about the premises and the predilections of the field.

Being brought up *in* the field, for example, may make one immune to certain ways of questioning it. The Australian scholar Elizabeth More who, like most of her Australian colleagues, came into "communication" from other disciplinary backgrounds, gives voice to a kind of uncertainty about her own identity in the field, which she characterizes as coming from certain rifts and disparities in the field itself. The kinds of questions that seem obvious to her may be unthinkable to those who grew up in the field. Should we be asking them, or can we, as she asks, afford not to?

Debates about "method" most often obscure underlying differences in conceptual/theoretical/ideological bias. James Taylor very deftly uncovers both levels in his retrospective on the "ethnographic" vs. "critical" debate. In doing so, he gives us insights into the kinds of "meta-" biases required to sustain either view, or perhaps to accept both as useful.

In my own essay, I've tried to raise a number of new–old matters of stance. Is the study of "communication" a "scientific" or an "operational" discipline? The difference lies in the assumption that if we could successfully learn everything we need to know "scientifically" about a Michelangelo, we would

thereby have a recipe for making either another Michelangelo or a Giaco-
metti.

"Empirical" originally meant being guided by practical experience and not
theory. By this definition, it is the members of organizations who are
"empirical" and those who do research on organizations who are not. We,
however, have perverted the term. In any event, what we are left with is the
question of whether or not people who are guided by "theory" can ever
understand people who are not guided by theory but by practical experience.
This is, in part, perhaps, what Frederick Steier and Kenwyn Smith are getting
at in their essay: Can we use a theoretical mode to catch and comprehend
people who are not in a theoretical mode?

Whether something makes sense or not, one characteristic of people who
want or need to be "organized" is that sense will be made of it. People who are
exposed to tables of random numbers can indeed "find" a pattern in them.
There are two essays on "sense making" in organizations included in Part II.
One is by Dennis Gioia and Cameron Ford, who explore the role of "tacit"
knowledge and of autocommunication in the process, which seems key to
much else. Peter Kellett comes at the same question from a combined
semiotic/phenomenological approach (and, in the process, perhaps raises the
additional question of the combinability of those two orientations).

We must address "culture," once again. It would be remiss, perhaps, not to
ask once again what culture has to do with the performance of organizations.
This is the question Pamela Shockley-Zalabak takes up, first reviewing
arguments pro and con, and then making some provocative observations of
her own. And James Everett undertakes to assay some of the implications of
the position that organizational cultures are forever evolving, never static,
and what bearing this may have on the context within which all communication takes place in organizations.

There are at least two ways of getting at the "drama-turgical" aspects of life
in organizations. One is from "below," from the perspective of language. Lori
Blewett and Randall Stutman consider "conventional" and "novel" metaphors
as a way of examining conflict in organizations—itself a topic of much
concern these days. The second is from "above," from the perspective of the
"scripts" that people get involved in and improvise on as they pursue their lives
in organizations. I. Mangham gives us a taste of what can be done with this
approach in his essay on "drama" in organizational life.

In all, it is as contemporary and as rich a set of veins as you could hope for.
We've made no attempt here to be exhaustive; there are other approaches, and
there are other versions of the ones that are represented here. If they seem
especially useful to the conceptual/intellectual enterprises that join us as
sometimes compatible, sometimes strange, bedfellows in our common interest
in the study of organizations and communication, we hope they will appear in
future volumes.

Julia Kristeva once made the following observation about "semiotics":

> Semiotics cannot develop except as a critique of semiotics. . . Research in
> semiotics remains an investigation which discovers nothing in the end but its
> own ideological moves, so as to take cognizance of them, to deny them, and to
> start out anew.[1]

In this, she puts herself squarely in the scientific—as opposed to the
scientistic—camp. If we substitute the word "communication" for the word
"semiotics" in her statement, we would see what we need to do. We could do
worse.

It is, in any event, the aim of this series to "take cognizance" of our
"ideological moves," and to ask not, "Is this an accurate description of what is
being described?" but rather, "Is this going to get us where we ought to be
going?"

---

[1]As quoted in my 1982 paper, "Human Nature: Of Communication, of Structuralism, of
Semiotics," *Semiotica, 41*(1/4), 25.

PART I

Some Questions about How the Field is Getting to Where It is Going

Organizational Communication: Continuing Dialogues of the Deaf?

Elizabeth More

The understanding of organization is inseparable from the organization of understanding. (Jeffcutt, 1994, p. 241)

Understanding is achieved when, for a moment, there are no more questions to ask. Understanding is the dead spot in our struggle for meaning: it is the momentary pause, the stillness before incomprehension continues; it is the brief relief from the doubt that is the norm. Thus understanding is a temporary state of closure. When we understand something we are effectively saying there is no more to ask, no more to question, all is revealed. But of course 'all' is never revealed and the sensation of certainty always passes. . . . Truth is not to be found in things or ideas but in the process of apprehending them. (Sless, 1986, p. 130)

The aftermath of positivism can produce a paralysing nihilism. Understanding, instead of causal explanation, may seem to be the new goal of science, but mere understanding is of questionable value. (Trigg, 1985, p. 84)

INTRODUCTION

The traditional primary epistemic approach to organizational communication — positivism — has been clearly interrogated in the recent history of the field. Putting it simply, it seems that organizational communication has for some time been focused on pragmatic empirical results — on explanation before understanding. Today that emphasis has been challenged in a newer approach to the field that stresses understanding first and foremost and one which, to some researchers and theoreticians at least, offers no right answers or solutions to be discovered. As Tompkins (1987) puts it: "It is no longer meaningful to speak of the truth or of science as the mirror of nature. Instead, we engage in conversation, in dialogue, and attempt to persuade each other of our claims" (p. 93). For him, whatever the case, compulsion is the only alternative to rhetoric, persuasion, and communication. The traditional division between the goals of explanation and understanding are clearly outlined by Smircich and Calas (1987):

> Traditionally, explanation and understanding are framed as opposite ways of knowing and pursuing inquiry. Explanation, as evident in positivist science, follows the model of the natural or physical world in which hypothesis testing, experimentation, verification or falsification, and generalizations are expected. Understanding, in contrast, relies on interpretations of subjective meanings; thus generalizations are not required or expected. Explanation takes the view of the world from the outside, while understanding takes the view of the world from the inside (Evered & Louis, 1981) [citation in original]. The two goals place objective and subjective, the physical world and the social world, in opposition. The ongoing debate between positivism and interpretivism highlights these oppositions. (p. 232)

In taking up issues already tussled over for some time in other fields of the social sciences, what has consequently emerged more recently in the field of organizational communication is a keen interest in the problem of knowledge and of epistemology and its social construction. It is as if, with some reference to developments in communication's sister disciplines, but often without reference to concerns closer by in other arenas of the communication discipline, some of the key scholars and researchers in organizational communication have come to agree that:

> Once we recognize that the practice of social science cannot be detached from philosophical assumptions about people's nature and their role in society, we should not despise it for this. Far from being an inadequate copy of "proper" science, it is wrestling with some of the most important questions facing mankind. Empirical social science must start from a properly articulated philosophical base if it is to be successful. The philosophy of the social sciences cannot be an optional activity for those reluctant to get on with the "real" empirical work. It is the indispensable starting-point for all social science. (Trigg, 1985, p. 205)

This seems in accord with the charter that Thayer (1986) has outlined for this series. The articulation and questioning of the philosophical base, of our theoretical assumptions and groundings, of our goals, is surely at the heart of our communication with one another in organizational communication at the micro level, and in communication science and social sciences in general at the macro level. This is a key determinant in the organization of ourselves, our communication enterprises, and our institutions. The reverse, as Thayer (1986) suggests, is also significant; the organization of ourselves, our enterprises, and our institutions being determinants of the way we communicate. This is rather like a sophisticated "egg and chicken" problem. The consideration of human consequences arising from this is vital but often apparently too difficult to grasp or even comprehend. This is in spite of the fact that the need to reflect seriously on such issues was already foreshadowed in a much earlier article by Redding (1979) in which he stressed the requirement for organizational communication scholars to critically analyze their own frames of reference.

If we are still asking questions about how the field is getting to where it is going, unfortunately the larger part of the question—what it is and where it is going—remains dazzlingly blurred!

In 1987 Greenbaum et al., pointing out that the area of organizational communication was the fastest growing of all areas in communication studies, maintained the youthfulness of the organizational communication discipline, outlining the key traits that characterised it as at an early stage of development:

- a precise definition of a domain is absent and core curricula are divergent, although we do have a general direction to the discipline;
- as a boundary spanning discipline many scholars cross the fields of both communication and organizatinal studies;
- the breadth and diversity of the field relates to the sources from which it draws—anthropology, psychology, information sciences, sociology and the like.
- specialisation in limited research facets of organizational communication does not encourage information sharing, cross fertilisation or integration of research amongst scholars;
- the instrumentation for conducting organizational communication research is underdeveloped.

Have we come any closer to a separate identity for the field today?

Even earlier, as part of a now classic volume, Roberts, O'Reilly, Bretton, and Porter (1977) bluntly made the statement that "organizational communication appears to be mired in an identity crisis," (p. 95) emphasizing particularly the communication failure that seemed to exist between organizational theory and organizational communication. I am not sure that the conclusions and suggestions made therein have been largely taken up, that the identity crisis has been resolved, nor that communication between organizational theory at large and organizational communication has improved greatly. Nor has the advice given by Redding (1979) been taken until very recently in the field and still by seemingly small numbers of researchers, scholars, and consultants.

Certainly it still seems to me that the field retains its identity crisis. This is supported by comments from Tompkins & Redding (1988), two leading scholars in the field. Distinctions and similarities in research and teaching among organizational behavior, organizational communication, business communication, managerial communication, communication management, employee and corporate communication, have largely still not been clarified (Leipzig & More, 1982; Irwin and More, 1994). This is especially evident in textbooks in these areas. Nor has the relationship of organizational communication to interpersonal, small group, and mass communication been often considered, in spite of the developments in new communications technologies that would seem to make such attention imperative. Indeed the still contentious issue of the centrality of communication to organizational life is now rarely debated.

Moreover, the identity crisis, if we admit it still exists, is itself paradoxical. On the one hand some would argue that it appears to have been partially alleviated by developments in new communications technology. On the other, it might well be argued that the crisis is renewed afresh by the almost wholesale adoption of philosophical and methodological approaches from outside the field, including much of the current work on such technology.

Not only may the field be grappling with an ongoing identity crisis, but as a social scientist (communicologist?), one initially trained in the humanities, I also constantly face the question of who I am. My own development and focus on the field has emerged from professional work and academic study in a variety of disciplines and fields — predominantly those of music, ballet, drama, history and philosophy of science, and thence into communication and management.

Previously I had naively imagined that I was on an intellectual journey, traveling sequentially in a straight knowledge and experience line — now I know differently. Nonverbal communication, the dramatistic approach, role theory and the presentation of self in communication, Kant-rediscovered and constructivist theory, information theory, communication management, decision theory, linguistics, textual analysis, media institutions, structuration, structuralists, poststructuralists, and so on all seem to be interdependent aspects of communication studies as well as numerous other arenas. Furthermore, a background in the humanities, once looked upon as being rather lowly by some, instead now provides a vital and useful way to pursue current trends in communication theory and research, including that of organizational theory and organizational communication.

This is perhaps nowhere more evident than in the work of Mangham (1986) and Mangham and Overington (1987), in which the central theme is an allegiance to the theatrical metaphor or model as a perspective on organizational life. Such a model, when applied to organizational life, is perceived by these social psychologists basically as a mechanism through which the constructed nature of action may be uncovered and demystified.

So indeed it seems that the humanities now also provide the analogies for theorizing about organizational culture (Winkler, 1985).

Having taken this particular route, and having watched the growing similarities occurring between the areas of organizational communication and mass communication, it seemed important to assess in terms of Thayer's (1986) brief what each could offer the other by way of experience, with an emphasis on which mass communication lessons might enlighten current developments in organizational communication. Cultural studies seem to be a central issue in both and, as in may social sciences, the problem of interpretation is considered by many now to be of central importance.

Looking at debates and paradigm dialogues in the field by comparing recent developments in organizational communication with more long-standing developments in mass communication seemed more reasonable than viewing them from vantage points outside the communication discipline itself. Nevertheless, it is worth remembering that it is, rather, from the outside that many might perceive current debates as having originated.

This chapter therefore takes Thayer's series charter as its basis, focusing on the academic enterprise and academic communication as key features to be explored in the field of organizational communication. It raises concerns primarily:

- about communication within the field of organizational communication
- about any uniqueness in the field and any contributions it has to make to others
- about communication between the field of organizational communication and some other fields within the communication discipline as a whole, particularly that of mass communication
- about the apparent directions that the field is now taking and might take in the future.

COMMUNICATION IN ORGANIZATIONAL COMMUNICATION

Paradigm Shifts

Paradigms and paradigm shifts. It seems that human sciences are today marked by their epistemological turbulence, by dissension. Much of that turbulence is characterized by the significant inputs from communication theory, linguistics, sociology, philosophy, anthropology, and so on to more traditional approaches to organization studies based in psychological orientations.

In the early, more positivist, days of organizational communication, the general approach was the championing of scientific methods (defining the essence of human rationality) to capture the reality of communication in the organizational context. The key assumption here was that social facts are objective reality — things.

Recent times in organization studies have seen an emphasis on language and the creation of meaning — social construction of reality and the coproduction of meaning — in a move away from open systems and contingency theories. Communication becomes central here in the creation and recreation of meaning as the social fabric of organization. The impact on the field of organizational communication is evident in a move from discovering laws about organizational reality to investigating the diverse ways in which individuals construct social reality and to the understanding of meaning in this context. Now organizational processes and structures, like television, can be indeterminate texts to be read. The emergence of the interpretive approach has thus grown to challenge that of the more traditional functionalist one. In addition, the critical approach, long established in European mass communication research, is now making its presence felt in the current literature of the field (Mumby, 1993).

Consequently, we can ask:

1. Is there a new paradigm in organizational communication?
2. Is there a paradigm shift?

If we agree with Kuhn's (1970) view of the process that the emergence of a new paradigm follows as

> a reconstruction of the field from new fundamentals, a reconstruction that changes some of the field's most elementary theoretical generalizations as well as many of its paradigm methods and applications. . . . When the transition is complete, the profession will have changed its view of the field, its methods, and its goals. (pp. 84–85)

then the answers seem to be:

1. No, in the sense that what has occurred is rather an adoption of paradigms evident elsewhere in the social sciences and humanities. Yes, in the sense that we have, if not a fully fledged paradigm, at least some new approaches within the field.

2. No, rather more the development of alternate paradigms. This can be compared with the field of mass communication where the differing paradigms rarely communicate.

Much of the literature labels major differences in terms of empirical and interpretive paradigms. However, others see the need to make further distinctions and label differences as functionalist, interpretive, and critical; as modernist, nauralistic, and critical Tompkins & Redding, 1988); or, pluralism, interpretivism, and criticism (Hawes, Pacanowksy, & Faules, 1988). In mass communication, empirical and critical approaches dominate, with the interpretive sometimes considered aligned with the critical or coming in a close third, now often in the domain of cultural studies. However, in the organizational communication field, empirical and interpretive approaches dominate, with the critical being a very minor newcomer as yet. Consequently, I propose in what follows to focus on the empirical and interpretive approaches rather than on the critical perspective. Perhaps we are then more in another preparadigm phase with different schools competing, the work of each guided by something akin to a new paradigm or a view of nature.

Where does this leave the identity of the field? Weick (1987) suggests that the theoretical base of organizational communication will only be improved by using organizational theory. Yet Tompkins (1987) emphasizes the greater degree of appropriation and translation of influential ideas in communication from other disciplines than in its contributions, suggesting that:

> It is important that our concept of communication is capable of transforming an eclectic approach developed under the rubric of social psychology into something of its own. Organizational communication gives indication of an imperial, if not imperious, attitude . . . the complex network of intertextuality we call organizational studies. (p. 76)

Is organizational communication indeed capable of contributing to its sister disciplines, or must we continue to be derivative and eclectic especially without learning from the experiences of other arenas? Will adoption of changes in other arenas lead to new theory and method, revealing how to see what we failed to see previously? What will occur as a result of an inversion of the empiricist approach in organizational communication with observations determining theory to one where methodology as theory of meaning determines observations? Do they actually change our conceptions of organizational reality and, more complexly, is the organizational reality itself actually changed? Surely these are some of the pressing questions needing closer attention at the forefront of our field now. It is fitting that in one major publication in the field (Goldhaber & Barnett, 1988), questions are at least posed concerning intellectual growth and scholarly commitment, about new theoretical ground being broken in defining the discipline, and about whether or not organizational communication scholars have furnished academic leadership offering research directions and challenges to colleagues.

Some of the same debates are already occurring in the broader field of organization studies, most still centering at large on the disputation between the empirical and critical traditions. This is particularly evident in the early input to the field provided by public administration studies (e.g., Harmon & Mayer, 1986).

In organizational communication, even in descriptive accounts, often a somewhat pejorative attitude seems to emerge towards changes in the field (Goldhaber & Barnett, 1988): "While the functionalist relies upon an empirical tradition and orientation, a perspective which relies more upon an anecdotalist's mode of thinking is growing in popularity among some organizational communication scholars and researchers" (p. 2). Others are openly defiant, claiming that the accumulation of world experience is more interesting than a theoretical interest in increasing disciplinary knowledge (Hawes, Pacanowsky, & Faules, 1988). In different ways, the very boundaries of disciplinary scholarship are called in to question.

Overall, however, in our field it seems that the concept of *better* views has given way to that of *different* views. This is a most serious matter, one for immediate and perhaps ongoing philosophical debate. Essentially it raises an evaluative dilemma. Can such views

> be measured against anything external to themselves, and therefore at least in principle be judged correct or mistaken, true or false? The alternative is that we are left with a succession of different theories, or conceptions of the world, with no means of determining which is better than the others. (Trigg, 1985, p. 13)

This dilemma is particularly conspicuous in the ongoing interest with the area of culture studies in organizational communication.

Culture research as a focus. Over the recent history of management and organizational studies in general there have been numerous and varied theories, paradigms, and approaches adopted. The diversity in the field, as Morgan (1986) asserts, is due to the differences in organizational images and metaphors that underlie ways of thinking about organizations; for example, those of organizations as machines, brains, political systems, instruments of domination, and as cultures.

The view of organizations as cultures is still a relatively new one in the literature and it has received considerable attention in recent time from a bevy of writers, both popular and scholarly, focusing largely on the arena of corporate culture. Such literature aims to provide another way of understanding the management and design of organizations, another way of helping organizational personnel to cope in the increasingly turbulent environment of our times. It differs markedly from much of the earlier works focused on the idea of organizations as functional machines, as systems or organisms akin to the human body — with input, throughput, and output. By contrast, the organizational culture literature emphasizes the idea of organizations as socially constructed realities sustained by ideas, beliefs, values, norms, rituals, myths, ceremonies, stories, and the like that are part of the creation and recreation of meaning that regulates organizational life. Such phenomena are symbolic expressions, the essential characteristics of an organization culture.

Indeed, as Bolman and Deal (1991) assert, culture lies within the symbolic frame, contrasting with more traditional management perspectives—the structural, human resource, or political. Understanding organizational life here is centered on understanding the processes of creating and recreating reality—shared meanings, understandings, and sense making. It is the shared interpretive schemas that inform action that provides the cornerstone for this view of organization. It empowers organizational members to take greater responsibility for their "world" through recognizing their contribution in constructing their realities (Morgan, 1986).

Sypher, Applegate, and Sypher (1985) provide a useful outline of numerous definitions and approaches within the rubric of cultural studies—both within interpretive and functionalist/management oriented arenas. Important points emphasized are:

- the need to expose inconsistent philosophical and theoretical positions forming the basis of current organizational culture research
- the significant differences occurring within the interpretive paradigm itself
- the way in which the new antideterministic approach of interpretive cultural concerns in organizational communication has communication not as a mere manipulable variable (as is the case with a positivist management approach), but as the focal process in organizational culture, here regarded as the basis of reality construction.

In organizational behavior, mass communication, and, more recently, organizational communication, there has been an increasing use of interpretive/critical approaches. This is well reflected, for example, in the early agenda setting work edited by Putnam and Pacanowsky (1983) and that of McPhee and Tompkins (1985), as well as in the first volume of this series (Thayer, 1986). Rather than being a shift to a new paradigm, however, as mentioned earlier, these perspectives stand side by side with the still dominant paradigm as is the case with organizational studies at large and in mass communication where, however, alternatives have had a longer period to establish their credibility.

Nevertheless, much of organizational communication has reached an ethnographic moment, focusing on the meanings generated through communication processes and texts generated by organizational members who are

actively centered in a field of inter-textual and interdiscursive relations
(Tulloch, 1990). The move is from a psychological emphasis on the individual
to a sociological one that insists on individual activity being meaningful only
as situated within the context of the institutional framework. It is further
argued that we need to move social observation out of the confines of
discourse: the ways of doing things or not doing them and "doing otherwise"
are important.

There has been criticism of the general traditional emphasis on a functionalist and managerial-centered perspective and one result has been a
refocus on other levels in the organization. Yet if we accept the newer
approach, it seems also imperative to conduct empirical research into the
reflexive constructions managers place on their own communication behavior
just as much as it is to explore those of other employees (as is done by
Mangham, 1986). Certainly from an interpretive perspective the ideological
grounds for not doing so would seem rather strained, especially given the view
that, finally, the concern is with 'producers' and 'readers' making innovative
'works' out of the received 'texts' of their lives (Tulloch, 1990).

Yet, whatever the focus:

> Over the past decade research aimed at understanding human behavior in
> organizational contexts has evidenced a move from more traditional theoretical
> frameworks (e.g., behaviorism, structural–functionalism, general systems the-
> ory) to the adoption of a wide variety of "interpretive" approaches. This
> theoretical shift has resulted in increasing numbers of organizational studies
> employing ethnographic, ethnomethodological, dramaturgical, symbolic inter-
> actionist, phenomenological, and hermeneutic perspectives. Much of this
> interpretive research has been grouped under the general rubric of "cultural"
> approaches to organizations. (Sypher, Applegate, & Sypher, 1985, p. 13)

The argument for the emphasis on culture seems accurate. What this actually
means, however, is now becoming more complex because of philosophical,
ideological, and methodological issues and a range of diverse perspectives
being brought to bear on the problem: "In effect the organizational culture
literature is full of competing and often incompatible views. Functionalist,
interpretive, and critical voices are all speaking at the same time. It resembles
what Burrell and Morgan would call paradigm wars" (Smircich and Calas,
1987, pp. 244–245).

Others (such as Ouchi and Wilkins, 1985) welcome the conflict and
confrontation in the organizational culture interest area while recognizing it
as a battle between the still dominant view in organizational theory research
and the growing minor one that advocates more naturalistic views of
organizational life.

Jeffcutt (1994) goes further, combining the analyses of organizational culture and symbolism under the heading of organizational interpretation. He argues this as a late-modern phase of organization studies, challenging traditional subordinations and priorities in theory and practice. This re-forming movement, he contends, constitutes part of the growing complexity and dislocation of organization theory "paradigm shifts." He contrasts this part of modernism in attempting to reveal the truth through a rational process of uncovering — interpretation — with postmodernism:

> The quest of organizational interpretation has thus become the "management" of uncertainty, in a search to re-establish order form the disorder (i.e., fragmentation and incoherence in the theoretical and empirical base of Orga-nization Studies) that earlier prophets and prophecies had been incapable of solving. . . . In contrast, the postmodern is both beyond and against the modern; being characterized by the interrogation, disruption and overturning of metanarratives which pursue privilege through the maintenance of hier-archies that seek authority through the censorship, suppression and proscription of other equally viable alternatives. . . . Postmodernism articulates a post-modern condition of undecidability and perpetual redefinition, rather than the nascence of the prioritizations of a fresh-elite. (pp. 237–239)

Postmodernism, drawn out later in the chapter, clearly complicates discussion of organizational culture, interpretation and communication. Yet the "battle-ground" is now made even more complex by expansion of the concept of culture into notions of diversity, cross cultural and polycultural approaches, through the work of scholars such as Hofstede (1991) and Albert (1992).

Paradigm Dialogues or Wars?

The culture focus provides grounds for ongoing questioning of whether we can indeed participate in dialogue and work together, or merely continue to engage in paradigm wars. Is there essential conflict and incompatibility between the differing paradigms, or can we accept the study of communica-tion from diverse perspectives with an effort to comprehend, synthesize, and appropriately utilize lessons from such perspectives? While there may be different responses to this important ongoing question, surely the issue itself is more than a debate about qualitative versus quantitative methods and rather one centered on culture in terms of cognitive, symbolic, and uncon-scious processes as the essential difference.

Burrell and Morgan (1979), as many still acknowledge, have provided a most useful outline of diverse approaches, dividing organizational studies into four paradigms, ('functionalist,' 'interpretive,' anti-organizational-'radical humanism,' and radical-'radical structuralism') which, they maintain, are mutually exclusive. Others such as Rosengren (1985, 1989), arguing for mass communication or the field more broadly, say this is not necessarily the case; while for Tompkins (1987), all organizational theory is merely "an extension of the classical concerns of rhetorical theory" (p. 77).

With communication academics working under different paradigms, using differing concepts, observations, and methodologies, and being devoid of theory-neutral observation and an objective world, we are left with (Trigg, 1985) "a competition between different visions of the world, some of which may overlap, but which cannot formulate their disagreements in any common language" (p. 14).

We can link Kuhnian (1970) conceptions with those of Feyerabend (1981), who stresses that our view of reality is determined by traditions and that, given the multiple competing traditions in our world, we can only judge truth in terms of relative validity within the tradition in which we locate ourselves. While it may be important to choose between competing alternatives, if we cannot find a basis in "the reality" for evaluating alternatives, and if we cannot communicate outside our traditions and paradigms, this surely is a disturbing communication situation! It certainly denies what the 1985 International Communication Association's "Paradigm Dialogues" was trying to foster, and what a few academics have been trying to achieve in a variety of arenas, ranging from organizational communication to communications policy — the integration of diverse approaches. This is the embrace of diverse perspectives that Krone, Jablin, and Putnam (1987) advocate, the comprehension and synthesis of organizational communication research from diverse views in order to generate new theories and increase the explanatory power of current ones.

But is this possible? The current evidence in most communication theory literature and in research reports seems to indicate otherwise. Scholars from one may go to the other, but the combination of the two is certainly not evident in the vast majority of our literature. At least, however, in organizational communication, there does not as yet seem the overt enmity evident in other communication fields where alternatives are often not even tolerated.

LEARNING FROM COMMUNICATION IN MASS COMMUNICATION

Paradigm Shifts?

Open hostility and the problems outlined previously here had been evident in the field of mass communication long before they were hinted at in organizational communication. The history of research emphases on effects studies, uses and gratifications, textual analysis, audience analysis and, more recently, communications technology and policy studies, have been placed firmly within the continuing debate between the so-called "empirical" and

"critical" schools for some time now (as well as other inimical camps—
positivist and Marxist specifically, structuralist and phenomenological theory
and research). This has been particularly true in mass communication, in the
ongoing "feud" between European and American scholarly traditions. Of
course, for European scholars, mass communication research *is* communication research, just as for these scholars organizational communication tends
not to be a field in its own right. Interpersonal and small group communication is also eschewed there. Generally, little consideration is given even to
the interesting question of the relationship of interpersonal communication
vis-à-vis mediated large-scale communication, and vice versa.

Here we find that (Rogers, 1985):

> The empirical and critical schools of communication research represent two
> quite different approaches. The former is typified by quantitative empiricism,
> functionalism, and positivism, while the critical school is characterized by a
> more philosophical emphasis, greater attention to the context of communica-
> tion, an early Marxist orientation, and a concern with who controls a
> communication system (p. 219). . . . Perhaps the central questions being asked
> today by critical scholars about communication are "Why?" or "Why not?" while
> the central research questions for the empirical school are "How?" and "How
> much?" (p. 225)

While the empirical schools have stressed what McCormack (1986) calls a sort
of cybernetic societal model with a focus on information and, more recently,
a cultural one focusing on meaning creation and symbols, in Europe the
emphasis has been essentially on a conflict model of society that centers on
ideological issues. Power has always been seen as central here, as have the
broad economic and political domains. In Europe the mass media are
considered agencies of social control, while in America they are seen more as
only one of many change agents or tools of persuasion, in spite of the long
history of the much-despised—by critical scholars at least—effects research
tradition.

While the eminent Kurt Lang (1979) denied the validity of what many
regard as an intrinsic incompatibility bewween the "positivism" of administrative communication research and the critical approach associated with the
Frankfurt school, today enormous differences are maintained, maybe even
nurtured. Such differences reflect conflicting political viewpoints—for example, the power elite view versus the pluralist one, to put it simplistically. As the
mass communication scholar Blumler (1982, p. 151) said over a decade ago,
some time before ICA's "Paradigm Dialogue" meeting:

> It is curious how the holders of certain positions in our field tend to restrict their
> appeal to already convinced devotees by arbitrarily narrowing the range of

phenomena they study or by turning a blind eye to their own philosophic soft spots. Cross-camp debate could become more mutually enlightening, at least, if attempts were made to break down some of these unnecessary barriers.

So from 1980 onwards, if not before, in the field of mass communication we have had calls largely for cross fertilization of ideas, most particularly by those scholars engaged in uses and gratifications research. Such calls have generally gone unheeded. Few visible large-scale effects or enduring efforts to follow such advice and exhortations are evident over a decade after such counsel was originally offered. This is in spite of the optimism of Blumler, McQuail, and Rosengren (1990) that former cross-paradigm antagonisms are cooling. Certainly they have not disappeared.

Instead, we still have estrangement of scholars in message analysis, audience, and cultural studies. Even the rise of new communications technology has not really brought the warring parties together, but merely served to once more accentuate the disparities between the empirical and critical schools of communication research and theory. The work of eminent scholars, such as Jay Blumler and Elizabeth Noelle-Neumann, who have endeavored to set the rest of the field a useful example by successfully employing multimethod research, has gone largely unheeded and uncopied.

Indeed antagonisms are still rife within particular paradigms domains themselves as the following appeal by a Finnish scholar serves to illustrate (Pietila et al., 1990):

> Given the communication barriers between the euro-American, French, and German lines of research, with paradigmatic soliloquies at their limits, there is a strong case for giving priority to dialogues in the field . . . a plea for multipurpose, complex, and critical . . . mass communication studies that are both intellectually open and rigorous. Although dialogue alone is not a sufficient condition for attaining this, we suggest that keeping the doors open for the dialectics underlying dialogical rationality should prevent the study of mass communication from disintegrating into a series of monologues or inner-directed endeavors to totalize the field. (p. 183)

As if in answer, Davis and Puckett (1992) propose a culture-centered paradigm for media research and scholarship, offering the opportunity to integrate much diverse work in the field, and providing a way of stemming the still current conflict between what they see as qualitative and quantitative scholars. They argue:

> for the utility of a "culture-centered" paradigm as a means of unifying scholarship in our field. . . . If future media research were more explicitly and self-consciously grounded in it, findings from very different types of analyses might be integrated and common problems might be addressed. Critics of our

proposal might argue that existing divisions in the field are giving rise to "heuristic dialogues." In our view, these dialogues too often consist of juxtaposed monologues (dialogues of the deaf). Within these, much effort is made to defend existing perspectives, but little is done to assess and build on common themes. Given the sterility of past debates over the nature of mass entertainment, we are skeptical that true dialogue will be possible without explicit acknowledgment of a common paradigm and a concerted effort to ground all forms of scholarship in it. (p. 9)

Paradigm Wars?

If there is still an identity crisis in organizational communication then, rather surprisingly for some at least, this also seems the case in communication studies overall. For example, Rogers and Balle (1985a) maintain: "We have a wide area in which to maneuver, and we still have not located effectively just where the theoretical center of communication study should be. That is an important task for the future" (p. 6). Others are openly critical that communication per se should see itself as a distinct disciplinary speciality, pointing to a supposed weak theoretical basis and its neglect of its underlying social theory, any cultural theory, or theory of power (Hall, 1989). Giddens (1989) emphasises, however, the centrality of communication studies to what social theory and social science are about.

Representing some of the arguments made in the organizational communication literature, Blumler (1985), discussing European–American differences in communication research, emphasizes the need to look at different approaches and sources for differences, and to learn from them. This is an avowed hallmark of this scholar's work, a view that he has held for some time now, going even so far as to outline the possibility of a critical-pluralist approach to political communication (1990). He believes that European scholars employ more mixed research methods than their American counterparts. This is a debatable point. What seems really the case is that nowhere are continuing major efforts being made to undertake such research, especially in terms of fleshing out what individual and combined approaches may best be capable of yielding across diverse paradigms.

In mass communication, the traditional American approach has been gradually infused with ideas from the European critical tradition. This has meant a move away, from 1960s onwards to the present, from the American dominant tradition, not only in mass media — effects-focused — but also generally in the social sciences, with the revived interest in Marxism, other arenas such as semiotics, cultural studies, sociolinguistics, structuralism, the influence of Foucault, and so on. Evidence of the reverse is not so clear.

Early on, Rogers and Balle (1985b) emphasize the intellectual strength that can be derived from more communication between European and American communication research scholars, despite the important differences that exist between the mass media on the two continents. They suggest that the empirical school should look more closely at

- the contexts of communication
- policy issues
- critical concerns in general

and that the critical school should particularly consider interpersonal communication, especially in relation to the opportunities of interactivity in new communications technologies. They believe that the historically evident antagonistic opposition between the empirical and critical school must cease. They think that the new communication techniques can speed the ending of this antagonism. Ten years later, certainly in the South Pacific, we see conflict maintained. Earlier divisions have merely been exacerbated along the Super Information Highway.

The European approach to communication emphasizes contextual issues — institutional structures and processes studied not in isolation from external social features. That is, the American tendency is to virtually equate communication science with microscopic, individual-level investigation, but what is clearly favoured in Europe are the more macroscopic levels of inquiry (Blumler, 1982). As Blumler et al. (1990, p. 133) put it more recently: "In several respects, European research reflects an interaction between historically rooted outlooks and current circumstances of economic advance, technological change, convergence of nations and acceleration of the European project."

Blumler (1985) himself doesn't call for reconciliation of division based on conflict of political philosophy. Nevertheless he continues to emphasize the need for more rewarding cross-camp debate by elimination of some of the unnecessary barriers that remain. A point highlighted is that, even while Adorno maintained that "no continuum exists between critical theorems and the empirical procedures of natural science" (quoted in Blumler, 1985, p. 193), he also acknowledged the legitimacy of, and even pointed out the necessity for, empirical inquiry.

A comparison between the beliefs of critical and empirical scholars merely reflects that there are too many misperceptions in each school about the other. Misconception is fostered by intellectual enmity and avoidance. It fails to come to grips with the view that, "in important ways, both the critical and empirical approaches to communication research necessarily entail the other" (Rogers, 1985, p. 233). Social theory needs empirical research just as does empirical research without social theory appear meaningless (McAnany, 1981).

The previous rancor and disputation between the two schools needs replacement by a recognition that each may have much to learn from the other and from an effort to make such cognition real in practice. Pluralism, though not of a naive kind, needs to prevail or current ferment will become total war, with fighting occurring among different sects and sectarians (Rex, 1978).

Rosengren (1985) maintained some time ago that Burrell and Morgan's (1979) classification and identification of the four paradigms has served to illuminate a twofold intellectual paradox:

> Those who can give the answers did not ask the questions; and those who asked the questions cannot provide the answers . . . The fact that questions raised in one paradigm may be given satisfactory answers by means of methodologies developed in another paradigm casts some doubt on the alleged incomparability of the four paradigms. Indeed, it may be questioned whether what we have are really paradigms at all. (p. 240-241)

He considered computer based programs such as LISREL and PLS, bridging the gaps between Burrell and Morgan's four paradigmatic antagonisms and, with Jensen (1990), offers a way forward with multi-method and cross cultural research and the possiblity of interdisciplinary theory development. Through these he thought "some highly interesting and provocative questions raised in the critical paradigms may thus be given answers that are falsifiable and replicable" (p. 255).

So, in mass communication there is a small but vocal body of scholars who regard the dimensions of Burrell and Morgan's typology as not absolute demarcations. Instead, they are perceived as continual pseudoconflicts, rather than real conflicts that cannot be solved. This group sees no problem in having questions raised in one paradigm and answered in another. They argue:

> The main hindrance to such movement probably is the interest which leading representatives or rival schools have vested in demonstrating to themselves, to their followers, and to their opponents that somehow they are radically different. In the long run, however, such claims cannot hold their own against empirical evidence . . . Thus there is a strong possibility that ferment in the field of communication research will be replaced by vigorous growth. (Rosengren, 1985, pp. 261-262)

Culture as a concern. In recent years the study of mass communication has become even broader in its focus, underlining the view that culture needs to be studied at a societal level as a macro phenomenon and often concentrating on the wide area of popular culture, an area that seems to be rising in regard more recently among American scholars. Because of the inextricable link between culture and communication, it is not surprising that culture has come to represent a problematic which is central to communication research of whatever paradigm, even though it has been particularly central to Burrell and Morgan's (1979) two more radical paradigms. In England the early work of cultural scholars such as Stuart Hall, and James Halloran's group at Leicester, were pivotal in representing this broader concern with culture, focusing on identifying ways in which practices are produced and reproduced. In explaining mass communication processes as part of everyday meaningful social activities, cultural studies emphasizes broad social and cultural practices. It asserts the worth of popular culture such as the study of television 'soap' operas.

One of the clear lessons organizational communication can learn from the struggles in the field of mass communication is indeed in this area of concern with cultural issues. Concentration by some scholars on the cultural studies arena has unfortunately often served to be divisive in terms of battles over methodology and ideology. Combined approaches may succeed where separate ones have hitherto failed or been largely unsatisfactory to one or other of the competing schools.

> Recent methodological advances within the dominant paradigm of communication research may facilitate the empirical study of the important questions about culture and ideology raised within the radical paradigms. Some of the questions about culture and ideology raised within the radical paradigms have been asked also within the dominant paradigm, as a result of intraparadigmatic developments . . . the serious study of culture will ultimately necessitate the systematic and sustained development of cultural indicators. Such development — mainly methodological in its thrust — may lead to a corresponding theoretical and empirical enrichment of the study of culture, not only in the social sciences but also in the humanities. A set of reliable and valid cultural indicators applied over time and space will permit comparative studies of culture at a higher level of precision than before. (Rosengren, 1985, pp. 246, 248)

A lesson that mass communication might well take from organizational communication is the need to look more closely at mass media organizations from diverse perspectives, including from the viewpoint of organizational communication itself. The reverse, looking at how organizations are portrayed in the mass media, could also apply. Indeed, the book by Vande Berg and Trujillo (1989), *Organizational Life On Television*, does just this. The authors are an interesting combination — Vande Berg is a mass media academic concerned with radio, television, and film, and Trujillo is an organizational communication academic. Both are concerned with the general values and patterns that prime time television dramas display and with the complex relationship between television and organizational life, a relationship they acknowledge is both interdependent and sometimes adversarial. The basic focus in this text is, however, the portrayal of organizational life on prime time television drama. The study is grounded in the belief that, (p. 3) "To the extent that television reflects and reaffirms organizational reality, these portrayals of organizational life on television drama may play a very important role in shaping our understanding and expectations of organizational America" (p. 3). The work succeeds in constructively erasing some traditional disciplinary and paradigmatic boundaries in communication studies and provides a fine example of the necessary intellectual boundary spanning that is vital for the continued growth of the communication discipline as a whole. Half a decade later it still remains a fairly isolated effort on the whole. Equally important is the emphasis on diversity, international and intercultural communication and the focus on media globalization (Casmir, 1993).

THE PROBLEM IN FOCUS

In discussing problems in both fields, we may take ethnography, often a basis for interpretive and critical theory, as an example of merely one trouble spot in our discussion. Ethnography focuses on describing interpretive practices rather than identifying the causes of actions. It explores the ways in which social phenomena are produced and reproduced through social agency, and its importance lies in taking the human actors' self-understandings seriously (Tulloch, 1990). The problem is that, even with adequate philosophical and theoretical preparation, the difficulty of translating programs into practice is still enormous. For example, there is the ongoing challenge of attempting to ground both mass and organizational communication studies without having the phenomena disappear.

Tulloch (1990) maintains that the 'ethnographic moment,' within an empiricist discourse, offers the possibility of consensus plus a way to overcome "unproductive" segregation through a return to sanity within specialist practice. For the 'subject/object' debate on the Left it provides another path. Without yielding to either the subjectivism of interpretive sociologies or postmodernist relativism, it tries to go beyond the 'object-centered' functionalism or structuralist-oriented analysis.

What is emphasized is the broader sense of popular reflexivity that can be captured by ethnographic study of day-to-day life in all of its institutional settings, in accord with Giddens' (1984, 1987) view of daily routine and consciousness. These are regarded as integral to the active reproduction of *all* institutionalized practices in which knowledgeable actors struggle to create their meanings.

Also stressed is the need for research perceptions of communication behavior to be from within the constituent actor's own cultural space rather than from somewhere outside. The rider is with reference to Giddens' (1984) discussion of the distinctions between mutual knowledge and common sense. Here the analytical emphasis is a realist one, highlighting the conditions of bounded knowledgeability within which human agents act.

McPhee (1989) and others have followed Giddens' lead in using a structurational approach to communication, emphasising the need to overcome traditional macro-micro polarity through seeing the mutual orientation existing between macro-structure and interaction concepts. He argues (p. 211) that "the structurational paradigm is unparalleled in its defensibility as a basis, and its fecundity as an inspiration and interpretive frame, for research."

Tulloch (1990) finally asserts that the task of the critical intellect is to make accountable the groups setting boundaries on the rationalization of action within historical contexts. This relates well to Morgan's (1986) point that:

> In studies of organizational culture, enactment is usually seen as being a voluntary process under the direct influence of the actors involved. This view can be important in empowering people to take greater responsibility for their world by recognizing that they play an important part in the construction of their realities. But it can be misleading to the extent that it ignores the stage on which the enactment occurs. We all construct or enact our realities, but not necessarily under circumstances of our own choosing. There is an important power dimension underlying the enactment process that the culture metaphor does not always highlight to the degree possible. When this is taken into account, the culture metaphor becomes infused with a political flavor. (p. 140)

Undoubtedly, there is much to agree with and applaud in these views. However, considered from a philosophical perspective, some manifestations of ethnography, concentrating on how participants in an organization view their everyday activities, leave little for the social scientist:

> The repudiation of causal accounts of how societies gain their character and the consequent distrust of any notion of rational standards allow little but the description of the varying viewpoints to be found and the recognition that the viewpoint of the social scientist provides one such example. (Trigg, 1985, pp. 84–85)

Here emphasis is laid on the move from empiricism and away from any paradigm of rationality, suggesting the possibility of reducing empirical methods to apparently pointless ritual. What may be regarded as key problems in the dominant alternative approach, advocated for some time as critical in mass communication and more recently as the interpretive in

organizational communication, are here summarized from an extensive
philosophical discussion (Trigg, 1985):

- Attacks on empiricism have removed the basis of our empirical knowledge
  while not putting anything in its place and leading to questions of
  knowledge, truth, reality, and reason being discarded. The greatest
  danger is that of denying the very possibility of rationality. Denying
  positivism and its strong idea of verification should not lead us to denying
  the possibility of truth.
- Instead of jettisoning the idea of rationality, it may be more profitable to
  admit that the methods of the physical sciences may be too restrictive as a
  model.
- We have moved from knowledge to belief; from truth to what is held to be
  true; from reality to individual's beliefs about reality; from questions of
  rational standards to diverse ways of individual reasoning; from justification to description; and, finally, from philosophy—epistemology at
  least—to sociology. Sociology, itself, investigates the construction of social
  reality by people rather than the nature of social reality. Because there is
  no sociological standard by which different forms of consciousness can be
  assessed they are accepted at face value.
- Emphasizing the incommensurability of theories leads to theories and
  traditions setting their own standards of rationality that are immune to
  criticism from outside.
- Problems exist in such approaches as ethnomethodology, where truth is
  denied in favor of examining multiple versions of the way our world is
  assembled. It is not that we have many windows on the truth: Rather, no
  truth is obtainable. Once we reach this point we have been caught in the
  paralyzing quagmire of relativism in the social sciences, a net that casts
  doubt on the value or purpose of any intellectual activity in general.
- Dangers are evident in the social sciences, ignoring the advances made by
  the physical sciences. Human sociobiology can present an example of
  building social sciences on physical ones without being reduced by them.
  Both sciences have commonality, not in empiricist methodology, but in
  the aim of discovering the nature of whatever reality the science is
  investigating.
- We need to adopt those values that are appropriate to the task at hand,
  whatever our presuppositions may be in our quest for knowledge.

Such views explore the consequences of the ongoing challenge to empiricism,
primarily from the stance that there is a great danger of jettisoning the very
possibility of rationality. The telling point is the possibility of a paralyzing
nihilism, the feeling that there are no answers, and the questionable value of

mere attempts at understanding. Yet, if there are no answers, if we are unclear about even the questions, and the rationale for our endeavors, where does that leave us as a community of scholars? Or, on the other hand, if the answers are already clear before we even ask the question, as may seem to be the case in some critical research, what use is the research?

What should concern us here is not explorations of differing paradigms and differing approaches to the field of organizational communication, but the need to keep some sense of balance in the field, a sense that has been hard fought over continuously in other fields. The concern, then, is a basic philosophical one, with what some have seen as the paralyzing impact that relativism has on the social sciences. Trigg (1985) elaborates this concern:

> It is one thing to assert that the physical sciences have no monopoly on truth, but it is another to jettison the concepts of truth, reality, and knowledge. It is one thing to resist a narrowly scientific paradigm for rationality, but it is another to widen the latter so that the most rigorous social scientist can be no more rational than the most superstitious tribesman. The only consequence of such a position is to cast complete doubt on the value or purpose of social science, or indeed of any intellectual activity. (p. 86)

New Communications Technology

That this is the case is again well evidenced in an emerging interest area that itself crosses the traditional boundaries between mass communication and organizational communication, and for some, even that of interpersonal and group communication: the new communications technology. It is an area that ought to be challenging traditional paradigms. Instead, myopaeia and conflict seem rekindled. Nearly a decade ago Rogers and Balle (1985b) observed:

> We see the new communication media as having a powerful influence on the nature of communication research. These new technologies make scholarly research on communication "a whole new ball game," unfreezing this research field from many of its assumptions, paradigms, and investigatory methods of the past. This challenge from the new media is impacting upon the nature of communication research in both Europe and America today. The common realization of these impacts on both sides of the Atlantic is a powerful force toward closer integration of European and American approaches to communication research. (p. 301)

Such integration sadly is not evident. In much of the American organizational communication research centering on such technology, there seems to be a return by some to the early days of media characteristics and effects research (see, for example, Rice et al., 1992; Cushman and King, 1993). However, one special issue of *Communication Research* (Steinfield and Fulk, 1987) on

"Theories of Organizations and Information Technologies" did offer an alternative approach. Here we find that to develop theory-guided research on information technologies we use not our own discipline's theoretical base, nor develop new theories, but work by analogy, borrowing theoretical frameworks generated in other contexts. The borrowings are from the disciplines of economics, sociology, psychology, and organization theory at large.

Steinfield's (1992) exploration of the theoretical underpinnings and development of computer-mediated communication in organizational contexts offers some novel directions. These are his emphasis on the interdisciplinarity of the field; the move away from the dominant paradigms of contingency theory to inclusion of critical mass and social influence models, focusing on the social context within which communication technologies are embedded as a basis for explaining adoption, use, and impact; and exploring new avenues in interorganizational communication, telecommunications infrastructures and achievement of organizational objectives.

The emphasis in European communication research is primarily on the policy dimensions, except in the so-called more "management"-oriented literature. Dominant paradigms determine the way in which such technology is generally considered, often in a myopic manner. The hoped-for increase in attempts to integrate European and American approaches to communication research and theory has not yet come about. The traditional lines of demarcation seem almost as firmly entrenched as ever in approaching this technology debate, whether from a mass communication or an organizational communication perspective. Shields and Samarajiva (1993) outline such competing frameworks for research in their exploration of four key approaches to understanding information-communication technologies and society: postindustrialists, industrialists, long-wave, and power theorists. They argue the need for, and possibility of, synthesis.

SOME OPTIONS

With reference to the interpretive/cultural approach in organizational communication, Sypher et al. (1985) have two key points of criticism — philosophical differences and methodological issues:

> Focusing on the choice between quantitative and qualitative methods as a defining feature of the "interpretive approach" denies researchers the flexibility to match method with theory. In the extreme it smacks of the "methodolatry" that has hindered the development of programmatic research in the social sciences generally. The major methodological issue is not which type ofmethod to use, but which method is most appropriate for the particular research question being asked. (p. 21)

Logic of Positions

Sless (1986), echoing some of the concerns expressed earlier by Thayer's work in the 1960s (see, for example, Thayer, 1987), proposes an elaborate solution to such difficulties. He does so in terms of articulating a comprehensive logic of positions in communication. Denying the fall into infinite regress, he maintains that no truths are attainable concerning the nature of any particular text: Rather, truth is found in the process of reading itself. For him (Sless, 1986):

> We find a clear sense of regularity and order which enables us to account for the changes at the level of the text itself . . . Thus my exegesis on the reading of texts should not be seen as an abandonment of all desire for order or understanding; on the contrary, it is a search for a better order of understanding . . . The landscape of communication is more like the surface of a giant trampoline than terra firma. When a trampoline yields as we walk across it the feeling may be one of uncontrollable and hence chaotic movement but we know that the trampoline is obeying strict physical laws of elasticity which do not change. The regularity is simply at a level which as walkers we have not yet grasped. (pp. 86–87, 129)

Such reading, is, of course infused with power considerations. Power, control, and politics have been central in European mass communication research for some time. Thankfully with the work of scholars such as Putnam and Pacanowsky (1983), McPhee and Tompkins (1985), Mumby (1988, 1993), Deetz and Mumby (1990), and Alvesson (1993), this has become infused, in a minor way at least, into organizational communication research.

A different logic of positions must also consider different meanings for culture and the issue of gender. Giving organizational communication a cross-cultural perspective, although absolutely imperative in the 1980s and 1990s, has really been unbelievably slow to take off. Albert and Triandis in 1987 made one of the first attempts, which was followed up later by Albert (1992) in delineating a newer perspective—what she called a *polycultural perspective*. There is a growing need for organizations to understand and manage within a polycultural environment, one that has culturally diverse populations. Organizations must deal with multicultural work forces and clients, internally and externally, domestically and internationally. She defines polycultural organizational communication as referring to multiple cultures, as "encompassing theory and research involving organizations in both international and domestic settings in which cultural differences operate" (p. 75). It encompasses both cross-cultural (comparing how organizational communication differs in diverse cultures or countries) and intercultural theory and research (that seeks to explore interactions between culturally diverse organizational groups or persons).

The 1980s work on organizational sexuality and gender as reported by Hearn et al. (1989), discussed by Gibson Burrell at the Dublin 1991 ICA Conference, and picked up in a volume edited by Mills and Tancred (1992), also provides a fertile and crucially underrated position from which to view our field. Mumby (1993) points out the lack of a real commitment to infusing the organizational communication literature with considerations of gender issues. This is echoed by Buzzanell (1994), who contends that the potential contributions of feminist organizational communication theory and research (such as innovative perspectives on organizing and gender relationships) remains largely unfulfilled.

CONCLUSION

Trigg's (1985) solution to some of the dilemmas outlined above is as follows:

> Part of the trouble is that empiricism relied heavily on the notion of experience of the world to the detriment of any emphasis on the world as such. Consequently, once the theoretical or even cultural influences on what seemed "raw" experience are exposed, it is difficult to recover any conception of the world or reality which does not itself seem to be merely a theoretical or cultural construct. Yet without such a conception, the hopelessness which leads some ethnomethodologists to give up ethnomethodology can soon set in. What is needed is a concept of objective reality which is divorced from the presuppositions of empiricism and which, as a consequence, is not tied too closely to the methods and findings of empirical science. The latter may be a source of knowledge, but its claim to be the *only* source has undoubtedly led many to intemperate opposition to the idea of knowledge or of objective truth.

It is possible that organizational communication may be the field to develop such a concept that may be applicable across all arenas of the field and avoid the dysfunctional debates that have occurred in mass communication. To do so it needs to avoid the tendency to work at the extreme ends of the two major paradigms in the social sciences. Without arguing for mindless and unfettered relativism, one can appreciate the view of Tompkins and Redding (1988, p. 27) that "all forms of inquiry are vital to continued progress in the study of organizational communication." (p. 89)

We need to think seriously about such warnings as follows:

> Human intellectual endeavour rapidly becomes pointless without the realist assumption that there is an independent reality for us to investigate. The demise of positivism with its strong notion of verification must not lead us to deny the possibility of truth . . . What physical and social science must hold in common

is not an empiricist methodology. Instead they must each hold fast to their aim of discovering the nature of whichever reality they are investigating.

Modern social science may expose some of the social roots of contemporary science but, once it suggests that all knowledge is the product of society, we shall be dragged down in the quagmire of relativism. The assertions of social science themselves purport to convey knowledge about society. A reflexive social science applying its findings to itself will soon destroy itself. Whatever our presuppositions, we are not thereby prevented from investigating how far they help or hinder us in our quest for knowledge. We must consciously adopt those values which are appropriate to the task in hand. (Trigg, 1985, pp. 202–204)

Today there seem to be numerous purposes in studying organizational communication, ranging from the more traditional social science ones of prediction and control to ones seeking to understand society as it is instead of how we want it to be. There are also questions of ethics and morality, and that of the purpose of understanding. Such issues are often ideologically based and need consideration as such. What can we learn from others in order not to make the same mistakes must be a pressing concern?

Lessons From Mass Communication

In this field, warring is currently evident in audience-level inquiry that is only now really emerging after being so long associated with the "bad name" of effects research. Its significance as an area of study is growing as Blumler (1985) suggested earlier on: "The study of mass communication as a social process without a well-founded investigation of audience response is like a sexology that ignores the orgasm" (p. 195).

In recent work, particularly on television research, there has been a resurgence of interest in audience studies, especially from an ethnographic perspective. Perhaps we can learn something from the extension that Tulloch (1990) speaks of in the following quotation, taking our investigations of organizational communication into arenas outside the normal organizational communication boundaries such as into homes, pubs, and the like:

Our argument here is for an *extension* of the ethnographic approach out of the domestic sphere into strategic conduct in all those institutional, professional, industrial, educational, and leisure spaces where pleasures and meanings contest in the construction of TV drama "texts." This should always be an examination of "politics" in so far as these interdiscursive spaces . . . are sites of hierarchy and power. But it will also be a description of "pleasures" as these relate to routine practices and to emotional solidarity. . . . Secondly, then, our argument is for ethnographic analysis always to be placed in the context of *structure* and power: at the macro-social level, and all of the micro-institutional levels as well . . . and, certainly not least, of the ethnographic research process itself.

Such suggestions offer possibilities to our field. It may be useful in adopting an interpretive approach to broaden our horizons by looking at actors' meaning construction in a variety of institutional arenas—that is, not only in organizations but also in other institutional settings.

Perhaps even more importantly, we should also do more of what some ethnomethodologists are doing with respect to traditional tasks of sociology— taking a more detailed look at the very way organizational communication is theorized, in ferreting out how communication processes and behavior are available to theoretical formulation and how that theorizing is done.

However important such suggestions may be, the key lesson is that the conflict still essentially there in the field of mass communication—between "American" and "European critical/cultural studies" approaches—should not be repeated in our field of organizational communication.

Combining Approaches

The special issue of the *Journal of Communication* in 1983, "Ferment in the Field" heralded the few years of overt introspection in the field, closely followed by the 1985 ICA conference, whose them was "Beyond Polemics: Paradigm Dialogues."

Dervin et al. could readily claim in 1989 that: Few of the issues raised in 1985 have been resolved: fundamental questions about theory, method, and purpose are still being asked. The term paradigm still has many meanings (p. 11). Writing in 1994 Buzzanell can clearly state that: In general, organizational communication theorists in the United States have inadequately questioned and critically assessed fundamental principles, constructs, and research methods underlying their theories (p. 339). This statement is both unfortunate in the sense that it can be made at all and also because such limitations extend much further than America—to Europe and the South East Asia–Pacific region.

Indeed what seems to have happened is that quite a few American communication scholars have incorporated European paradigms and perspectives (see, for example, McPhee's, 1989, work) but there is little evidence of the opposite happening.

It has been suggested (Hawes, Pacanowsky, & Faules, 1988) that "all our positions, in reality, can and do inform one another, and can and do undermine one another, but for very different reasons" (p. 52). Yes, it is necessary to acknowledge, in our communication discipline as a whole, the problems that stem from the obvious conflict and perceived ideological incompatibility of different positions. Nevertheless, in spite of relevant philosophical and theoretical issues, it seems important to combine quantitative and qualitative approaches—to utilize paradigm diversity by combining perspectives—in order to improve our analysis, understanding, and explanation of organizational communication. The best way to do so is still very debatable. Researchers such as Sypher, Applegate, & Sypher (1985) suggested that "the soundest approach to using multiple methods is to move from qualitative to quantitative analyses" (p. 23), which supports Rosengren's earlier mentioned (1985) emphasis in mass communication on the use of LISREL and PLS to overcome the barriers promoted by traditionald demarcations between paradigms and methodologies.

In such combined efforts we should do our utmost to avoid reinventing the wheel, especially so far as mistakes and enmity are concerned and, to paraphrase Garfinkel (1967), to do communication research that does not lead to the disappearance of the phenomenon.

We need to be clear, with the growing popular emphasis on the alternative approach, whether we are actually tracking a path from "the world-as-it-appears to the world-as-it-really-is-in-itself" (Sharrock & Anderson, 1986, p. 10). Or, are we stuck in the initial groove by the wholesale rejection of rationality? Perhaps, after all, we do need to take account more seriously of Sless's (1986) notion of a logic of positions, although one could do with more cogent methods for overcoming difficulties once this notion is accepted.

We should, however, grapple with the problems Deetz (1994) raises, indicating the ways in which our associations and publications compartmentalize and ignore theoretical perspectives that span numerous domains:

> While the dialogue and ferment of the past decade gave an opening for new conceptions, the sterility of phenomena-/topical-centered research leaves paradigm dialogue a mere pluralism. Only in dealing with choice making regarding problems in the necessary contingent conditions of social life does the difference of different modes of explanation stand out and make a difference. Mere paradigmatic pluralism makes it impossible to adjudicate conflicting knowledge claims and values because they reference not the common social problem but the incommensurable technical language and procedures of their makers. (p. 571)

Combining also means we have to ask anew what the tasks of academe and the critical intellect are. Previous concerns under the dominant paradigm were those of productivity, competence, and the like. What now? The ethnomethodologists suggest that the gap between research and phenomena is as important as the gap between theory and research (Sharrock & Anderson, 1986). It seems to me equally important that we add another gap—that between research and affect on the world outside of academe, the last part of Thayer's (1986) brief for the series. This has sadly been too often ignored.

The Postmodernist Influence

What about the postmodernism, mentioned earlier, that has already for some time been argued over both in literary and mass communication studies? It seems to be entering organizational communication now (along with that other "trend" in organization studies — population ecology) with the emphasis on "postparadigmatic" thought (seen, for example, in Jablin, Putna, Roberts, & Porter, 1987). What may its impact be in this field?

Smirich and Calas (1987) suggest that:

> In postmodernity, the aim of the minor voices is not to stay around until they become dominant, but to maintain an opening from which to question the totalitarian attempts (to provide integrative, all-encompassing, worldviews that explain, and explain away, everything) of those who want to become or to stay dominant . . . If we extend the possibility of multiple interpretations to include the research writer and the research reader, we see that no one will ever have the "ultimate truth of the matter" . . . "Truth or falsity" (and the system of inclusion/exclusion created through disciplinary boundaries) is just a "manner of seeking." (p. 249)

We should not deny the usefulness of a multiplicity of interpretations, nor encourage the belief that there is an all-encompassing world view that explains everything. Nonetheless, surely we need to be wary of ending up in a quagmire of postmodernist "blues," with feelings of academic impotence and a further desire to escape into the "pleasures of contemplation":

> In their collective evolution, these new perspectives [i.e., Kuhn, Feyerabend, Althusser, Lacan, and Derrida] have issued in ways of seeing the world which, by and large, militate against our acting in it . . . Despite their self-proclaimed radicalism . . . the characteristic mode of these new perspectives is one of contemplation: in their relativism and in their obsessional epistemological ambivalence, in the rejection of historical modes of analysis, and — at their termini — in their embrace of intellectual nihilism and irrationalism, they opt for noninvolvement, for social abstention, for an inner emigration from an unbearable present and a problematic future. (Mellor quoted in Tulloch, in press, p. 9)

We seem to be drowning in the arguments about the best theories and methods of the social world on the one hand and the more recent concerns with whether indeed it is possible that this social world can be "theorized" at all. For organization studies as a whole, many would agree with Mangham's (1986) espoused problematic that "most books about the conduct of individuals in organizations seem to me to have been written by people who have read other books about the same thing. Most are parasitic, feeding on concepts and ideas deriving from others; some are cannibalistic, devouring entirely their own species" (p. vi). On top of this, we have others suggesting that in communication itself as a field we are merely recreating many other disciplines anew within one parent discipline, or, indeed, that we still have not tackled the task of formulating our mission (Peters, 1986). As Deetz (1994, p. 568) argues:

> If we are to make our full social contribution, we have to move from studying "communication" phenomena as formed and explained psychologically, sociologically, and economically, and produce studies that study psychological, sociological, and economic phenomena as formed and explained communicationally.

Where does this lead us in terms of the issues of concern pointed out in the introduction to this chapter?

- Concerning communication in the field of organizational communication, we need to be careful not to let it degenerate, particularly by virtue of new approaches regarding organizational culture, into the same bedrock of disputation plaguing the field of mass communication. Many of the sensible suggestions made by Paisley (1984) about improving communication in the Communication Sciences need to be heeded. Diversity and pluralism need to be defended, and working together from differing paradigms needs to be encouraged.
- Concerning the possibility of any unique offerings that the field of organizational communication might make to communication studies in general, the field needs to remember that while networking in the traditional sense was thought to be a vital factor in the past, it is unclear now what our unique contribution is — certainly the work on culture (and power) to date has generally been more often derivative than innovative and original. What is to be our role and our contribution as a field of communication studies? What will we add to current debates on organizational quality, reengineering, change management, and learning?
- Concerning communication between organizational communication and other communication fields — we will need to consider especially work on the new communications technology (still not much evident in texts and curricula in the organizational communication field generally), just as mass communication scholarship might consider the possible breakdown of paradigms that may eventuate from such technology research and theory.
- Concerning the apparent directions of the field, it seems imperative that we don't continue to have reruns of things in other communication arenas — the new wine in old bottles syndrome — particularly:
    1. in the developing shift of emphasis from a functionalist paradigm into an interpretive, or possibly critical, approach
    2. in terms of the pitfalls becoming evident in postmodernist thought.
- Concerning something that goes beyond theoretical navel gazing, we should heed the call by those such as Craig (1989) and Smeltzer (1993) for

the cultivation of communicative praxis, for managerial application, not just trendy research. Here organizational communication can learn from the mass communication discipline — little notice is taken of this field by policy developers and government per se, perhaps only in the more popular areas of television violence and the like. As DeWine and Daniels put it (1993, 338): "Organizational communication researchers have an obligation to contribute significantly to human existence and should not shrink from that task."

So, at a time when communication is regarded by so many as central to contemporary and future organizational and social life, setting ourselves up in continuing limited and parochial intellectual compartments would surely be an inexcusable error. It would serve only to retard any real maturation and growth that the 1980s "ferment in the field" was intended to generate. We need more than the occasional signs of contact between different research domains and traditions or, as Deetz (1994) puts it:

> Many feel that we have had our paradigm dialogues, displayed our mutual respect, and that it is time to go back to our work (and our associations with each group's preferred other disciplines. But identity is not just something one gets; it is best thought of in terms of constant invention regarding changing environments . . . to be continually self-reflective as a field in regard to our current environment. (p. 565)

Unification is not the necessary end aim. But certainly we need to reap the benefits of the sort of dynamism and innovation that more truly fruitful coexistence and mutual learning could offer. Some synthesis could increase opportunities for formulating more comprehensive theories, better systems of description and explanation and understanding, and perhaps even more useful input into organization communication practice on a global scale.

REFERENCES

Albert, R. (1992). Polycultural perspectives on organizational communication. *Management Communication Quarterly, 6*(1), 74–84.

Alvesson, M. (1993). Cultural–ideological modes of management control: A theory and a case study of a professional service company. In S. Deetz (Ed.), *Communication yearbook/16* (pp. 3–42). Newbury Park, CA: Sage.

Blumler, J. (1982). Mass communication research in Europe: Some origins and prospects. In M. Burgoon (Ed.), *Communication Yearbook 5* (pp. 145–56). New Brunswick, NJ: Transaction Books.

Blumler, J. (1985). European and American approaches to communication research. In E. Rogers & F. Balle (Eds.), *The media revolution in America and in Western Europe* (pp. 185–199). Norwood, NJ: Ablex.

Blumler, J., Dayan, D., & Wolton, D. (1990). West European perspectives on political communication: Structures and dynamics. *European Journal of Communication, 5*(2-3), 261-284.

Blumler, J., McQuail, D., & Rosengren, K. (1990). (Eds.). Editorial. *European Journal of Communication, 5*(2-3), 131-134.

Bolman, T., & Deal, T. (1991). *Reframing organizations.* San Francisco: Jossey-Bass.

Burrell, G., & Morgan, G. (1979). *Sociological paradigms and organizational analysis.* London: Heinemann.

Casmir, F. (1993). Third-culture building: A paradigm shift for international and intercultural communication. In S. Deetz (Ed.), *Communication yearbook/16* (pp. 407-428). Newbury Park, CA: Sage.

Craig, R. (1989). Communication as a practical discipline. In B. Dervin, L. Grossberg, B. O'Keefe, & E. Wartella (Eds.), *Rethinking communication. Vol. 1. Paradigm issues* (pp. 97-122). Newbury Park, CA: Sage.

Cushman, D., & King, S. (1993). High-speed management: A revolution in organizational communication in the 1990s. In S. Deetz (Ed.), *Communication yearbook/16* (pp. 209-236). Newbury Park, CA: Sage.

Davis, D., & Puckett, T. (1992). Mass entertainment and community: Toward a culture-centered paradigm for mass communication research. In S. Deetz (Ed.), *Communication Yearbook/15* (pp. 3-34). Newbury Park, CA: Sage.

Deetz, S. (1994). Future of the discipline: The challenges, the research, and the social contribution. In S. Deetz (Ed.), *Communication yearbook/17* (pp. 565-600). Newbury Park, CA: Sage.

Deetz, S., & Mumby, D. (1990). Power, discourse, and the workplace: Reclaiming the critical tradition. In J. Anderson (Ed.), *Communication yearbook/13* (pp. 18-47). Newbury Park, CA: Sage.

Dervin, B., Grossberg, L., O'Keefe, B., & Wartella, E. (Eds.). (1989). *Rethinking communication. Vols. 1 and 2.* Newbury Park, CA: Sage.

DeWine, S., & Daniels, T. (1993). Beyond the snapshot: Setting a research agenda in organizational communication. In S. Deetz (Ed.), *Communication yearbook/16* (pp. 331-346). Newbury Park, CA: Sage.

Feyerabend, P. (1981a). *Philosophical papers. Vol. 1, realism, rationalism and scientific method.* Cambridge: Cambridge University Press.

Feyerabend, P. (1981b). *Philosophical papers. Vol. 2, problems of empiricism.* Cambridge University Press.

Garfinkel, H. (1967). *Studies in ethnomethodology.* Englewood Cliffs, NJ: Prentice-Hall.

Giddens, A. (1984). *The constitution of society.* Cambridge: Polity Press.

Giddens, A. (1987). *Social theory and modern sociology.* Cambridge: Polity Press.

Giddens, A. (1989). The emerging synthesis. In B. Dervin, L. Grossberg, B. O'Keefe, & E. Wartella (Eds.), *Rethinking communication. Vol. 1. Paradigm issues* (pp. 53-65). Newbury Park, CA: Sage.

Goldhaber, G., & Barnett, G. (1988). Foreword. In G. Goldhaber & G. Barnett (Eds.), *Handbook of Organizational Communication* (pp. 1-3). Norwood, NJ: Ablex.

Greenbaum, H., DeWine, S., & Downs, C. (1987). Management and organizational communication measurement: A call for review and evaluation. *Management Communication Quarterly, 1*(1), 129-143.

Harmon, M., & Mayer, R. (1986). *Organization theory for public administration.* Boston: Little, Brown and Company.

Hawes, L., Pacanowsky, M., & Faules, D. (1988). Approaches to the study of organization: A conversation among three schools of thought. In G. Goldhaber & Barnett G. (Eds.), *Handbook of Organizational Communication* (pp. 41-53). Norwood, NJ: Ablex.

Hearn, J., Sheppard, P., Tancred-Sheriff, P., & Burrell, G. (Eds.). (1989). *The sexuality of organizations.* London: Sage.

Hofstede, G. (1991). *Cultures and organizations.* London: McGraw-Hill.

Irwin, H., & More, E. (1994). *Managing corporate communication.* Sydney: Allen & Unwin.

Jablin, F., Putnam, L., Roberts, K., & Porter, L. (Eds.). (1987). *Handbook of organizational communication.* Beverly Hills, CA: Sage.

Jeffcutt, P. (1994). The interpretation of organization: A contemporary analysis and critique. *Journal of Management Studies, 31*(2), 225-250.

Jensen, K., & Rosengren, K. (1990). Five traditions in search of the audience. *European Journal of Communication, 5*(2-3), 207-238.

Krone, K., Jablin, F., & Putnam, L. (1987). Communication theory and organizational communication: Multiple perspectives. In F. Jablin, L. Putnam, K. Roberts, & L. Porter (Eds.). *Handbook of Organizational Communication* (pp. 11-17). Beverly Hills, CA: Sage.

Kuhnian, T. (1970). *The structure of scientific revolutions* (2nd ed.). Chicago: University of Chicago Press.

Lang, K. (1979). The critical functions of empirical communication research: Observations on German–American influence. *Media, Culture and Society, 1,* 83-96.

Leipzig, J., & More, E. (1982). Organizational communication: A review and analysis of three current approaches to the field. *Journal of Business Communication, 19*(4), 77-92.

Mangham, I. (1986). *Power and performance in organizations: An exploration of executive process.* Oxford: Basil Blackwell.

Mangham, I., & Overington, M. (1987). *Organizations as theatre: A social psychology of dramatic appearances.* Chichester: John Wiley & Sons.

McAnany, E. (1981). Change and social structure in mass communication: An overview. In E. McAnany, J. Schnitman, & M. Janus (Eds.), *Communication and social structure: Critical studies in mass media research* (pp. 3-20). New York: Praeger.

McCormack, T. (1986). Reflections on the lost vision of communication theory. In S. Ball-Rokeach & M. Cantor (Eds.), *Media, audience and social structure* (pp. 34-42). London: Sage.

McPhee, R. (1989). Organizational communication: A structurational exemplar. In B. Dervin, L. Grossberg, B. O'Keefe, & E. Wartella (Eds.), *Rethinking communication. Vol. 2. Paradigm exemplars* (pp. 199-212). Newbury Park, CA: Sage.

McPhee, R., & Tompkins, P. (Eds.). (1985). *Organizational communication: Traditional themes and new directions.* Beverly Hills, CA: Sage.

Mills, A., & Tancred, P. (1992). *Gendering organizational analysis.* Newbury Park, CA: Sage.

Morgan, G. (1986). *Images of organization.* Beverly Hills, CA: Sage.

Mumby, D. (1988). *Communication and power in organizations.* Norwood, NJ: Ablex.

Mumby, D. (1993). Critical organization communication studies. The next 10 years. *Communication Monographs, 60,* 18-25.

Ouchi, W., & Wilkins, A. (1985). Organizational culture. *Annual Review of Sociology, 11,* 457-483.

Paisley, W. (1984). Communication in the communication sciences. In B. Dervin & M. Voigt (Eds.), *Progress in communication sciences,* Vol. V. Norwood, NJ: Ablex.

Peters, J. (1986). Institutional sources of intellectual poverty in communication research. *Communication Research, 13*(4), 527-559.

Pietila, V., Malmberg, T., & Nordenstreng, K. (1990). Theoretical convergences and contrasts: A view from Finland. *European Journal of Communication, 5*(2-3), 165-185.

Putnam, L., & Pacanowsky, M. (Eds.). (1983). *Communication and organizations.* Beverly Hills, CA: Sage.

Putnam, L., & Packanowsky, M. (1983). *Communication and organizations. An interpretive approach.* Beverly Hills, CA: Sage.

Redding, W. (1979). Organizational communication theory and ideology: An overview. In D.

Nimmo (Ed.), *Communication Yearbook 3* (pp. 309–341). New Brunswick, NJ: Transaction Books.

Rex, J. (1978). Threatening theories. *Society, 15*(3), 46–49.

Rice, R., Chang, S., & Torobin, J. (1992). Communicator style, media use, organizational level, and use and evaluation of electronic messaging. *Management Communication Quarterly, 6*(1), 3–33.

Roberts, K., O'Reilly, C., Bretton, G., & Porter, L. (1977). Organizational theory and organizational communication: A communication failure? In L. Porter & K. Roberts (Eds.), *Communication in organizations* (pp. 95–117). Harmondsworth, Middlesex, England: Penguin.

Rogers, E. (1985). The empirical and critical schools of communication research. In E. Rogers & F. Balle (Eds.), *The media revolution in America and in Western Europe*. Norwood, NJ: Ablex.

Rogers, E., & Balle, F. (1985a). *Introduction to communication research In Europe and America*. In E. Rogers & F. Balle (Eds.), *The media revolution in America and in Western Europe* (pp. 1–17). Norwood, NJ: Ablex.

Rogers, E., & Balle, F. (1985b). Toward integration of European and American communication research. In E. Rogers & F. Balle (Eds.), *The Media Revolution in America and in Western Europe* (pp. 297–307). Norwood, NJ: Ablex.

Rosengren, K. (1985). Communication research: One paradigm or four? In E. Rogers & F. Balle (Eds.), *The media revolution in America and in Western Europe* (pp. 236–266). Norwood, NJ: Ablex.

Rosengren, K. (1989). Paradigms lost and regained. In B. Dervin, L. Grossberg, B. O'Keefe, & E. Wartella (Eds.), *Rethinking communication. Vol. 1. Paradigm issues,* (pp. 21–39). Newbury Park, CA: Sage.

Sharrock, W., & Anderson, B. (1986). *The ethnomethodologists*. London: Tavistock Publications.

Shields, P., & Rohan, S. (1993). Competing frameworks for research on information–communication technologies and society: Toward a synthesis. In S. Deetz (Ed.), *Communication yearbook/16,* (pp. 349–380). Newbury Park, CA: Sage.

Sless, D. (1986). *In search of semiotics*. London: Croom Helm.

Smeltzer, L. (1993). A de facto definition and focus of management communication. *Management Communication Quarterly, 6*(4), 428–440.

Smircich, L., & Calas, M. (1987). Organizational culture: A critical assessment. In F. Jablin, L. Putnam, K. Roberts, & L. Porter (Eds.), *Handbook of organizational communication* (pp. 228–263). Beverly Hills, CA: Sage.

Steinfield, C. (1992). Computer-mediated communications in organizational settings. Emerging conceptual frameworks and directions for research. *Management Communication Quarterly, 5*(3), 348–365.

Steinfield, C., & Fulk, J. (Eds.). (1987). Theories of organizations and information technology. [Special issue]. *Communication Research, 14*(5).

Sypher, B., Applegate, J., & Sypher, H. (1985). Culture and communication in organizational contexts. In W. Gudykunst, L. Stewart, & S. Ting-Toomey (Eds.), *Communication, culture, and organizational processes*. Beverly Hills, CA: Sage.

Thayer, L. (1986). *Organization — communication. Emerging perspectives 1*. Norwood, NJ: Ablex.

Thayer, L. (1987). *On communication: Essays in understanding*. Norwood, NJ: Ablex.

Tompkins, P. (1987). Translating organizational theory: Symbolism over substance. In F. Jablin, L. Putnam, K. Roberts, & L. Porter (Eds.), *Handbook of organizational communication* (pp. 70–96). Beverly Hills, CA: Sage.

Tompkins, P., & Redding, W. (1988). Organizational communication — Past and present tenses. In G. Goldhaber & G. Barnett (Eds.), *Handbook of organizational communication* (pp. 5–33). Norwood, NJ: Ablex.

Triandis, H., & Albert, R. (1987). Crosscultural perspectives on organizational communication.

In F. Jablin, L. Putnam, K. Roberts, & L. Porter (Eds.). *Handbook of organizational communication,* (pp. 264–295). Beverly Hills, CA: Sage.

Trigg, R. (1985). *Understanding social science.* London: Basil Blackwell.

Tulloch, J. (1990). *Television drama: Agency, audience and myth.* London: Routledge

Vande Berg, L., & Trujillo, N. (1989). *Organizational life on television.* Norwood, NJ: Ablex.

Weick, K. (1987). Theorizing about organizational communication. In F. Jablin, L. Putnam, K. Roberts, & L. Porter (Eds.), *Handbook of organizational communication* (pp. 97–122). Beverly Hills, CA: Sage.

Winkler, K. (1985). Questioning the science in social science: Scholars signal a "Turn to Interpretation." *Chronicle of Higher Education, 30*(17), 5–6.

2

Contrasting Perspectives on Nonpositivist Communication Research

James R. Taylor
Geoffrey Gurd

A highlight of the 38th annual International Communication Association conference, in New Orleans, was a debate entitled *"Resolved: That ethnography is a better way of understanding organizational communication than is critical theory."*[1] In this chapter, we argue that there is what might be called a "debate within a debate": one which pits interpretive research against positivist, and a second, within the interpretive perspective, which opposes ethnographic practices to critical. The chapter is organized into three parts: we begin by examining the factors that explain the rejection of positivism, and the emergence of a trend towards interpretivism; we then present the debate between ethnography and critical theory; and, finally, we offer an alternative explanation. The rejection of positivism, we argue, follows on from the realization that research, from data collection to theoretical interpretation, is a form of translation; positivism has encountered difficulties both because of its reliance on operationalization of variables and its choice of theoretical language. The contrasting points of view within interpretivism can thus be seen as alternative solutions to the problem of translation. The central section of the chapter is in part a literal presentation of the arguments developed in the New Orleans debate and in part a reflection based on it. In the final part of the chapter, we turn to address what we conceive to be a (if not *the*) central question facing communication researchers in the field of organizational studies today: how to reconcile the two perspectives developed in the debate, that is, how to go from micro to macro, and from macro to micro?

---

[1] Speaking for the affirmative were John Van Maanen, professor of organization studies at the Sloan School of Management of the Massachusetts Institute of Technology and author of the recent *Tales of the Field,* and Charles Bantz, associate professor of communication at Arizona State University, while the negative was represented by Dennis Mumby, author of another recent book *Communication and Power in Organizations: Discourse, Ideology and Domination,* now with the Department of Communication at Purdue University and Stanley Deetz, of the Department of Communication, School of Communication, Information and Library Studies, Rutgers University. A similar debate is reported in Hawes, Pacanowsky, & Faules (1987).

The chapter concludes by examining the epistemological problems inherent in communication research, and proposes a reexamination of the problem of scientific objectivity from within a communicational perspective.

THE LIMITATIONS OF THE POSITIVISTIC MODEL OF RESEARCH

The recent awakening of interest among communication researchers in interpretive methodologies such as ethnography and critical theory (Putnam & Pacanowsky, 1983; Frost, Moore, Louis, Lundberg, & Martin, 1985; Lincoln, 1985; Thayer, 1986, 1987) indexes a growing impatience with the strictures of positivism, in all of its manifestations (behaviorism, operationism, functionalism, inductivism, abductivism, logical empiricism, falsificationism, etc.).

Like a well-worn family recipe book, the positivist approach to research once seemed to promise that, providing you followed the steps faithfully, you were guaranteed, if not truth, at least publishability. The recipe went more or less like this:[2]

1. find (a) new variable(s)
2. translate it (them) into indicators
3. develop a test situation and take measurements
4. analyze — statistically — the results
5. write the findings up for publication
6. go back to step 1.

What has kept this version of "normal" science from degenerating into automatism — a kind of plug-in methodology — is what Kuhn (1970) has called its "puzzle-solving" character. Experienced researchers know that to come up with variables that will produce an acceptable signal-to-noise ratio, when the data are analyzed, means developing finely tuned intuitions, based on an intimate knowledge of the literature and at least considerable familiarity with the object of study; the operationalization of variables and the measuring of

---

[2] The oversimplication is deliberate. Of course, modern positivism is not just a "cookbook methodology": To quote Lakatos, (1978), "Popper's 'logic of scientific discovery' is a theory of scientific rationality; more specifically, a set of standards for scientific theories. Originally people had hoped that a 'logic of discovery' would provide them with a mechanical book of rules for solving problems. This hope was given up: for Popper the logic of discovery or 'methodology' consists merely of a set of tentative (and far from mechanical) rules for the appraisal of ready articulated theories. All the rest he sees as a matter for an empirical psychology of discovery, outside the normative realm of the logic of discovery." The criticism of positivism that follows is meant to apply equally to the "modified" version described by Lakatos as well as to the oversimplified "straw-man" caricature outlined earlier.

responses has, in turn, developed into something resembling a cottage industry, mediated by multilateral trading agreements in questionnaire formats, experimental designs, intervention strategies and content analysis schemes, and with the increasing use of computers, statistical analysis aspires to the level of a high art form. Raising grants and getting into the journals are talents all by themselves (Savan, 1988). Social scientists, like their cousins in the physical sciences, can take pride in their hard-won professionalism.

The problem is that thoughtful people in the field have now begun to wonder whether the investment in skill was really worth it — whether the enterprise may not itself have been wrongly conceived.

Behind the practice of the positivist methodology lies, of course, a concept of the nature of society, of knowledge, and of how to access knowledge systematically. Stated crudely, the theory assumes that beneath the superficial confusion, if not chaos, of social life, there lie deep regularities, if only they can be uncovered. Finding the key to unlocking the hidden patterns is equivalent to locating a *system* in them. A system, to quote Ashby (1956), is merely a "list of variables." The *objects of study* are not themselves the systems, if only because "every material object contains no less than an infinity of variables and therefore of possible systems" (p. 39). The scientific method thus boils down to the search for consistency: varying the list of variables until a set turns up that exhibits a "single-valued transformation" (behaves with predictable regularity, in other words). Nature, the positivist must assume, is explicable to the extent that it displays machine-like behavior (Deutsch, 1951, 1963): The trick is to isolate the pattern of behavior in the observable data. What makes a random list a system, then, is its being the *right* list.[3] When there are competing theories as to which is the "real" system, however, the scientist is confronted with a decision as to what qualifies as the *best* description. While such a question has no absolute answer, it is often assumed that, in a probabilistic world, the discipline of statistics is the scientist's best friend. The question as to which is the best list can then be transposed into the determination of which "explains the most variance." This is about as far as positivism can go without becoming embroiled in the contentious issue of competing paradigms (Kuhn, 1962), where statistics as a rationale for choice

---

[3] Cf. Ashby (1952): "Because any real 'machine' has an infinity of variables from which different observers (with different aims) may reasonably make an infinity of different selections, there must first be given an observer (or experimenter); a *system* is then defined as *any set of variables* that he selects from those available on the real 'machine.' It is thus a list, nominated by the observer, and is quite different in nature from the real 'machine.' " A not dissimilar argument is made by Weick & Daft (1983) but in a different context: They claim that the determination of an organization's "real" environment is a function of the questions the organizational decision maker asks. Reality has many faces, all of them equally valid, depending on who is observer.

has no further role to play: Statistics assumes you already know something about the contours of the universe you want to infer to.

The base language of science, in this view, is mathematical—a set of abstract statements that link variables together relationally (although perhaps probabilistically), through the operation of functions (or more generally, mappings or transformations). As mathematical entities, these statements have in and of themselves no referents at all (they are semantically uninterpreted abstractions, in other words) but because mathematics and formal logic stand with respect to each other in a determinate relationship, and because formal logic mimics some of the properties of natural language, it has seemed feasible to turn ordinary natural-language statements about the empirically experienced real world into mathematical statements, and vice versa (Blalock, 1969; Boudon, 1971/1974, 1979; Carnap, 1947/1956; Coleman, 1964; Collins, 1976; Galtung, 1969; Hempel, 1966; Kaplan, 1964; Lave & March, 1975; Quine, 1960; Rapoport, 1953; Simon, 1957; Stinchcombe, 1968; Underwood, 1957; Woodger, 1939).

It is this "translation," on which the whole enterprise of positivist science rests, that has turned out to be the source of its recent troubles, especially where the social sciences are concerned, because the ugly question has been raised as to whether the researchers have been actually engaged in *discovering the system in the phenomena* (as the positivist position must assume)—or simply *giving events a name to fit a preconceived framework or causal construction, or a priori model.* The journey from abstraction to concrete experience and back has proved to be more perilous than anyone predicted. It is no longer even clear that formal logic (and hence mathematical modeling) is the "natural" language of social science.

The positivist approach is vulnerable to two kinds of criticism, which we will call (with apologies to Carnap, 1947/1956) the problems of *extension* and *intension.*

The Problem of Extension

Variables, being mathematical in character, are not measured directly, but must instead be translated into *indicators,* or observable features of reality, such as gestures, answers to questions, transactions, artifacts, and so on, to which a name has been given (towards the goal of categorization). The difficulty with reliance on nominally identified indicators is that ordinary language is infected with fuzziness: Words and expressions, where speech is concerned, are what the ethnomethodologists have taught us (Handel, 1982, citing Bar-Hillel, 1954) to call "indexical" (i.e., they depend on knowledge of context for the determination of their exact meaning).

The operationist is caught on the horns of a dilemma: Resorting to strict behavioral operationism (of the kind which used to be unconditionally advocated by purists such as Underwood, 1957) so cuts down the field of research as to lead to trivialization (if not to complete semantic vacuity), while a more casual operationism produces measures that may reflect less the realities of the social world than the subjective interpretive preferences of the individual researcher, however much they masquerade under a cloak of "inter-coder reliability" or "blind" experimentation.[4] When a batch of studies now ends up producing contradictory findings (as is frequently the case), there is no sure way to decide whether the contradictions are the consequence of undefined variation due to as yet unknown variables (the desirable case, since this can be seen as a stimulus to further research) or simply hermeneutic noise. It is of no help to insist that the "same" questions were asked, or the "same" experimental conditions replicated, because this begs the question as to whether the respondents *heard* the same question, or the subjects *perceived* themselves to be in the same experimental setting. Because research is context-bound, its products are themselves contingent on nonreplicable circumstances: The research act is more relativistic than earlier theorists were prepared to admit. The nature of the communication medium linking the social scientific researcher to informants is such as to forever block an exact imitation of the physical sciences. The latter has no need to try to compute into the interpretation of results the intelligence of the objects he or she studies (since material objects have none) and *their* interpretation of the situation of research (although see Callon, 1986; LaFour, 1994).

At some point, the distinction between science and opinion becomes problematical; what is most evidently left separating them is the positivist rhetoric, perhaps best exemplified by statements about "statistical significance."

The initial assumption of positivism was that, whatever the scientist lost in idiographic richness of observation typical of the "natural" or Darwinian

---

[4] One of the authors recalls having once sat in on a coding session in the context of a content analysis of violence on television. The program being analyzed was a series called "Sanford & Son," starring Redd Foxx, and the theme was what could be plausibly interpreted, under at least one reading, as an affectionate, if not loving, relationship between a man and his grown-up son, although mediated by a running dialogue of mutual insults. In the research project in question, verbal as well as physical violence was recorded. The result was to register "Sanford & Son" as one of the more violent programs on television, a "result" that, for those who recall the show, is likely to somewhat strain our credulity, given the other television fare then available. The point is that, whether or not the researcher was right, and shows like this may be less innocent than they appear, the coding of a "violent" act calls into play, inevitably, assumptions about context and intention that are tied to the circumstances of the act, and depend on the background knowledge of the person doing the interpretive coding. No amount of definition will circumvent the problem, if only because the definitions must also themselves be framed indexically, so that redefining the definitions accomplishes no more than to set one off on an infinite regress (Handel, 1982).

attitude, would eventually be more than compensated for in exactness, and nomothetic generality. Given the apparently insurmountable difficulties of operationalization, this assumption no longer looks so tenable, and the loss of freshness that follows from the adoption of an operation-tied research philosophy appears to be an even more serious impoverishment than it once did. In this respect, social science has something to learn from the experience of artificial intelligence, where it has also become painfully evident that the initial dream of a "general problem solver," using the same logical tools as positivism, has had to be qualified by the recognition that what might be called the "competitive advantage" of natural intelligence over artificial, namely skill in pattern recognition, is not easily captured in systems of formal logic (Dreyfus, 1979; Dreyfus & Dreyfus, 1986). By analogy, the worst knock of all on the positivist approach may be that it has succeeded in blocking the spontaneous pattern recognition abilities of the empirical investigator, to no great end, by filtering the research experience through an artificial apparatus of surveys, experimental and quasiexperimental designs, content analytic schemes, and Q-methodologies, whose combined effect has been to bind — to, in effect, reduce to the state of helpless prisoner — the Gulliver of unaided human intuition within the cords of a lamentably Lilliputian technology.[5] The putative compensating gains in "generalizability" somehow never materialized.

The Problem of Intension

Concepts have *extensions* to the extent that they permit us to refer to, and to classify, the objects in the world around us. They have *intensions* in that they link into a semantic network composed of other concepts with which they share affinities, and from which they are differentiated (Bar-Hillel, 1964; Carnap, 1937, 1956; Quine, 1960). The underlying rationale for the intensional dimension of concepts was initially explicated in its contemporary form by the father of modern linguistics (de Saussure, 1984), who argued that no concept can have any meaning at all until it figures as a component in a network of polar contrasts, and family resemblances, which he called its "associations." How we cut the world up into recognizable objects and events is not unilaterally determined by the universe of external phenomena, as Hume thought, but is a consequence of the paradigmatic *structuring* of the repertory of symbols we use to decode experience. Every culture has its own

---

[5] The good researchers go right on using their normal skills of pattern recognition, all the while doing the right genuflection in their published papers by making sure that they have meticulously (and visibly) followed the methodological canons of their discipline. The gap between actual practice and literary fiction was dignified by Kaplan (1964) under the terms of "logic-in-use" versus "reconstructed logic."

way of carving up the continuum of perceptual and auditory data (Leach, 1964; Tyler, 1969; Whorf, 1956). The semantic system thus produced is *fundamentally* arbitrary, and hence culture-bound. Its roots are historical, not strictly logical. To the extent that we use words at all, we function within a culturally defined semantic matrix.

The scientist is no freer of this straitjacket of language than anyone else, and his or her choice of variables cannot easily be abstracted from it. Innocent-sounding words like "cooperative" and "competitive," "passive" and "aggressive," are like iceberg tips to the semanticist: Their meaning is mostly to be found in their connections ("associations") to an invisible mass of hidden assumptions that informs them and gives them their representational power. Perception is not synthetic, built up little by little out of isolated facts (which is the essence of the positivist method), but is dominated by global metaphorical images of how the world is (Lakoff & Johnson, 1980; Morgan, 1986; Ortony, 1979). It is these metaphors that inform the concepts, and not the other way around (Gregory, 1966). Operationism assumes that the concepts of the theory can be held down to their *denotations,* that is, to their extensional referents, word by word; whether we like it or not, a word, once we start to use it, also takes on *connotations,* which, since they stay unstated, figure in the interpretation of results in a manner that puts them beyond the conscious control of the researcher, however pure the latter's motives may be. This becomes not just uncontrolled, but uncontrollable, variance.

The nub of the problem is the assumed primacy of syntactics over semantics, which the Vienna Circle postulated (and has been reaffirmed many times since, notably by the early Chomsky). Syntactics is concerned with the principles of construction of statements. Positivism *must* employ statements, because statements (of a peculiarly restricted kind, as we shall see) are what can be translated into mathematical form, and ultimately into computations: Quantificational operators (of the so-called "predicate logic") which distinguish between the singular and the general are seen to support the goal of the analyst to infer probabilistically from a sum of individual cases to a population—to move from the particular to the universal, that is, from instances to laws.[6] The difficulty which this poses is that statements, although they *can* be treated, syntactically, as isolates, inevitably also figure as components within larger discursive structures, where they operate as *semantic* functions in a suprasentential combinatorial system (Chabrol, 1973; Dik, 1981; Lévi-Strauss, 1963; Propp, 1958). The domain of semantics envelops

---

[6] Cf. Nagel (1986): "The distinction between more subjective and more objective views is really a matter of degree . . . A view or form of thought is more objective than another if it relies less on the specifics of the individual's makeup and position in the world, or on the character of the particular type of creature he is. The wider the range of subjective types to which a form of understanding is accessible—the less it depends on specific subjective capacities—the more objective it is."

that of syntactics, and informs it. While the exact nature of these overarching semantic units is less than perfectly understood, it seems likely that they are fundamentally narrative in character (Greimas, 1966a, 1966b, 1970, 1973, 1976a, 1976b; Prince, 1973; Taylor, 1978, 1989). As such, their effect is to infuse even the most commonplace statement of fact with a hidden import of value, of normative assumptions about intentionality and cause, and of quasimythical beliefs in the origins of things (Maranda, 1972). By downgrading the importance of the semantic dimension, the positivist engages in a sleight-of-hand: While he or she seems to be limiting explicit claims to (empirically verified) statements of fact, he or she is actually affirming (or reaffirming, really) a belief in the unstated, presuppositional part of the structure from which the sentences are derived, and on which they depend for their meaning. The attempt to bring semantics down to a sentential frame only creates confusion. One cannot even *think* about influence, or persuasion, or aggression without grounding the ideas in implicit semantic structures that transcend the limits of the sentence. When a researcher reports results (in the form of statements) about the success or failure of some interpersonal strategy that has been studied in a particular organizational environment, he or she is always doing much more: He or she is reinforcing an unstated belief in the reality of a narrative universe within which such statements make sense. Sentences, we have come to understand, say more than what they explicitly state (Barwise & Perry, 1983; Garner, 1971; Keenan, 1971; Kempson, 1975): they also affirm their presuppositions!

Let us consider how this semantic "interference" operates, in practice.

The statements that figure in positivist accounts of social reality constitute, to a linguist, a subclass, which describe relations between nominalizations, as in: "Familiarity breeds contempt." There are two problems here. First, nominalization involves a linguistic transformation which serves to *suppress* information (by a deletion transformation), particularly as to the identity of the embedded-sentence subject and direct object. Suppose, in the spirit of positivism, we had set out to discover if "division of labor" serves to increase "solidarity," and in turn encourage "consensus" and discourage "deviance" (Blalock, 1969, Boudon, 1974, both citing Zeterberg, 1965). We are, in other words, in search of a law. We collect data about particular cases, and we summarize the result into statements containing nominalizations. These nominalizations—"division of labor," "solidarity," "consensus," and "deviance"—now hide as well as reveal: They, for example, mask the identity of *who* divided *whose* labor, and *who* was "solidary" with *whom*, and *who* consented or agreed with *whom* and *who* deviated from *what*. The elements in the situation that did not happen to be part of the researcher's focus are all left to our imagination (for more thorough discussion, see Kress & Hodge, 1979). The researcher's implicit theory of society is now more than an organizing principle for the choice of variables: It has become a template to conceal, as well as to reveal. To go from concrete situation to abstract nominalizations is to go beyond summarizing, or inferring. It is to *interpret.*[7]

The second problem is that, while the initial aim of positivism was to make a link between experience (the empirical) and abstraction (the lawful), nominalizations, in the context of a sentence, are *not* just generalizations: they are *functional units in syntactic structures that are informed by semantics.* Nominalizations take on intrasentential functional meanings (Chomsky, 1965) that are *not* part of the positivist program, and subtly corrupt it — a kind of clandestine semantic fifth column operating deep within the territory of logical syntactics.[8] In the positivist system, statements that record actual states and events, with the main actors left in, are not supposed to figure in the explanatory vocabulary of general conclusions. Unfortunately, language does not work this way. Sentences that have nominalizations in their subject and direct object nodes still make attributions which involve a concept of agency, and of actors.[9] It is just that now the *abstractions* have become the "actors."

---

[7] One of the unfortunate side effects of the abstracting procedure is to render much of the social scientific literature on organizations not very useful for actual practitioners. For example, to learn that "in post-industrial organizations the diffuseness of influence on decisions will be greater," or that "the heterogeneity and size of 'formal' decision-making units will be less in terms of personnel but greater in terms of resources" (Huber, 1984) is not very useful to a manager confronted with adapting his/her organization to changing circumstances. Huber's theory of postindustrial organizations *explains* what is happening in general, but is not *predictive* in the particular case. In this respect, he is quite typical of mainstream contemporary positivist theorizing in the domain of the social. Some of the important connections are left unspecified. Whatever else you could say about Newton, at least his mechanics predicted the time of arrival of Haley's comet, exactly. If, as some say (Medawar, 1984), social sciences are weak on prediction, then they may have to be evaluated in terms of their *explanatory,* and not their *predictive,* value. We shall return to this issue later.

[8] The *categorial* meaning of a formative (or word) is fixed across syntactic contexts: It is what we would usually think of as figuring in the dictionary definition; the *functional* meaning of a term is an effect of the placement of the word into the context of a sentence structure: It depends on the matrix of connections which a sentence establishes. Formal logic is also concerned with functionality, in that it also distinguishes between *arguments* and *operators.* The operators are not, however, subcategorized in the same way as the verbs of ordinary language, and the selection restrictions on arguments are quite different. What we are discussing here is the unspecified interference that occurs when statements in ordinary language are translated into statements in "scientific" language. This interference is generally ignored in treatments such as those of Blalock or Boudon.

[9] There are different explanations that have been offered for the phenomenon. For example, Fillmore (1966, 1968) argues that what might be called the "slots" in a sentence (Dik, 1981) are marked by *case;* Gruber (1965, 1967) and Jackendoff (1972, 1983) postulate a system of *thematic relations* which semantically informs syntactic sentence structure; while Halliday (1970, 1976) distinguishes between *grammatical* and *logical* categories, and uses the term "participant functions" to describe what Fillmore calls "case." The problem with formal logic, as it has been used in the positivist lexicon, is that it confounds grammatical and semantic function, and thus fails to capture the intuition that "factual" sentences are in fact conveying more information than they seem to on the surface. In this manner, systematic bias is introduced into the positivist methodology.

"Division of labor" becomes an active force to which we ascribe, at the level of semantic interpretation, intentionality, and even something of a personality, with the result that the (anonymous) people who did the division in the first place take on legitimacy, as mere instruments of an underlying causality. If the "language" of science were *really* restricted to statements such as

$$(\forall x)(\forall y)x \rightarrow y$$

there would be no problem, at least until we discovered that x refers to "division of labor" and y to "solidarity," whereupon we would be tempted to see this as "meaning" that division of labor causes, or leads to, or encourages, solidarity, at which point we have exceeded the positivist mandate to an unmeasurable extent.

There is still a further problem. A linguist would note the absence in the vocabulary of positivism of another kind of sentence, sometimes called a "modal" (Greimas, 1973), which lets us in on the feelings, attitudes, doubts, and needs of the *person making the assertion*. In the positivist universe, the researcher remains a shadowy figure, lurking somewhere behind the screen of abstract nominalizations that his/her method throws up. Again, because something is not said explicitly does not mean it is not thereby said. Ross (1970), for example, argues that all surface sentences are derived from deep structures containing a performative verb (cf. Taylor, 1978). Since deleted elements in a sentence are still present as "traces" (Baker, 1988; Chomsky, 1982; Pollard & Sag, 1987) and can figure in its interpretation (the equivalent in programming is the way a "default" condition works), it follows that even when the researcher is silent about his or her own intentions and attitudes, he or she is still speaking—with the voice of "scientific" authority, as it turns out. It has not gone completely unremarked that such a low profile can be advantageous when the researcher is a comfortable, middle-class professional—not infrequently with a management-paid contract in his or her pocket!

How humans (scientists included) really reason is not captured in the austere syntax of the positivist grammar. The barren language of formal logic is not an adequate instrument for recording scientific knowledge (any more than a computer program can *really* encapsulate an expert's knowledge; cf. Dreyfus & Dreyfus, 1986). Formal logic simply lacks the requisite variety.[10]

---

[10] For one thing, classical formal logic of the sort used in the positivist tradition has no recursive (self-embedding) property, without which its generative potential is severely limited. Barwise & Perry (1983) put it this way: "The importance of situations has been obscured by another tradition stemming from Frege, a tradition we might call semantic holism. This is the idea that in the reference of a sentence, as Frege puts it, 'all that is specific is lost.' This idea has been projected into the very definitions of logical notions that philosophers and linguists grow up with. It has led some to *a perplexing condescension toward most sentence-embedding constructions of language* [emphasis added] and has made the very possibility of a semantics based on situations seem suspect." Of course, the recursive property of language leads to other problems (Hofstadter, 1979).

The insistence on limiting scientific assertions to the emasculated cripples of strict logic is an act of faith, a component in a positivist ideology, with historical roots in a movement within mathematics (led by men such as Boole, Frege, Moore, Russell/Whitehead, Hilbert, Wittgenstein, Brouwer, Tarski, Carnap, Ayer, and Quine). It is not a scientific imperative. The positivist pretension to have built a "purer" scientific language is based on the misapprehension that you can use just a little bit of language, and not all (thus "getting rid" of the unwanted subjective, metaphorical parts). In language as in life, however, it's hard to be just a little bit pregnant!

The Quest for a Better Methodology

Positivist-inspired methodologies have thus come under fire as a result of two kinds of restriction they impose: (a) limitations on what can be recorded in a research situation to what can be justified on the basis of an operationalization of a *priori* variables, and (b) limitations on what is considered acceptable as theory to a collection of statements that can be turned into predicates of formal logic by a simple procedure of substitution.

Not surprisingly, the seeking of nonpositivist approaches has also branched into two lines of exploration—on the one hand, towards a more naturalistic philosophy of data recording with emphasis on the spontaneous insights of the researcher (in a context of emerging goals), and on the other towards a more consciously self-critical investigation of the role of language in the construction of theory and the relationship of the researcher to his or her research. The "new" directions turn out, in fact, to be among the oldest in the social sciences: Both ethnography and critical theory, in one form or another, go back in history about as far as positivism itself. Their historical letters patent (and their predilection for a science based on interpretation) are, however, as we shall see shortly, about all that they share in common. If the decline of positivism marks a "paradigm shift," as some think (Lincoln, 1985), it is assuredly not because its alternative is crystal clear.

THE GREAT DEBATE: ETHNOGRAPHY VERSUS CRITICAL THEORY

. . . And speaking for the affirmative[11]

Ethnographers have a way of disarming you by the simplicity of their account of what they do.

---

[11] The summary that follows is based, by and large, on the presentations of John Van Maanen and Charles Bantz at the New Orleans conference, mentioned earlier. We have, wherever possible, used their own words. The reader should, however, be warned that we have

An ethnography, in John Van Maanen's view of things, for instance, is merely a written account of a culture.[12] It is not a method, or a theory, or a technique, but an outcome, a result. It is (and this is fundamental) based on the first-hand involvement of the researcher in the situation, community or world that he or she describes, normally as a result of prolonged contact with it — a "long stay." The purpose of the account that results from this personal implication is to translate the interests and concerns of one people, one culture, into those of another. The goals of ethnography are always *multiple* — in that the account they write of their experience may aim to evoke, to instruct, to open up, to enlighten, to amuse, to translate, to provoke, even on occasion to sabotage — and highly *situated,* depending as they do on the "unfolding" of a study as it takes place in the field. The accounts of the ethnographer thus reflect the influence of the scene that is being investigated, and the group of people that are trying to be portrayed, but they also index the commitments of the ethnographer, which are by no means always neutral, ranging as they do all the way from trying to give a dispassionate, realistic description of the society being observed (a somewhat dated goal), to being confessional (where the nature of the communicative link to the community studied is the center of the account's concern), to being critical (where culture is perceived by the ethnographer to be a "set of self-congratulatory ideas that a people have about themselves"), to being "redemptive" and even romantic. The conduct of research is thus characterized by an attitude, which, on the whole, tends to be critical of both the culture it describes and the culture towards which it aims its descriptions. The involvement of the ethnographer with the community is, in any case, itself part of the matter of study: Ethnography has a strong tendency to be self-reflective.

The means of ethnography are as seemingly straightforward as its goals: They follow on logically from the mission itself, which is always first and foremost to translate. An adventure in ethnography begins with participant observation, although such a characterization of the ethnographer's method is "more of a definition of the researcher's situation than it is an index of what people really do." The steps that will eventually lead to translation always involve discourse; the conduct of the project is realized in the first place in the form of a dialectic between the researcher and the researched. The ethnographer learns by *dis*orientation, by the "*de*centering" that results from leaving a culture of origin and being plunged into another where the familiar has turned into the strange. Understanding comes through questioning and

---

also taken liberties in rearranging the material, abridging it, and substituting our own version on certain points. In the spirit of their presentation, it would be better to think of this summary as *our* "translation" of what *they* said. This will hopefully absolve Messrs. Van Maanen and Bantz of blame for any infelicities which may have crept into the text and simultaneously let them know that their injunction to put convincing the audience first did not fall on deaf ears.

[12] See also Van Maanen (1988) for an expanded version of his views on ethnography and Van Maanen & Barley (1985) for a discussion of organizational culture.

dialogue, taking the form of a dialectic, in that it involves both the learner and the poeple whose culture the ethnographer wants to come to be able to describe; it does not come from the meticulous combing of library sources, or from deep knowledge of "sacred texts." Ethnography involves talking to people, using a primitive technology which consists mainly of writing materials (pen and paper), and involving a group of people the researcher wants to investigate. It is a "lone wolf," not a collective, enterprise: one person alone amidst others, normally for an extended time (a year or so). It takes place in the ordinary places where people congregate; the offices, the corridors, the factories, the outside locations, the streets, the playgrounds, the cafeterias and the bars — in the world that is studied, that is, and not in the ethnographer's world. And it hasn't changed much, according to Van Maanen, in more than 100 years!

The object of ethnography, it is not to be forgotten, is to publish an account that will be read and understood by as many people as possible — to, above all, convince people that the portrait of the people that are examined is authentic — real. To penetrate, *and be penetrated by,* a particular culture, is the means to that end.

As a discipline, ethnography makes no pretense to stand on a higher plateau of objectivity. On the contrary, it positively rejoices in its biases: It is, to quote Van Maanen, "shot clean through, unavoidably, unmistakably, with historical, political, and cultural mediations and constraints." As for any other kind of activity, ethnographers are products of their history, their time, and their culture. What prevents ethnography from sinking into self-indulgent subjectivism is that it is somewhat, if not indeed obsessively, self-aware of the mediations its practitioners have to deal with. In part this is because the creation of a written account which the people studied can themselves relate to and accept as authentic is to submit oneself to a special kind of discipline whose effect is to force the researcher's attention back onto the interpretive processes which contributed to the description that eventually came into being.

If discussion of methods, in any technical sense, does not figure greatly in the ethnographer's *apologia,* neither does theory, at least not in the usual way. It is not that the researcher does not arrive in the field equipped with theory, says Van Maanen, but rather that not much "makes the round trip." The nature, aims, and direction of what can be studied, when in the field, tend to shift, sometimes slightly, sometimes radically, as a result of the confrontation with a culture which seems to march to a different drummer than the researcher has been used to. The theory the researcher started with tends, at this point, to seem jejune — if not downright naive. Theory, in the sense that an ethnographer is likely to use the term, is more useful after the field work is underway, or even completed. Then it becomes a way of abbreviating, of centering, of organizing and trying to make sense out of data rather than something that had to be tested or something that was used to direct the study beforehand.

It is even tempting to speculate, on the basis of Van Maanen's testimony, that the most consuming methodological questions, for an ethnographer, arise not with respect to data collection, but in how to tell the story that has emerged through the field experience. The ethnographer's goal being to *convince,* what convinces, it can be argued, is neither data, nor theory, but *rhetoric.* The ethnographer is therefore constantly preoccupied with how to write in a way that other people will take as authentic, or meaningful and instructive, or amusing and provoking—to persuade as wide an audience as possible that what they are reading is a faithful description of life as it is lived in some real place, in some real time, by some real people. The power to convince, to an ethnographer, comes down to "getting it right" and getting it right has as much to do with skill in telling a story, in relating events, as it does with what goes into the story. Not surprisingly, therefore, contemporary ethnography seems to be preoccupied with the issue of authorship. The ethnographic researcher, unlike one trained in the positivist tradition, is repelled by anonymity. Instead he or she is more apt to employ Foucault's distinction, to distinguish between authors and writers. Authors, said Foucault, generate a tradition, a way of seeing things and of doing things; writers work inside that tradition. Ethnography is about *insight.* Ethnographers worry about how to concoct the symbols that will best tell a story of a culture, and narrate the life of a society. The theories that interest them sometimes seem to be less theories of society than theories of meaning, of description, and of representation.[13]

The Ethnographic Approach Compared to the Positivist

To compare the ethnographer's way of going about doing research with the positivist's is to discover how important one single assumption can be. The difference is this: *Unlike the positivist, the ethnographer does not believe there is any special, privileged scientific language.*[14]

---

[13] Two recent texts that provide an overview of anthropology's concerns with representation and description are Clifford & Marcus (1986) and Marcus & Fischer (1986).

[14] Although it should perhaps be noted that this has not always been a unanimous, or even the prevailing, view in ethnographic circles; cf. Bateson (1972): "In every case the anthropologist is concerned not with mere description but with a slightly higher degree of abstraction, a wider degree of generalization. His first task is the meticulous collection of masses of concrete observations of native life—but the next step is not a mere summarizing of these data; it is rather to interpret the data in an abstract language which shall transcend and comprehend the vocabulary and notions explicit and implicit in our culture. *It is not possible to give a scientific description of a native culture in English words; the anthropologist must devise a more abstract vocabulary in terms of which both our own and the native culture can be described* [emphasis added]." Bateson's view now

From this one divergence of opinion, all the other differences flow.

For one thing, since the data come to the researcher in the form of ordinary language, and the report is published in ordinary language, it follows that the essence of social science is *translation*. Positivism also involves translation, but it doesn't sound (and indeed *isn't*) the same when it comes out as "operationalization of variables." When the language of reporting is homologous to the statements of formal logic, skill in writing up a report is reduced to mastering the formalisms of a restricted technical language (and hence suppressing the personal style of the reporter). If the language of reporting is natural, then the writing skills of the reporter are all important.

The style of anonymity favored by the positivist tradition makes no sense when everything rests on the authorial presence of the reporter, that is, the skill of the translator. Here again the example of artificial intelligence is revealing: Translation is one domain which resists all attempts to reduce it to machine language, other than for extraordinarily restricted uses. The translator's task depends to an exceptional degree on intuition, on sensitivity to pattern and mood, on skill in composition. It is hard to characterize what makes a good translator, and even harder to isolate the processes that go into translating. The translator must not only understand the host language, down to its finest nuances, but must possess a gift of expression equal to, if not sometimes greater than, that of the source in order to reproduce not just the main sense but the overtones of the original. When the "language" to be translated is a whole culture, the task is even more complex — and even harder to describe formalistically. (Small wonder, then, that ethnographers such as Van Maanen concede that in certain respects their craft partakes more of an art than a science.)

Similarly for the choice of what to observe and to record: If the responses of the informants are to be reduced to the dry language of computation, selection of data sources is dictated by an iron logic; if they are to be reported in natural language, the eyes and ears of the investigator are tuned to those details that are not only typical, but *telling*.

Similarly again when it comes to explanation: If your idea of system is that of a structure of equations, then your attention is focused in one way; if you think of system in more metaphoric terms, then perhaps you should even be using a different term, such as that longstanding favorite in anthropology, "pattern."[15] If your reporting is limited to statements, then you have a very

---

seems dated, and the more naturalistic methodology which Van Maanen describes indexes more than just a change of fashion within a single discipline: It is part and parcel of the rethinking of the nature of research, and the role of the researcher, leading up to the present debate.

[15] It should perhaps be noted that ethnographers such as Van Maanen tend to refer to themselves as "poststructuralists." Anthropology has traversed a long period of fascination with system-ness, although its conception of structure was by no means identical with that of positivism (Boudon, 1968/1971). Much (but by no means all) of this work originated in the study of family, or "kinship," arrangements, and for some time it seemed that there might be some deep

different conception of what you are about than if you think of yourself as telling stories (assuming the latter to be the "natural" unit of ordinary language). It is thus hardly surprising that the theoretical preoccupations of ethnography have latterly begun to center on theories of description and of representation, because ethnography, being all about interpretation (which is just a synonym for translation), can presumably advance in scientific precision only to the extent that it can understand its own analytic imperatives: The finality of the whole enterprise of science being determined by how it reports its results (data collection being a mere ancillary to that ultimate objective). It thus behooves ethnography to understand, they think, what kinds of accounts "count" as acceptable, what kinds do not, and why.

Ethnography, and the learning of how to do it, seems to hark back to the era before Frederic Taylor persuaded the industrializing world that methods of work which are explicitly "scientific" are to be preferred to skills that are passed on by personal example from generation to generation. If the ethnographer talks little about the techniques of research, it seems to be because he or she still adheres to a premodern view that professions are best mastered through apprenticeship. The discipline, in this view, comes not from the fact that the criteria are written down, but rather that in a tight world of professionals everyone can *tell* the difference between who is good, and who isn't. This is a corporatist idea going back to an earlier epoch, an idea which is at a polar extreme from positivism. Logical positivism was historically, we recall, one branch in a stream of intellectual development leading to computerization, and hence to the suspicion that knowledge development will one day end up as just another industrial process.

There is one respect, though, in which positivism and ethnography (or at least the Van Maanen version) do stand shoulder to shoulder: In their passion for the empirical, their belief in the primacy of the experiential, their respect for the situational — and their distrust, verging on phobia, of the abstruse and the theoretically high-falutin'.

The ethnographer has in one sense resolved the problem of extension, since the problem vanishes once the scientist is limited to natural language (whose "extensions" are outright connotative to begin with, and make no pretension to denotational exactness), but by doing so they open up another, which they seem to have only begun to address in what Van Maanen called the "temples" of ethnography, as part of a recent "questioning the way description is done": the problem of intension.

Questioning the way description is done is the lifeblood of critical theory.

---

underlying logic that drives social formations into determinable configurations. This work culminated in the imaginative constructions of Claude Lévi-Strauss (which Geertz, 1983, calls a "higher cryptology"), and now has somewhat petered out (if for no other reason than that no one could presumably hope to emulate such a towering edifice of pure theory more than once a century!)

. . . And Now, Speaking for the Negative[16]

Critical theory runs the risk of appearing to the layman to be as forbidding as ethnography is beguiling. This is not just due to its occasional habit of resorting to obscure language (an inheritance from its philosophical forebears), but also to its message: What it advances clashes (and is meant to clash) with our commonsense notion of how the world is.[17] To put it in a nutshell, critical theory claims that the social fabric of culture that envelops us is not as **WYSIWYG** as we thought: what you see is *not* always quite what you get![18]

Dennis Mumby,[19] for example, quotes Geertz (1973) to the effect that man is "an animal suspended in webs of significance he himself has spun" (and which we would ordinarily think of as his culture). Where Mumby asks us to take leave of Geertz's vision is in seeing the construction of meaning—the spinning of the web—as a social process, and one which exemplifies, and sustains, power relations between different social groups. As he puts it: "After all, a spider's web is not simply an intricately constructed aesthetic product of nature; it is itself a site of struggle. The very existence of the web structures and instantiates a certain script that is played out over and over again in the predatory relationship between the spider and its prey. In the same way, culture is not only an intricately weaved web of meanings; it also functions to instantiate the struggles and conflicts between social groups that underlie those meanings."

The objective of the critical theorist, to stay within the metaphor, is to show how to decode the script of the struggle indexed by the innocent-looking web, on the one hand, and to alert the fly to what is really going on, on the other. The fly, of course, is us (and so is the spider)! The first part of this

---

[16] This section is based on presentations of Dennis Mumby and Stanley Deetz.

[17] The term "commonsense" recalls the ethnomethodological (and phenomenological) preoccupation with what Husserl (1962) called the "natural" attitude, or standpoint: We accept as unquestionable the world of facts that surrounds us. Experience is a consciousness, and of an "intentional" object (i.e., one on which our attention is focused, in a purposive way), and what we are conscious of we quickly come to *take for granted* as just existing. Husserl thought it was possible to suspend belief in the existence of the world out there, by bracketing it. The critical position, in some sense, is an attempt to accomplish such a "bracketing." The object is less to *construct* social reality, than to **de***construct* it, and hence to see it in a new way. The reader will observe that even this crude approximation of Husserl's position illustrates the layman's problem of penetrating a way of thinking that is very different from that which supports everyday speech.

[18] For those interested in pursuing some of the critical approaches, and especially recent attempts to incorporate postmodern theories into organizational studies, see, among others, Hall (1985), Alvesson (1987), Burrell (1988), Cooper & Burrell (1988).

[19] We are again making the attempt to summarize the arguments developed in the New Orleans debate, in this case of the adherents of critical theory, but we have to admit that the task is complicated by what we perceive to be significant differences of emphasis in the presentations of the two members of the side (particularly with respect to the centrality of class). The reader is thus strongly advised to go back to the sources themselves, and in particular Deetz, 1982, 1983, 1984, 1985, 1986, 1992; Deetz & Kersten, 1983; Deetz & Mumby, 1985; Mumby, 1988).

program is thus to develop a "theoretical grounding which makes explicit the interdependence between deep structure power relations and the meaning-configurations that emerge in a given organizational setting" (the making explicit of the link between systems of power and communicative practices being seen as an "act of interpretation" on the part of the researcher). The second is to adhere to "an emancipatory philosophy."

The process of interpretation is not limited to the researcher, however: Interpretation is omnipresent in social life. The goal of the researcher is *not* to produce yet one more interpretation—this one definitive ("an absolute reading"), presumably because it is more "scientific" than the others, which is the goal of positivism—but rather "to draw attention to the act of interpretation itself, and to show how certain dominant 'readings' become incorporated into the meaning of social and discursive practices."

Stated slightly differently, we could think of people as being constantly implicated in making interpretations (which inevitably result in commitments of various kinds) but they don't *see* themselves as making interpretations (in their own view, they are just living). They have no perception of how the business of interpreting in which they are engaged entraps them within configured arrangements where they come out at a disadvantage with respect to others who have got themselves into positions of dominance, and therefore of exploitation. Meaning, argues Mumby, *inevitably* gets played out in the context of power relationships. Giddens, for example, speaks of the phenomenon of "dialectic of control": Merely by virtue of the fact that people enter into relationships with each other, even at the level of the dyad (let alone between people in wider organizational contexts), they also enter into a situation which inevitably comes to be "inscribed and instantiated" by power. The idea of an emancipatory philosophy is to make them understand that this happens: "to create a disjuncture between the social actor and the received, dominant interpretation of events," "to undermine the veneer of a stable, natural reality which positions and fixes the social actor once and for all in a particular relationship to the social formations which s/he inhabits" and "to problematize the act of meaning construction and expose the degree to which dominant ideologies can produce a sense of experiential closure, and hence acceptance of the *status quo*."

In the context of organizational research, as the latter remark suggests, the short-term objective of critical theory is to free us from the tyranny of management-oriented studies which do not allow various interests to be heard from or interpretations to be voiced.[20] "Critical theory . . . is a way of unpacking the management oriented, arbitrary privileging of certain meaning constructions in organizations."

---

[20] This objective harks back to the original mission of the Frankfurt school; adherents saw themselves as critics of administrative ideology, and they have greatly influenced contemporary critical thought.

The validity of research is therefore not to be assessed on grounds of verifiability or verisimilitude, as we expect in more conventional functional frameworks, but is legitimate to the extent that it produces social transformation (which occurs when people become able to engage in self-reflection and can reevaluate their conditions of existence). The business of the researcher in this process is to discover, and point out, "the systematically distorted ideological meaning structures that articulate organizational reality." The ultimate goal of critical theory is *praxis*: "practical action informed by the attainment of both conceptual and theoretical insight."

As all this suggests, critical theory is deeply reflexive in its approach to the study of social phenomena: It is engaged in an *interpretation of interpretations,* and preoccupied with the conditions of social interaction in which interpretation occurs. It is, to quote Deetz, concerned with the relationship between knowledge, and the production of knowledge, and the formation of a community, and the continued development of that community, and how that relationship is founded upon the basis of power and unequal representation of interests.

The Critical Theorist's View of Ethnography

Because it is critical, its aims, and modes, come out most clearly when it is juxtaposed against more affirmative approaches, such as ethnography. Here, for example, is how Deetz sees the dangers in pretending to translate the culture of one society into that of another, through an act of personal authorship:

> While I am sympathetic when I listen to ethnographers, when they say let's interpenetrate the world of our subjects and allow the goals of research to be established in interaction with them, I would nevertheless like to hear what those goals are, and how they are articulated. I would like to see some understanding of the relationship between how knowledge is produced and how meaning is formed in society. It is all too easy to accept the argument that the goals of research are situatioinal, that they arise in the field, that we should not be too quick to determine what the goals of our research are, that we must not presume *a priori* that an organization is this or that until we are in the organization. Unfortunately, it is an argument which falls flat because there is no answer to the question of at what moment and in what way the goals *are* determined. What are the power relationships at play at that moment in the field when the goals are established, for example? At what point do the rhetorical talents of the author, substituting for the sophistication of a method, begin to determine what is being translated from a particular site? Anyone who is effective at speech knows how easy it is for the speaking skill to take over in the determination of what is said. Ethnographers must also know that at times writing *becomes* the method. They must agree how easily skill in expression can be substituted for understanding of the people. I do not see in the case made for ethnography how those two issues

are sorted out, or why it is that the ethnographer's own pressures to get funding for works on projects and to produce manuscripts that are publishable does not enter into that dialog, with the result that translating the culture of one's subjects is equivalent to adding lines to the vita. It is important that we understand at what point and in what way we make the determination of those goals. It isn't enough to say they are "emergent"—that they will emerge in some fashion if only we set out in the field and allow these things to take place.

Critical theory tries to establish what such goals might look like: what we believe to be the relationship between knowledge and social formation and what sort of criteria might be utilized in our understanding of real human situations. How we apply those criteria to make decisions about what we study or report ought not to be based upon the ability to tell a good tale but the ability to participate in a human struggle—a struggle that is not always vicious but is always present—a struggle to engage in the production of meaning, and to participate in the construction of meanings that affect our lives. That is what we get from an emancipatory philosophy: not a doctrine, but rather a touchstone, a guidance, a way of thinking through the real choice-making that a person in the field must make—indeed every researcher must make—in what is, after all, the construction of knowledge.

It is important to recognize that in any organization, no matter how modest, there are real structures of power. That is not to say that power is vicious but it *is* to say that even when power is benevolent it may also be the most destructive. We are not talking about bad people trying to do other people in. We are talking about a managerial logic, a technological way of thinking that engulfs even managers, and traps them into engaging in productive activities and decision-making that at times do not even represent their own interests. We are talking about self-examination, a way of looking into our *own* situation to help us to uncover the kinds of power configurations that exist there. Look at something as simple as engaging in debate. One of the questions that might be asked from the philosophical perspective of critical theory is whether engaging in a debate does not begin to structure issues in such a way as to privilege certain kinds of points of view over others. That to me is a meaningful issue: the conventional debate format is precisely *conventional*, it is arbitrary, it privileges. Academic conferences and conventions, generally, privilege people who engage in work in certain ways. That is something we need to examine, even in organizations as innocent as professional associations.

Consider the ethnographer's concept of text. It is not real people who are represented in the pages of an ethnography—that is an illusion—it is a story. What we want to examine is not simply the story, but at what point the story moves away from the people who are there (and the ability of those people to represent their own interests) and starts to take on a life of its own. A story can of course be very powerful, as a persuasive tale of a human situation. Consider a television program such as "Sixty Minutes." The power of "Sixty Minutes" is a power not simply of representation; it is the power of a documentary tale that misguides and misleads, precisely because it leads us to have feelings about events based upon the presumption that "this is real." But everyone who reflects even minimally upon "Sixty Minutes" knows that "this" is not real. This is entertainment. This is another episode in a struggle for ratings. This is the attempt to acquire an audience, for a corporate author to take on *authority*. Its authority is not an equally distributed authority, nor is any ethnographer's tale. Every story is from a point of view and represents an interest. Our point is that the representation of interest itself ought to be made thematic. The ethnographer's tale, like "Sixty Minutes," ought to be put forward for examination based upon what types of power configurations and interests become represented, embedded, and reproduced in such a tale. It is precisely the belief, which is the rhetorical ploy of the ethnographer, that the tale is real, and natural, that hides from us the fact that there are alternative tales, that there are interests not being represented. If we were to accept Van Maanen's position, we would conclude that the successful ethnographer is precisely the ethnographer who keeps us from seeing, who stops us from telling more tales, from being able to produce counter-narratives representing different types of interest, from having access to the plurality of voices that always exist where human beings interact together.

It is not that the critical theorists are psychotherapists of a special sort. Nor is it that the public is self-duped. We all of us struggle to gain self-understanding. We struggle to gain that understanding against the power relationships in which we must work. We do that as individuals; we do that as a public. Without historical self-understanding, we do not understand ourselves. We do not understand what meanings we are producing and reproducing. We do not know what we as real people are doing. It is not that we are crazy and in need of therapists; it is that we are human and exist in very complex cultural and power relationships. Those power relationships are difficult to sort out. It is incredibly difficult to understand privilege, whether it be something as trivial as a recency–primacy effect or the way we engage in conventions and even more difficult yet when we look at people trying to find careers in organizations. We spend the majority of our lives and gain a substantial part of our identity working in organizations. It is important for us to understand what we are doing therein in terms of the production of a sense of identity, the production of decisions, and in the production of products. All of us know that power relationships are significant in organizations. We know that. That's trivial. What is not trivial is trying to understand the place of those power relationships and the effect that they have and the manner in which they are produced in stories within organizations, produced within the culture—*and reproduced by ethnographers presenting stories from the field.*

The notion of deep structure is an attempt to understand what underlies and generates the social production of meaning. Each of us has theories that are generative: they structure our conceptions, our ways of looking and thinking about issues. The critical theorist is saying "Let's look at the structure of those theories that we have as human beings, that we have as researchers, and see how they participate in the structure of meaning. We must critically examine those theories in the light of power relationships and in the light of the representation of interests, if anyone is to have a voice." It is not to say that we want to privilege the critical theorist's voice, but that critical theory gives us an opening to remove the centering of any one voice so that every voice may come to understand itself and articulate its needs in a social context. If ethnography can show that it is a part of the critical task, if it can enhance self-understanding, then it has succeeded. But an ethnography that does not understand what self-understanding is, and that cannot talk about the conditions under which self-understanding is produced, and the way that self-understanding either perpetuates or changes social relationships, fails. That's the question we are left with. I do not give you missionary zeal; I give you an idea that we ought to be guided in the manner in which we do research by a concern for power relationships and the representation of real people's interests in real life situations. That's what we are struggling to do.

In Rebuttal: "The Empirical Strikes Back"

The essence of the *différend* separating the two schools is shrewdly articulated by Charles Bantz as follows:

> The thing we object to is the *presumptive position* which the critical theorist takes. The critical theorist argues for "allowing voices" to be heard; they say there should be no special privileging of any meaning construction in an organization. But are we to believe that it is the critical theorist who is in a position to go into an organization and somehow "allow" voices, which presumably have no ability to express themselves because they are oppressed, to be heard?
>
> The flaw with critical theory is that it seeks precisely to privilege a particular set of meaning constructions that are those of the critical theorist's rather than those of the participants in the organization. There is an orthodoxy involved in their argument that is built upon texts, and upon *texts,* and upon **texts.** The result is, on the one hand, an absence of authorial voice — who is it that is doing the writing? — and on the other a missionary zeal which says we have the texts, we are taking them to the people, and with our texts we will emancipate them. The difficulty with this is the notion that the people involved do not have the ability to accomplish that, that these people cannot examine and express their own voice. In spite of the presumptive relationship between the critical theorist and the organization, there is an absence in their writing of organizations, of people and of communication. It *is* possible that there are voices in organizations which find difficulty in expressing themselves, but we take exception to the presumption that is that the critical theorist who is necessary to emancipate them. Critical theory has positioned itself away from the organization, away from communication and away from the real activity. Surely, in studying communication and organizations, we need first of all to be aware of them. We need to be involved in them. We have never denied that critical approaches can be useful. We deny the critical theorist positioning himself at a point which says only he is privileged to decide.

Van Maanen's rebuttal is even more blunt, and considerably more colorful!

> The point about text is that we get the holy trinity, which right now seems to be Habermas, Dilthey and Gadamer, replacing Marx, Weber and Durkheim, and God knows who it will be in the future. The theory changes, and the authorities change, with the fashions. It's channeling for Habermas, or for Giddens:

translating what Giddens has written, translating what Habermas has written, for us poor *hoi polloi*. We are told there is deep structure, hidden and unseen, which is apparently supposed to index some non-obvious property of social life. But the issue is not the deep structures of power . . . No ethnographer worth their salt could do their work without talking about the structures of power and the distribution of influence inside and outside organizations. . . . The issue is the subterfuge that there is a grand theory at hand. . . . The gods can talk together, we are supposed to believe, the meta-theorists can talk together and carry on conversation that is useful. But those theorists had better not talk to the people out there. Because the people don't know what they are saying. It takes a theorist to understand what they are saying. That's an olympian conceit, hard to match anywhere in the social sciences.

We are not talking here about theory, but about ideology, for which the sweeping statements of the critical theorist are but a disguise. Ideology is something we can accept and embrace, or we can reject, as we see fit, but that is not how it is presented to us. Instead it's passed off as a theory. "Hegemony"! "Domination"! There's a codebook at work here. When you see "hierarchy," that indexes "domination," when you see "specialization," that's "dispersement of interests" or "exploitation of labor," when you see "automation," the code says "de-skilling." You read the codebook, and the ideology is clear. It's cold, it's chilly, it's "emancipatory"—and it's offputting! There isn't much fireworks: there's no presentation of a real world. It's an airless, closed system, a bloodless telling. We had all better look out. Here come the critical theorists, along with the missionaries, and the O.D. people! They're out to change us, to make us better, to take us back to Lake Woebegone! . . . It's a Wizard of Oz world: remove the curtain and the little wizard will be revealed. Somehow the structures of domination, and of signification, will instantly be changed merely by revealing that they exist. Well, as we all know, that's a fairy tale.

So Whose Position is Really "Presumptive"?

It can hardly have escaped the reader's notice that each side's rebuttal of the opposing position is a mirror image of the other's: Each accuses the other of having tried to occupy a "presumptive position," to use Bantz' expression. From the point of view of critical theory, it is the ethnographer who "presumes," through the intervention of an "authorial" voice, to interpret a culture. This blatant glorification of the authorial voice seems to the critical theorist to be a regression to pure romanticism: a reincarnation of Byron in Greece! On the other hand, to the ethnographer, the presumption of the critical theorist comes in abrogating to him/herself the right to pass judgment on the act of interpretation itself, as if he or she had privileged access to some overreaching "higher" wisdom of what makes an interpretation right or wrong. Each is concerned with interpretation, but they see it from different standpoints. Unsurprisingly enough, therefore, each accused the other during the debate of being on the side of the missionaries. The debate did in fact turn on the issue of power — the power of the researcher, or who should have the last word.

The debate thus leaves us, the audience, with a question: How are we as practicing communication researchers to evaluate its outcome, and its meaning for us?

There is no easy answer to that question, but in the concluding part of this essay on method, we offer one view, our own, on the issue, for whatever it may be worth.

AN ALTERNATIVE CONCEPTUALIZATION
OF THE INTERPRETIVE PERSPECTIVE

"Organization/Communication": The Odd Couple

The phrase "organizational communication" incorporates, we argue, a choice of perspectives, from which no one working in the field is exempt: It cannot be wished out of existence. The difference between an ethnographic approach to the study of organization, and one based on critical theory, is not therefore a mere accident of history, nor will it eventually disappear as fashions change, and the influence of Goffman, Geertz, and Garfinkle, on the one hand, or Foucault, Gadamer, and Habermas, on the other, fades from the forefront of intellectual history. The labels may evolve; the need to choose will remain.

What we would ask you to consider are certain semantically linked couples, which together form a system, and, we believe, underlie the present debate.

The first such couple is *structure/process*. Notice that, with respect to time-dependent phenomena, there is really no way to assign logical priority to either of these two concepts, because each figures in the definition of the other. A *structure* is the "manner in which a building or organism or other complete whole is constructed" (the Concise Oxford Dictionary) or the "manner of building, constructing, or organizing . . . the arrangement of all the parts of a whole" (Webster's New World Dictionary). When the "whole" to which these definitions refer is in the sphere of the dynamic, then the "manner of constructing or organizing" is a process. A *process*, on the other hand, is a "course of action, proceeding, esp. method of operation in manufacture, printing, photography, etc.; natural or involuntary operation, series of changes" (the Concise Oxford) or "a continuing development involving many changes: as, the *process* of digestion . . . a particular method of doing something, with all the steps involved" (Webster's New World). In other words, what turns a chaotic sequence of events into a *process* is its structured-ness (its "method"); on the other hand, in the world of the dynamic, where the pattern of an object unfolds over time, there can be no structure without process: The *structure* of something can hence be perceived only as an abstraction, that is, the manner in which the interacting parts of something (a conversation, for example) are composed to form a whole.

The couple *language/speech* (or *langue/parole,* in de Saussure's classic formulation) has a parallel structure. What makes speech more than just a sequence of random sounds is the structure which supports its production (which linguists have traditionally formalized as a "grammar"); a "language," however, is a collectively owned property which has no existence other than in its expression through speech.

The couple *organization/communication* is of the same order.

An organization does not exist in the realm of the physical: It can be neither seen nor heard, touched nor smelled—directly. Its existence is made known to us indexically, through its artifacts: the buildings it occupies, the symbols that give it its name, the documents that mention it, the people who carry out its rituals and costume themselves according to its norms. Nobody doubts its existence, even where their experience of it is mediated by their communicative experience—and by nothing else. Everybody accepts uncritically the *idea* of organization, and governs his or her own life on the assumption of its reality, even though all they know of it, in the concrete, is what can be gleaned from their daily communicative experience.

On the other hand, to enter into communication is to become organized. Communication *necessarily* (by definition even) involves precedence: coming before and coming after, in the simplest of cases; precedence, as Jay Haley has pointed out, is the basis of hierarchy (Haley, 1976). To come before and to come after, in a regular way, is to be organized.

This idea, that communication and organization are not so much different things as different ways of thinking about the same thing, is not new. As far back as 1916, for example, Dewey (1916/1944) wrote as follows: "Society not only continues to exist *by* transmission, *by* communication, but it may fairly be said to exist *in* transmission, *in* communication."

When von Neumann and Morgenstern (1964) published their theory of games (a game being one mode of communication), they distinguished beween a game in its *extensive* form (where its processual naure, with its many stages, taking the form of choice points, is emphasized) from a game in its *normal* form (where the resulting structure of an ongoing competitive/cooperative relationship is made to stand out) or its *canonical* form (where the structure involves more than two participants in some form of coalition).

Similarly, until at least the time of Allport,[21] social psychologists saw *attitudes* and *behavior* as making up a couple: Behavior being but the visible

---

[21] Cf. Allport, 1935: "An attitude is a mental and neural state of readiness, organized, through experience, exerting a directive or dynamic influence upon the individual's response to all objects and situations with which it is related."

manifestation of the latent tendency to react in a certain way in a certain situation (attitude), and *vice versa*. Even though later, in the 1950s, psychologists began to decontextualize the idea of attitude, by making it a property of cognitive formation, rather than of communicative readiness, this movement, as Steiner (1974) has pointed out, was merely part of the more general detaching of behavioral social psychology from its situational moorings; more recently, people who study behavior *in situ* have been trying to reinstate the link (by observing, for example, the different behavior, and by implication *attitude*, manifested by police officers towards recalcitrant rubbydubs, depending on whether or not there is an audience present at the time of the interaction) (Handel, 1982). One way of viewing an organization, indeed, is simply to see it as a constellation of attitudes, which people learn and which they themselves take to be the way to guide the performance of whatever "roles" they see themselves as carrying out in the organization, which is therefore simultaneously a constellation of behaviors.[22]

Similarly, economics also employs a distinction between a "micro" (i.e., transactional, or process-based) and a "macro" (i.e., institutional, or structure-based) perspective.

Two Modes of Theorizing: Micro → Macro versus Macro → Micro

There is no *a priori* reason to privilege the concept of "organization" over that of "communication," or, in other words, a "macro" approach over a "micro" (or vice versa). One vision of reality is intrinsically equal to the other. The consequences of one way of proceeding versus the other are, however, monumentally important when the question is how to do research. This was what the New Orleans debate was all about. There is a choice to be made, macro → micro, or micro → macro. What we want to explore here are the

---

[22]Putnam and Stohl (1988) note the tendency to think of groups as if they were "containers." In this view, people are either in or not in, a not very realistic conceptualization. The classical sociological theory of roles suffers from much the same disability. Putnam and Stohl point out the difficulties in delineating any one consistent definition of a "group"; exactly the same problem is to be found in definitions of "role." These definitional difficulties are reminiscent of Wittgenstein's discussion of a "game": He shows that a "game" is not a single unitary phenomenon but instead stands for a family of ideas. Treating concepts such as "group" and "role" in the same manner, as a family of ideas, seems to us to be a productive way to go. If we thought of being part of a group, or taking on a role, in the same frame as playing a game, we would avoid many conceptual traps: People are simultaneously members of many groups, and play many roles, without experiencing dissonance. A main advantage of this change of perspective is to transform our idea of organization away from that of a rigid set of roles (or job descriptions) such as we might expect in a conventional organization chart, and toward the more fluid, and realistic, notion of an interlocking set of attitudes underlying the manifest behaviors to be observed in actual organizational communication.

consequences of going in one direction versus the other—selecting, in other words, which is to be *figure,* which *ground*: communication or organization.

Macro→Micro: From a Theory of Organization to the Study of Communication

Since organizations are abstract objects,[23] we can access them only through conceptualization—in effect by metaphor. Morgan (1986) has put together an inventory of the several ways by means of which theorists have tried to capture the essence of "organization." In this century, particularly, the machine metaphor has had a good run, both in its pristine precybernetic version and later as a theory of "adaptive systems," where the kind of emergent structure is seen to be "contingent" on the nature of the "environment." Other models of organization have borrowed from the biology of organisms, and the psychology of the human brain. Whichever metaphor is chosen, there is one thing common to all these conceptual approaches: a commitment to discovering in the empirically-discovered communication patterns of people in organizations evidence of their organizational "function," as required by the model. Weber's ideal-type of a bureaucracy had everyone memoing and speaking to each other in buttoned-down, laconic monotones *(sine ira et studio).* The classical theorists had people "following channels." The school of contingency theory had communicational style varying with environmental uncertainty. The cyberneticists developed putative (and complicated) information-flow networks. And the critical theorists, if we are to credit their opponents in the Great Debate, see the exercise of power and the exploitation of interests manifested in the littlest of eyeblinks.

What this risks leading to is tautology.

Consider the notion of power.

Power is a property of organization, not of communication. It is an abstraction, a nominalization, a way of catagorizing the observed communication reality of precedence, by putting a label on it. This means that its identification, in concrete circumstances, depends on how the observer has conceptualized power to begin with, and thus in turn on his or her *image* of organization. When two observers, who start with different images, or who are living out different roles, now look at an actual sequence of interaction, they may make different attributions of the power relationships exemplified therein, precisely because their starting model of organization was

---

[23] Which does not make them less real: It was Whitehead who seems to have introduced the notion of a "fallacy of misplaced concreteness" (i.e., the fallacy of arguing that relations between objects are less real than the objects themselves).

different.[24] Let us suppose that the *participants* to the interaction perceived there to have been consensus achieved, while the *observer* considered the consensus to be an illusion and to mask an underlying "deep" structure of exploitation, and hence of exercise of power. The latter may therefore speak of "false consensus" (Mumby, 1988). What is he or she now to do? If he or she were to intervene, and to substitute his or her interpretation of the transaction (by whatever means, such as persuasion, involving a re-*presentation* of the episode), the result would not be just to have given precedence to one image of the situation (the observer's) over another (the participants') but to have thereby instated a new relationship of power, this time involving the participant and the observer(s), and a *relationship of power, furthermore, as defined by the observer's own image of what a power relationship is*. The circularity is complete.

In the language of the Palo Alto school, the effect of such an intervention, should the observer be tempted into it, would be to create *a double bind:* To say to someone "emancipate yourself" is thereby to render emancipation impossible, since the effect of the injunction is precisely to create a dependence of the emancipatee on the emancipator (Watzlawick, Beavin, & Jackson, 1967). This is the emancipatory paradox. The critical theorist is now him/herself, furthermore, caught in a double bind: To be silent is to be inconsistent with one's own philosophy, but to speak is to contradict it!

This is not a difficulty which inheres in the reflexive position as such (what might be called, to coin a phrase, the "Gödel trap"), but one which follows from the *combination* of thinking in a reflexive mode *and* the decision to adopt an *a priori* notion of organization, and hence of power, of class, and of interest. Once you have decided that power is present in communication, you are bound to find it, and nobody can contradict you, because you have defined it that way. But it does mean that the researcher, in pointing out hegemony, is therefore made guilty of reinstating hegemony, even by his or her own definitional terms!

Gramsci's problem does not yield itself up to easy solution.

The difficulty with *macro→micro* approaches is that there is no possible way to disconfirm them: Since an organization is an idea which exists in the realm of the abstract, we can perceive it only through a conceptual filter, which is what not only structures our image of it, but also provides us with the categories by means of which to decode our practical experience. Power, for example, is not a property of process, but of the inferential structure underlying process. Whenever we know what we are going to find ahead of time, our research ends up reinforcing our prejudices. What we understand

---

[24] The example of the coding of "Sanford & Son," cited earlier, is relevant in this context.

the ethnographers to be pleading for is fewer prejudices to start with. That strikes us as a reasonable wish.

Micro → Macro: From the Study of Communication to a Theory of Organization

But we now confront a new difficulty.

Ethnographers tend to study society in the small. Suppose they are right. Suppose that organization is actually a local phenomenon: a structuring of communication patterns in the essentially face-to-face situations ethnographers most often report on. Formal communications in *large* complex organizations, in this view, would consist of those exchanges, written or spoken, whose function is to *sustain the illusion* of an overarching structure, but their effect would be largely ceremonial: presidential announcements largely ignored, or reinterpreted in practice, and accounting systems where what is reported and what actually happens are so different as to index a generalized phenomenon of recoding, all leading to an uncoupling of senior management (caught up in its own political games) from the hurly burly of daily organizational life at the lower levels. What makes this world work is what Weick (1976, 1982), borrowing from Ashby (1956/1979), calls its "loose coupling": The residual ambiguity of a loosely-coupled system allows the reality and its symbolic representation to coexist more or less harmoniously even in the face of the most flagrant contradictions.

There is a good deal of evidence in favor of this view. If it is right, this would provide at least a *prime facie* justification for a largely theory-free ethnography of *local* practice (by and large its main preoccupation).

However, the ethnographer risks being caught as certainly as the critical theorist in a dogmatic trap, for suppose that organization is *not* strictly a local phenomenon: In this case, a description of local practice would be as artificial as any other representation, since it has escaped the Scylla of too much theory to be dashed upon the Charybdis of not enough. (It is surely reasonable to believe that organization transcends the strictly local. Otherwise, how would we explain that a police station, even allowing for local idiosyncrasies, operates pretty much the same in Duluth as it does in Saskatoon or Ocala, or indeed in Coventry and Helsinki and Osaka.) The difficulty which confronts the theory-hostile ethnographer is how to take account of the higher-order regularities that appear when organization in the large is considered. Are we not supposed to try to capture that greater pattern in our scientific net?

Ethnography, from the outside, has often appeared ambivalent on the question of theory. When we listen to a Van Maanen plead eloquently for a moratorium on theorizing, for example, it is difficult not to recall that he represents the same discipline that produced a Radcliffe-Brown, a Goodenough, and a Lévi-Strauss. It is hard not to suspect him of being a member of a generation in reaction against the previous overemphasis, in his own field, on theories (which he calls its "proud towers") — a generation that would like to get back to an earlier, less sophisticated, and more authentically American tradition of native — and *naïve* (in a good sense) — empiricism. And it is difficult not to suspect that just because he now publicly abjures theorizing, this does not mean that he has really given it up!

The ambiguity arises because of the notion of "theory" itself. We would like to suggest that there is a way of thinking about Theory (with a capital letter, that is; not "theories," in the plural) that clears up the confusion. The argument turns on the notion of situation. The researcher in the field finds him/herself in a situation. Indeed, it can be argued that reality always consists of situations (Barwise & Perry, 1983): We are in them, we see them, and we have attitudes toward them. What gives the situation meaning is the ability of the person in it to see *relations* between the situation he or she is now in, and other situations with which he or she is already familiar, or to perceive, as Barwise & Perry (1983) put it, "uniformities across situations." When ethnographers began to study other cultures, for example, one of the things they concentrated on (Barnes, 1971) were extended families (known, technically, as "kinship systems"), precisely because they already had a notion of family, and it was easy in a strange environment to pick out variations on a pattern with which they were familiar. Theory building takes off when the researcher starts pulling out of real situations, across the range to which he or she has been exposed, directly or indirectly, *invariants,* or *uniformities:* This is a conceptualization which is based on the recognition of individuals, properties/relations, and locations that seem to vary systematically across situations, and thus lead the observer, progressively, to a notion of *abstract* situations (Barwise & Perry, 1983). At this point, theorization always runs the risk of developing an existence autonomous of the data, and we understand Van Maanen to be reacting to exactly this tendency in anthropology, where the exquisite abstractions of a Lévi-Strauss, bringing to its culmination a half-century of classification of kinship systems, left mere observation far behind, and soared into the conceptual stratosphere. It is important to note, however, that there never was a point of *no* theory. Indeed, all that theory is, in the sense we are using the term here, is the set of notions of situation that we already possess (for most of us, consisting of abstractions based on ordinary experience, inherited within our own culture) which permit us to pick out from a new situation that which is meaningful, or informative. As each of us enlarges our experience, we also enlarge the repertoire of situations we have to draw on that allows us to explain what is now before us: This is what gives the experienced professional his or her competitive advantage, in ethnography as in chess. Reading the meaning of a situation is an act of coding, and information is what we extract from the situation that allows us to translate it into our own available set of interpretations (Bateson, 1952; Dretske, 1981).

Theory, therefore, is simply the language of representation of situations made available to us to encode experience. Positivist theory would have had us postulate a kind of Newtonian universe of forces and material causes (now so out-of-date that even the physical sciences have relegated it to the periphery of their concerns), into which we were supposed to code our data. Neo-Marxist theory still concentrates on a situational image in which the appropriation of the means of production, and the structuring of classes, figures large. The ethnographer simply uses the models of situation with which he or she is familiar as a result of a life experience to decode his or her own participant observation of a strange society. But that's not to be theory-free.

To concentrate on direct observation is not, indeed, to be inoculated against the maladies of theorization. Some of the problems of kinship study arose, it is well to recall, not because of too much abstract theorization, but because the field investigators oversimplified to fit the data into their own ideas of family (Schneider, 1984). Similarly, although Van Maanen cites with approbation Margaret Mead as one of the ethnographers who could write convincingly about societies she had visited (and it is certainly true that Mead was a teller of tales of great talent), it is no longer clear that her first, and most famous, "tales" really illuminated so much the society she visited, Samoa, as they did the society she came from, and its preoccupations with eugenics, the "nature/nurture" debate, the changing character of relations between the sexes, and with sexual behavior generally, in a post-Freudian world. Her tales, it has even been argued (Freeman, 1983), were really driven by theory and it was, paradoxically enough, their *theoretical* content, striking as it did a chord in the society of the time, which explains their popularity, and not their narrative beauty: The fact that her stories were not explicitly represented to the public as theory did not make them less so. The result was not to reveal Samoan society to us, but to hide it behind a new kind of romantic screen, as surely as Paul Gauguin did for Tahiti, and Dorothy Lamour for the rest of the South Seas islands, however different her intention and methods, and hence to turn our attention away from the larger world trends enveloping all these societies, part of a transformation too great to be understood through the lenses of a set of small-scale studies of individual "cultures."

All science ultimately faces a double challenge: how to investigate phenomena too small to be seen with the naked eye, and too large. We are concerned here with the "too large," or perhaps the too complex. It is a problem that cannot be solved in the social sciences by manufacturing telescopes. To observe complexity in the social world requires instead what de Rosnay (1975) calls a "macroscope" — which is another way of saying "theory." The problem with studying *organizations* empirically, using the ethnographic approach, is that our conclusions have to be based on the testimony of a set of people, *each of whom has only a partial view of the whole.* To put together a set of individual perceptions, each biased by the limitations of its singularity of point of view, into something resembling a coherent unified picture, is not just a matter of shrewd observation: Like the blind man encountering an elephant, the organizational analyst is inevitably reduced to relying on theory (in the absence of which his or her conclusions are restricted to treating organization in its local manifestations). Large organizations are not simply constellations of small organizations. They have a pattern that cannot be directly apprehended, but must be divined by imagination. Their complexity, furthermore, is achieved through an abstracting process which is played out in their communications. It is not just that we have to rely on abstractions to visualize them, but that the abstracting was what went into their making (Callon & Latour, 1981). They can thus only be understood through the use of models which take account of the abstraction process. This, to us, is the Achilles heel of the ethnographer: his or her suspicion of the kind of theory which explains structures that are real, even though they are abstract. What the physicists have taught us is that without theory you sometimes can't even see the world in front of your face.[25] Social science is pretty much in the same fix.

The issue, though, is what kind of theory.

The Epistemological Bias of Communication Theory

We claim that communication theory has a unique role in the playing out of the tension between macro and micro perspectives.

All social scientific knowledge (indeed perhaps all knowledge) is gained through the resolution of a single problem (Nagel, 1986): "how to combine the perspective of a particular person inside the world with an objective view of that same world, the person and his viewpoint included." How that problem is attacked determines what kind of science we are dealing with. *Micro/macro* is a variant on the theme of *subjective/objective*.

A typical way of proceeding, in the broad positivist tradition of the social sciences, has been to ask a sample of individuals, chosen at random from a population, to report on their perspectives (through answers to questions— possibly, but not necessarily, as a result of being placed in a controlled experimental framework). The passage from "perspective of a particular

---

[25] Einstein is quoted (Campbell, 1986) as comparing a physicist's knowledge about the world to an attendant in a cloakroom who can read a number on a ticket, and know it matches a number he or she already holds, and can thus use it to retrieve a coat, even though there is nothing about the number that has the property of "coatness." Einstein was thus emphasizing the indispensable role of theory in the scientific endeavor. To understand organization, theory is also necessary, and for the same reason. The data do not provide their own explanation. The problem of the ethnographer seems to be exactly opposite to that of the physicist: The empirical is *too* present.

person inside a world" to "objective view of that world, the person and the viewpoint included" is then accomplished by the use of the probabilist calculus, on the grounds that each observation represents an *independent,* autonomous personal view on an essentially *shared* collective experiential world. The independence of the sampled perspectives is a *sine qua non* of inquiry, in that without it statistical analysis encounters such technical difficulties as to threaten the validity of the whole operation. The parametric assumption of a fixed, commonly accessible reality (such as a television program), combined with that of subject heterogeneity, is what validates the computation of indices such as the population mean and variance.

This manner of conducting research is founded on the assumption that (a) people are subjects, and (b) society is an object composed of a set of individuals, each characterized by properties, the links between them being transsubjective. The *process* by which (a) is transformed into (b) is taken to be summation (commonly called "induction"). In this research tradition, inherited from (a) psychology (a theory of subjects) and (b) sociology (a theory of individuals as social objects), a process of communication is assumed, but not in general explained.[26]

In organizational communication research, the conventional subjective-to-objective logic breaks down. For one thing, perspectives are not multiple and autonomous; they are intrinsically interrelated, in a manner analogous to a figure/ground relationship: One person's opinion becomes the background against which another's is made visible. The reported perspective of someone in an organizational setting—the data in a conventional project—cannot be treated like some freelance news report from a foreign correspondent—the cool testimony of a mere visiting observer; It is part of an *accommodation,* a *functional element* in a *system* of perspectives. The "freelancer" (or organizational informant, to bring the language closer to home) must now be seen to be, not an uninvolved outsider, but someone reporting on a situation which is in part the outcome of his or her own presence. Organizations are not external to the individual in the same way as a television program. *The organization is created in the very act of reporting on it.* Research, for example, which reports by giving attributions of causality, based on the positivist model of separation of the observer from the object observed, is subverted because the attributions are themselves a component in an organizational perspective.[27] To take a sum of

---

[26] The network theory of communication is one attempt to reconcile the two levels of object abstraction: the nodes being taken to be equivalent to the subjects, the pattern of links to the society, and the "messages" to the communication process which serves to translate one into the other. Networks models thus trivialize the problem of perspectives (Taylor, 1993).

[27] This was the dilemma of the human relations school of management: Their attributions of the sources of employee motivation became a source factor *contributing* to employee motivation as soon as their interventions were interpreted to be an instance of "management manipulation" (Meyer, 1977).

perspectives en route to an evaluation of population parameters, is, in these circumstances, to embark on a nonsense operation, however sophisticated the computational mechanics. The world is "shared" in a quite new sense, in that one member's perspective constitutes the environment for another, so that while the perspectives certainly complement each other, they do not do so additively. They *interact*. That interaction is an *intrinsic* part of organizational reality, and not merely a correctable deviation from the norm. At this point, collecting data on individual perspectives is a starting point for the conduct of research quite different from the positivist model. Communication theory comes at the subjective/objective (and hence micro/macro) dichotomy in a new way.

To begin with, it assumes that, to quote Nagel (1986), "The distinction between more subjective and more objective views is really a matter of degree."

Subjective and objective are seen to be poles of a continuum, not a binary dichotomy. Such an assumption begins to make sense as soon as we realize that the subjective is not a Cartesian experience ("I think, therefore I am") that *precedes* communication, and is then *subsequently* conveyed by it to contribute to an objective view, but rather that, as George Herbert Mead argued, the subjective *and* the objective are both born in the act of communication, and continually regenerated within it. In this view, *both* the individual and the society emerge in communication; Neither predates communication. This is not to claim that all human experience is comprehended by what passes within communication; there are, for one thing, flashes and feelings that never get captured in language (or any other medium of communication), and on the other, a vaguely intuited access to a larger reality that forever eludes our capacity to state in words. All we claim is that the phenomenal experience of the individual does not *become* "subjective" until it is expressed in communication (and thus translated into language). It is still inchoate. What we can claim as *objective* knowledge is also constrained within the bounds of the communicational universe. We claim further that this subjective/objective recreation is not something incidental to the communication act — a kind of by-product — but intrinsic to it: The nature of the language medium is such that the subjective point of view cannot possibly be expressed except as a counterpoint to the objective, and *vice versa*. We can't practice our tennis against a backboard without a backboard, but a backboard only becomes a backboard through its capacity to structure the subjective experience of hitting a ball. Similarly, we struggle to formulate an expression which will "objectify" our subjective experience; and as we do, we frequently encounter the response "I think what you mean to say is . . ." Our subjectivity emerges in communication; it is not autonomous of it. Conversely, every subjective experience comes to be framed within what the individual takes to be the objective reality of his/her situation and that again is determined only as a counterpoint to the subjective experience. All thought is framed in the language of dialogue. All organizations, great and small, have their origin in the ebb-and-flow of conversation. We struggle to build both subjective and objective knowledge as part of a single process: The "me-generation" (preoccupation with self) emerged concurrently with the "it-generation" (the triumph of science and technology).

The interpretive approach to research, as we see it, constitutes a break with a logic which must assume, as positivism does, a *well-defined frontier* between the universes of the subjective and the objective. Because philosophy itself, like the traditional social sciences it supported, never had a proper theory of communication — and, conversely, held to a theory of knowledge that was noncommunicational — its realization in formal logic perpetuated a fallacy, and it is this fallacy which is at the heart of the positivist dogma.

Practically speaking, in organizational research, the transition from "more" subjective to "more" objective, which is the task of science, is one which more closely resembles the enterprise of someone doing a jigsaw puzzle than it does an exercise in statistical analysis. For one thing, the researcher is confronted with the issue of *intersubjectivity,* which is to say understanding how representations of the world function within a universe where they both affect and are affected by other people's perspectives. The individual subjective experiences can only be turned into an objective view of the whole by discovering the pattern in them, and a pattern which takes account of the context-dependent, or situated, nature of representation.

Towards Theoretical Triangulation

What then can we learn from ethnography and critical theory (and indeed positivism)?

In one sense, the Great Debate was not really about communication at all. It was yet one more skirmish in a long war of attrition pitting one branch of sociology against another: one (often called *Anthropology*) that studies *other* societies, even where the "other" society being studied is a subculture of our own, and another (called *Sociology*) which studies our *own* industrial society, but from a particular point of view, sometimes known in the past as *dialectical materialism.* The debate was a confrontation of images, one centered on *culture,* the other on *praxis.* Both schools have absorbed a great deal of what we have learned in the past generation or so about the way symbolic systems work, including their recursive property, and can thus talk in a sophisticated language *about* communication, but neither is principally concerned *with* communication, as such.[28] Communication, to both, is the arena in which the social drama gets played out.

---

[28] The functionalist branch of social theory was not more helpful. It may be true, to use Simon's (1957) formalization of Homans as an example, that the "level of interaction" in an organized group affects and is affected by its "cohesiveness," which in turn affects and is affected

As communication researchers, on the other hand, our task is to understand, to document, and to develop theories about how interaction is configured, how it exemplifies the commitment-making process that leads to and supports social formation, how it is represented in the symbolic descriptions we use to account for it and to create a world of meaning for ourselves, and how it relates to the constraints of work, as the world goes about its tasks. To this end, we can learn from both critical theory and ethnography, and even positivism.

We can benefit, for example, by giving the critical position an attentive hearing on the issue of how meaning is constructed. In every science but ours, it makes some kind of sense to think of our observational tools and our instruments of measure as a (perhaps imperfect) window interposed between us and what we want to understand, since the object of study can be presumed to exist independently of the perceptual filter. In organizational research, however, what we study has been created by the very instrumentation that we use to study it. An organization is not a physical object, but a *logical* one. How we structure the set of interactions which compose the organization depends on how we conceptualized an interaction to start with. We structure *interaction* using the same logical procedures that we use to structure our *representation of interaction*. Critical theory renders us an inestimable service in reminding us that the making of *organizations* and the making of *theories about organizations* are part and parcel of the same process: Business schools don't just study organizations—they invent them!

We should consider organization, in other words, not as a container within which communication occurs, but as itself a communication structure whose patterning (unlike for the lower animals) is not just a matter of sequence, to be discovered by observation, but involves a complex interaction between doing and representing: It is reflexive.

Critical theory should, however, leave us skeptical to the extent that it is only a means by which to slip the metaphor of class relations in by the back door.

Similarly, we need to continually bear in mind that communication occurs within a culture, is sustained by it, and expresses it. If nothing else, the ethnographers have rendered us an immense service by calling into question the legitimacy of the organizational metaphor—any metaphor, so long as it is not grounded in observation. In so doing, they brought qualitative research methods back into vogue, since the use of quantitative methods, it may not

---

by the "degree of uniformity" of its opinions, but to describe organization using variables such as "level of interaction," "cohesiveness," and "degree of uniformity" is to describe the *products* of communication, and *not the communication itself*. One reason the study of process languished after promising initiatives in the 1930s and 1940s (Steiner, 1974) was that positivism was an inappropriate language for communication science.

have been noticed, supposed that we already understood what organizations were. We too have to start by looking. *Really* looking. Not just "collecting data." Our task is equally the construction of pattern, through a procedure of discovery that depends greatly on intuition and creativity.[29]

We may even want to take a fresh look at positivism, but in a different way. Positivism, beginning with Comte, borrowed a claim of the physical sciences (McMullin, 1988) to have eliminated the distinction between "explanation" and "prediction." The social sciences have not fared well in prediction: Even economics and experimental psychology, on the most charitable reading, have at best a mixed record of success. Were we now to unhook explanation from prediction, positivist research would then become just another branch of interpretivism. How to compare the *explanatory* powers of positivist theory, as opposed to its predictive, against other interpretive alternatives, is a question which does not seem to us to have a cut-and-dried answer: The interpretive advantage of conventional positivist science resides in its capacity to formalize. Mathematics, as a tool of abstraction, continues to have considerable advantages over commonplace conceptualizations. Intuition and theory stand to each other in a dialectical relation. Where we are weak, in the communication sciences, is on the side of theory.

Social science used to make much of the virtues of "methodological triangulation," but methodological triangulation assumed that we already knew how to frame explanations. Perhaps the time has come to sing the praises of "theoretical triangulation," in that the discovery of better explanations of the communicational basis of organization is the challenge we now face.

A POSTSCRIPT

Positivism has been getting it in the neck lately. Given its long run, we can be perhaps pardoned for sparing our sympathy. Newtonian-inspired models of society no longer inspire us, and formal logic has lost its magic in an era when a logic machine sits on almost every desk. But before we discard it as a weathered relic of a bygone era, we should remember that positivism was born as a reform movement, in reaction against the tyranny of theories whose justification was limited to the prestige of the people who voiced them. The best-known work of Karl Popper, the man who did the most to make positivist

---

[29] Modern rationalism arose in opposition to an older, Aristotelian theory of science, which took as its starting point intuition, schooled by experience (McMullin, 1988). The social sciences seem to be returning to something like this original idea, which was, it should recall, most strongly rejected by the sciences of the physical, whose reasoning positivism imitated (Benton, 1977).

science dominant in America (although he was apparently not himself a charter member of the Vienna Circle, nor even in full accord with its precepts, cf. Lakatos, 1978, Feyerabend, 1981), was, after all, entitled *The Open Society and Its Enemies*. Whatever its faults, positivism enjoined us to always test our ideas against experience, and when there was a discrepancy between the two, to change the ideas to make them fit the reality and not the other way round. Positivism taught us to be skeptical of totalitarianism, in all its forms. That is perhaps a message which we would do well not to forget, as we set about exploring alternatives to it. If there is one conclusion that can be drawn from the Great Debate, it is that *no* theory now offers a complete solution to our problems, or is likely to in the near future. The conduct of research, like most activities, has to be guided by a measure of common sense, an ongoing commitment to act responsibly and a certain trust in our own professional judgment — none of which are factors that can be ever quite inscribed into a formal system.

REFERENCES

Allport, G. W. (1935). Attitudes. In C. M. Murchison (Ed.), *Handbook of social psychology* (pp. 798–844). Worcester, MA: Clark University Press.

Alvesson, M. (1987). *Organization theory and technocratic consciousness*. New York: De Gruyter.

Ashby, R. (1960). *Design for a brain*. London: Chapman and Hall. (Original work published 1952)

Ashby, R. (1979). *An introduction to cybernetics*. London: Methuen & Co. Ltd. (Original work published 1956)

Baker, M. C. (1988). *Incorporation: A theory of grammatical function changing*. Chicago: The University of Chicago Press.

Bar-Hillel, Y. (1954). Indexical expressions. *Mind, 63*, 359–379.

Bar-Hillel, Y. (!964). *Language and information: Selected essays on their theory and application*. Reading, MA: Addision–Wesley.

Barnes, J. A. (1971). *Three styles in the study of kinship*. Berkeley: University of California Press.

Barwise, J., & Perry, J. (1983). *Situations and attitudes*. Cambridge, MA: Bradford Books/MIT Press.

Bateson, G. (1972). Social planning the concept of deutero-learning: A comment on Margaret Mead's "The comparative study of culture and the purposive cultivation of democratic values." *Science, philosophy and religions, Second symposium*. New York: The Conference on Science, Philosophy and Religion. Reprinted in *Steps to an ecology of mind*. New York: Chandler. (Original work published 1942)

Benton, T. (1977). *Philosophical foundations of the three sociologies*. Boston: Routledge & Kegan Paul.

Blalock, H. M., Jr. (1969). *Theory construction*. Englewood Cliffs, NJ: Prentice-Hall.

Boudon, R. (1971). *The uses of structuralism* (Originally published in French under the title *A quoi sert la notion de structure?*) London: Heinemann.

Boudon, R. (1974). *The logic of sociological explanation*. Harmondsworth, Middlesex, England: Penguin. (Original work published 1971)

Boudon, R. (1979). *La logique du social*. Paris: Hachette.

Burrell, G. (1988). Modernism, postmodernism and organizational analysis 2: The contribution of Michel Foucault. *Organization Studies, 9*(2), 221–235.

Callon, M. (1986). Some elements of a sociology of translation: domestication of the scallops and the fishermen of St. Brieuc Bay. In J. Law (Ed.), *Power, action and belief* (pp. 196–233). Boston: Routledge & Kegan Paul.

Callon, M., & Latour, B. (1981). Unscrewing the big Leviathan: How actors macro-structure reality and how sociologists help them to do so. In K. Knorr-Cetina & A. V. Cicourel (Eds.), *Advances in social theory and methodology: Toward an integration of micro- and macro-sociologies* (pp. 277–303). Boston: Routledge & Kegan Paul.

Campbell, J. (1986). *Winston Churchill's afternoon nap: A wide-awake inquiry into the human nature of time*. New York: Simon & Schuster.

Carnap, R. (1937). *The logical syntax of language*. London: Routledge & Kegan Paul. (Original work published 1934)

Carnap, R. (1956). *Meaning and necessity: A study in semantics and modal logic*. Chicago: University of Chicago Press. (Original work published 1947)

Chabrol, C. (Ed.). (1973). *Sémiotique narrative et textuelle*. Paris: Larousse.

Chomsky, N. (1965). *Aspects of the theory of syntax*. Cambridge, MA: MIT Press.

Chomsky, N. (1982). *Some concepts and consequences of the theory of government and binding*. Cambridge, MA: MIT Press.

Clifford, J., & Marcus, G. E. (1986). *Writing culture: The poetics and politics of ethnography*. Berkeley, CA: University of California Press.

Coleman, J. S. (1964). *Introduction to mathematical sociology*. New York: The Free Press of Glencoe.

Collins, L. (Ed.). (1976). *The use of models in the social sciences*. London: Tavistock.

Cooper, R., & Burrell, G. (1988). Modernism, postmodernism and organizational analysis: An introduction. *Organization Studies, 9*(1), 91–112.

Deetz, S. (1982). Critical interpretive research in organizational communication. *The Western Journal of Speech Communication, 23*, 139–159.

Deetz, S. (1983). Keeping the conversation going: The principle of dialectical ethics. *Communication, 7*, 263–288.

Deetz, S. (1984). The politics of the oral interpretation of literature. *Literature in Performance, 4*, 60–64.

Deetz, S. (1985). Critical–cultural research: New sensibilities and old realities. *Journal of Management, 11*(2), 121–136.

Deetz, S. (1986). Metaphors and the discursive production and reproduction of organization. In L. Thayer (Ed.), *Organization ↔ Communication: Emerging perspectives* (pp. 168–171). Norwood, NJ: Ablex.

Deetz, S. (1992). Democracy in the age of corporate colonization: Developments in communication and the politics of everyday life. Albany: State University of New York Press.

Deetz, S., & Kersten, A. (1983). Critical models of interpretive research. In L. Putnam & M. Pacanowsky (Eds.), *Communication and organizations: An interpretive approach* (pp. 147–171). Beverly Hills, CA: Sage.

Deetz, S., & Mumby, D. (1985). Metaphors, information, and power. *Information & Behavior, 1*, 369–386.

de Rosnay, J. (1975). *Le macroscope*. Paris: Editions du Seuil.

de Saussure, F. (1984). *Cours de linguistique générale*. Paris: Payot. (Original work published 1916)

Deutsch, K. (1951). Mechanism, teleology, and mind: The theory of communications and some problems in philosophy and social science. *Philosophy and Phenomonological Research, 7*(2).

Deutsch, K. (1966). *The nerves of government: Models of political communication and control*. New York: The Free Press of Glencoe. (Original work published 1963)

Dewey, J. (1944). *Democracy and education*. Glencoe, IL: The Free Press. (Original work published 1916).

Dik, S. C. (1981). *Functional grammar*. Dordrect, The Netherlands: Foris Publications.

Dretske, F. I. (1981). *Knowledge and the flow of information*. Cambridge, MA: Bradford Books/MIT Press.

Dreyfus, H. L. (1979). *What computers can't do: The limits of artificial intelligence.* New York: Harper Colophon. (Original work published 1972)

Dreyfus, H. L., & Dreyfus, S. E. (1986). *Mind over matter.* New York: The Free Press.

Feyerabend, P. K. (1981). *Problems of empiricism* (Philosophical Papers, Volume 2). Cambridge, London & New York: Cambridge University Press.

Fillmore, C. J. (1966). Toward a modern theory of case. In Reibel & Schane (Eds.), *Modern studies in English.* Englewood Cliffs, NJ: Prentice-Hall.

Fillmore, C. J. (1968). The case for case. In E. Bach & R. T. Harms (Eds.), *Universals in linguistic theory* (pp. 1–90). New York: Holt, Rinehart & Winston.

Freeman, D. (1983). *Margaret Mead and Samoa: The making and unmaking of an anthropological myth.* Harmondsworth, Middlesex, England: Penguin.

Frost, P. J., Moore, L. F., Louis, M. R., Lundberg, C. C., & Martin, J. (1985). *Organizational culture.* Beverly Hills, CA: Sage.

Galtung, J. (1969). *Theory and methods of social research.* New York: Columbia University Press. (Original work published 1967)

Garner, R. (1971). "Presupposition" in philosophy and linguistics. In C. J. Fillmore & T. D. Langendoen (Eds.), *Studies in linguistic semantics* (pp. 23–44). New York: Holt, Rinehart & Winston.

Geertz, C. (1973). *The interpretation of cultures.* New York: Basic Books.

Geertz, C. (1983). *Local knowledge: Further essays in interpretive anthropology.* New York: Basic Books.

Gregory, R. L. (1966). *Eye and brain: The psychology of seeing.* New York: McGraw-Hill.

Greimas, A. J. (1966a). Éléments pour une théorie de l'interprétation du récit mythique. *Communications, 8,* 34–65. Republished by Éditions du Seuil in 1981 under the title *L'analyse structurale du récit.*

Greimas, A. J. (1966b). *Sémantique structurale: Recherche de méthode.* Paris: Larousse.

Greimas, A. J. (1970). *Du sens: Essais sémiotiques.* Paris: Éditions du Seuil.

Greimas, A. J. (1973). Les actants, les acteurs et les figures. In C. Chabrol (Ed.), *Sémiotique narrative et textuelle* (pp. 161–176). Paris: Larousse.

Greimas, A. J. (1976a). *Sémiotique et sciences sociales.* Paris: Éditions du Seuil.

Greimas, A. J. (1976b). Entretien avec A. J. Greimas sur les structures élémentaires de la significatioin. In F. Nef (Ed.), *Structures élémentaires de la signification* (pp. 18–26). Paris: Presses Universitaires de France.

Gruber, J. S. (1965). *Studies in lexical relations.* Doctoral dissertation, Massachusetts Institute of Technology, Cambridge, MA.

Gruber, J. S. (1967). *Functions of the lexicon in formal descriptive grammar.* Santa Monica, CA: Systems Development Corporation.

Haley, J. (1976). *Problem-solving therapy.* New York: Harper Colophon.

Hall, S. (1985). Signification, representation and ideology: Althusser and the post-structural debate. *Critical studies in mass communication, 2*(2), 91–114.

Halliday, M. A. K. (1970). Language structure and language function. In J. Lyons ed., *New horizons in linguistics* (pp. 140–165). Harmondsworth, Middlesex, England: Penguin.

Halliday, M. A. K. (1976). *Halliday: System and function in language.* (Selected papers edited by Gunther Kress). London: Oxford University Press.

Handel, W. (1982). *Ethnomethodology: How people make sense.* Englewood Cliffs, NJ: Prentice-Hall.

Hawes, L., Pacanowsky, M., & Faules, D. (1987). Approaches to the study of organizations: A conversation among three schools of thought. In G. Goldhaber & G. Barnett (Eds.), *Handbook of organizational communication* (pp. 41–53). Norwood, NJ: Ablex.

Hofstadter, R. (1979). *Gödel, Escher and Bach: An eternal golden braid.* New York: Basic Books.

Huber, G. P. (1984). The nature and design of post-industrial organizations. *Management Science, 30*(8), 928–951.

Husserl, E. (1962). *Ideas: General introduction to pure phenomenology,* (W. R. B. Gibson, Trans.) New York: Collier. (Original work published 1931)

Jackendoff, R. S. (1972). *Semantic interpretation in generative grammar.* Cambridge, MA: MIT Press.

Jackendoff, R. S. (1983). *Semantics and cognition.* Cambridge, MA: MIT Press.

Kaplan, A. (1964). *The conduct of inquiry: Methodology for behavioral science.* San Francisco: Chandler.

Keenan, E. L. (1971). Two kinds of presupposition in natural language. In C. J. Fillmore & T. D. Langendoen (Eds.), *Studies in linguistic semantics* (pp. 45–54). New York: Holt, Rinehart & Winston.

Kempson, R. M. (1975). *Presupposition and the delimitation of semantics.* New York: Cambridge University Press.

Kress, G., & Hodge, R. (1979). *Language as ideology.* Boston: Routledge & Kegan Paul.

Kuhn, T. S. (1970). *The structure of scientific revolutions.* Chicago: University of Chicago Press. (Original work published 1962)

LaFour, B. (1992). *Aramis: ou l'amour des techniques.* Paris: La Découverte.

Lakatos, I. (1978). In J. Worrall & G. Currie (Eds.), *The methodology of scientific research programmes* (Philosophical Papers, Volume 1). Cambridge: Cambridge University Press.

Lakoff, G., & Johnson, M. (1980). *Metaphors we live by.* Chicago: University of Chicago Press.

Lave, C. A., & March, J. G. (1975). *An introduction to models in the social sciences.* New York: Harper & Row.

Leach, E. (1964). Anthropological aspects of language: Animal categories and verbal abuse. In E. H. Lenneberg (Ed.), *New directions in the study of language.* Cambridge, MA: MIT Press.

Lévi-Strauss, C. (1963). *Structural Anthropology.* New York: Basic Books.

Lincoln, Y. S. (Ed.). (1985). *Organizational theory and inquiry: The paradigm revolution.* Beverly Hills, CA: Sage.

Maranda, P. (Ed.). (1972). *Mythology: Selected readings.* Harmondsworth, Middlesex, England: Penguin.

Marcus, G., & Fischer, M. (1986). *Anthropology as cultural critique.* Chicago: University of Chicago Press.

McMullin, E. (1988). The shaping of scientific rationality: Construction and constraint. In *Construction and constraint* (pp. 1–47). Notre Dame, IN: University of Notre Dame Press.

Medawar, P. (1984). *The limits of science.* New York: Oxford University Press.

Meyer, M. (1977). *Theory of organizational structure.* Indianapolis: Bobbs-Merrill.

Morgan, G. (1986). *Images of organization.* Beverly Hills, CA: Sage.

Mumby, D. J. (1988). *Communication and power in organizations: Discourse, ideology and domination.* Norwood, NJ: Ablex.

Nagel, T. (1986). *The view from nowhere.* New York: Oxford University Press.

Ortony, A. (Ed.). (1979). *Metaphor and thought.* New York: Cambridge University Press.

Pollard, C., & Sag, I. A. (1978). *Information-based syntax and semantics: (Volume 1) Fundamentals.* Stanford University: Center for the Study of Language and Information.

Prince, G. (1973). *A grammar of stories.* The Hague and Paris: Mouton.

Propp, V. (1958). *Morfologija Skazki* [Morphology of the folktale]. Bloomington, Indiana: Indiana University Research Center. (Original work published 1928)

Putnam, L., & Pacanowsky, M. (1983). *Communication and organizations: An interpretive approach.* Beverly Hills, CA: Sage.

Putnam, L., & Stohl, C. (1988, May/June). *Breaking out of the experimental paradigm.* Paper presented at the 38th Annual Conference of the International Communication Association, New Orleans, LA.

Quine, W. V. O. (1960). *Word & object.* Cambridge, MA: MIT Press.

Rapoport, A. (1965). *Operational philosophy.* New York: John Wiley & Sons. (Original work published 1953)

Ross, J. R. (1970). On declarative sentences. In R. A. Jacobs & P. S. Rosenbaum (Eds.), *Readings in English transformational grammar* (pp. 222–272). Waltham, MA: Ginn.

Savan, B. (1988). *Science under siege.* Montreal & Toronto: CBC Enterprises.

Schneider, D. M. (1984). *A critique of the study of kinship*. Ann Arbor: The University of Michigan Press.

Simon, H. A. (1957). *Models of man*. New York: John Wiley & Sons.

Steiner, I. (1974). Whatever happened to the group in social psychology? *Journal of Experimental Social Psychology, 10*, 94–108.

Stinchcombe, A. L. (1968). *Constructing social theories*. New York: Harcourt, Brace & World.

Taylor, J. R. (1978). *A method for the recording of data and analysis of structure in task groups*. Doctoral dissertation, Annenberg School, University of Pennsylvania, Philadelphia, PA.

Taylor, J. R. (1993). *Rethinking the theory of organizational communication: How to read an organization*. Norwood, NJ: Ablex.

Thayer, L. (Ed.). (1986). *Organization↔Communication: Emerging perspectives I*. Norwood, NJ: Ablex.

Thayer, L. (Ed.). (1987). *Organization↔Communication: Emerging perspectives. II*. Norwood, NJ: Ablex.

Tyler, S. A. (Ed.). (1969). *Cognitive anthropology*. New York: Holt, Rinehart & Winston.

Underwood, B. J. (1957). *Psychological research*. New York: Appleton–Century–Crofts.

Van Maanen, J. (1988). *Tales of the field: On writing ethnography*. Chicago: The University of Chicago Press.

Van Maanen, J., & Barley, S. (1985). Cultural organization: Fragments of a theory. In P. J. Frost, L. F. Moore, M. R. Louis, C. C. Lundberg, & J. Martin (Eds.), *Organizational culture* (pp. 31–54). Beverly Hills, CA: Sage.

Von Neumann, J., & Morgenstern, O. (1964). *Theory of games and economic behavior*. New York: John Wiley. (Original work published 1944)

Watzlawick, P., Beavin, J. H., & Jackson, D. D. (1967). *Pragmatics of human communication: A study of international patterns, pathologies, and paradoxes*. New York: W. W. Norton.

Weick, K. (1976). Educational organizations as loosely-coupled systems. *Administrative Science Quarterly, 21*(1), 1–11.

Weick, K. (1982). The management of organizational change among loosely-coupled systems. In P. S. Goodman (Ed.), *Change in organizations: New perspectives on theory, research and practice* (pp. 375–408). San Francisco: Jossey–Bass.

Whitehead, A. N. (1925). *Science and the modern world*. New York: MacMillan.

Whorf, B. L., & Carroll, J. B. (Eds.). (1956). *Language, thought and reality: Selected writings of Benjamin Lee Whorf*. Cambridge, MA: MIT Press.

Woodger, J. H. (1939). *The technique of theory construction* (Volume II, Number 5, Foundations of the unity of science). Chicago: The University of Chicago Press.

PART II

Sensemaking In Organizations:
Two Views

3

Tacit Knowledge, Self-Communication, and Sensemaking in Organizations*

Dennis A. Gioia
Cameron M. Ford

At its essence, life in organizations is fundamentally a sensemaking experience. Attempts to impute meaning to events, to fit day-to-day incidents into some structure of understanding, to sustain a workable interpretation of potentially important occurrences — in short, to make sense of one's experience — is arguably *the* central concern of organizational life. Although people are often unaware of their own sensemaking processes, such processes are pervasive, ongoing, and neverending. Sensemaking is a complex endeavor involving the self in a reciprocal exchange with other organization members, contexts, and situations, and it is both the process and product of the construction of meaning for organizational events. Moreover, these personally and socially meaningful interpretations of "what's going on" are guides to action in organizations. Thus, sensemaking holds a prominent place in any attempt to understand the nature of organizations and the experiences and actions of the people who comprise them.

How is sensemaking accomplished? Perhaps not surprisingly, communication, in its myriad forms, constitutes the main means by which people make sense of organizational life (see, for instance, Gioia, Donnellon & Sims, 1989; Putnam & Pacanowski, 1983). In many ways, sensemaking is an interpersonal communicative process: One negotiates the construction of meaning with other organization members (cf. Blumer, 1969; Goffman, 1967; Nonaka, 1994; Ritti, 1986; Weick, 1995). Yet not all understanding is developed in this way. Other important aspects of sensemaking that have been notably underattended in the study of organizational communication and behavior involve *intra*personal phenomena such as intuition, introspection, affective reflection, and other forms of self-communication.

---

* We would like to thank Don Ford and Dean Gioia for helpful comments on a previous version of this chapter.

When such processes are taken into account, sensemaking is seen as a personal as well as an interpersonal phenomenon. In this chapter we will concentrate almost exclusively on the personal, individual aspects of sense-making. We do so, in part, because work on sensemaking has been dominated by social interactionist views. Despite their obvious relevance, these views have tended to overshadow the significance of internal experience. As a consequence, the importance of individual processes has been either obscured or underplayed in treatments of sensemaking in organizations.[1]

Some of the internal communication processes with which we will be concerned involve the active, conscious manipulation of knowledge and information. Other self-communication processes, however, employ knowl-edge that is "tacit" and not easily available to active consciousness. For our purposes, *tacit knowledge* is abstracted, personal knowledge that cannot be brought *directly* into active awareness.[2] An exploration of the structure and process of such knowledge demonstrates why it is so difficult to bring these tacit understandings into conscious awareness. Yet it also suggests methods of communicating-with-self that can permit organization members to adapt, improve, and exploit this vast store of knowledge in their sensemaking and action taking. To state our overarching thesis and to preview the architecture of our argument, we can summarize our basic position as follows:

A significant element of sensemaking is accomplished by using tacit personal knowledge. Such knowledge is retained in the form of cognitive structures (schemas) that have been developed on the basis of experience and learning. Once such experiential knowledge becomes organized and abstracted into schematic form, it can no longer be represented directly in active consciousness. Understanding and action are then accomplished by "automatic" information processing. To more actively manage one's own sensemaking and action taking (by guiding the conscious alteration of existing knowledge structures) requires that one be able to access one's own tacit knowledge. Using self-communication techniques, organization members can not only gain access to, but also some

---

[1] We adopt this individually oriented position while recognizing that sensemaking nonetheless occurs within, and is substantially influenced by, the social milieu (i.e., individual exprience occurs within a setting that has social, organizational, and cultural history, as well as immediate social influence). Thus, the individual human experience can never be divorced from the social context (just as the social context cannot be divorced from individual experience). Nonetheless, an explication of the individual processes can provide insight into the *internal* experience of the individual sensemaker within the social context.

[2] There exist a number of differences in the use of the term "tacit knowledge." The major distinctions can be noted according to whether the term refers to personal or social knowledge that is typically unavailable to active consciousness (à la Polanyi, 1958, 1966; Garfinkel, 1967) or to context-specific knowledge that is not explicitly taught, but is "picked up" through experience (Sternberg & Wagner, 1986). In addition, popular usage suggests that it is knowledge that people have, often know they have, but rarely talk about for personal or political reasons. In this paper we are concerned predominantly with tacit knowledge in the former sense.

influence over, this storehouse of personal knowledge that usually operates out of conscious awareness.

Given that managers and other creative decision makers in organizations often talk about the accomplishment of work in terms of intuition, instinct, insight, and instantaneous judgment, it is evident that they make sense of situations using cognitive processes of which they are not fully aware (Ford & Gioia, 1995). Organization members know that they do not always engage in "rational" decision processes, but they do not know quite *how* they do it. We will attempt to show that processes such as intuition are based on "legitimate" knowledge and information processing and that these cognitive processes are essential to sensemaking.

This chapter, then, is devoted to an exploration of tacit knowledge and sensemaking in organizations, with particular attention focused on the role of self-communication processes. The purpose of self-communication is not only to aid self-sensemaking and understanding, but also to guide active learning about the structure of one's own tacit knowledge, with the goal of changing it to facilitate more effective organizational action.

SENSEMAKING

A straightforward but not so simple question arises as a consequence of our initially stated position: What do we mean by sensemaking? From one perspective it is simply the recognition that people in organizations are more or less constantly engaged in explicit or implicit attempts to understand what is happening around them. For the most part, events usually occur pretty much as they always have, expectations are thus confirmed, and no novel action is required. The existing implicit understanding of experience sustains some previously arrived at understanding, and organizational life goes on in the accustomed fashion. Only when some event occurs that violates expectations is explicit action necessary (whether active thought, emotional response, or behavior). Under these conditions, active, conscious attempts to establish an altered sense of the situation are engaged (Weick, 1995).

Of course, because these explicit attempts to understand one's experience are relatively few and far between, it often appears that sensemaking is a fairly rare activity. However, sensemaking and social comprehension depend as much on the reaffirmation of an existing construction of reality as on the reconstruction of reality. For that reason, sensemaking is perhaps more accurately understood as an ongoing, even continual activity. Indeed, everyday life in organizations is a repetitively re-enacted "accomplishment," wherein a given interpretation is either implicitly sustained or explicitly revised via some form of communication or negotiation (Donnellon, Gray, & Bougon, 1986; Garfinkel, 1967; Handel, 1982).

Fundamentally, sensemaking involves an individual or group's effort to impute *meaning* to experience. Given that the creation of meaning is a notably human phenomenon and is never intrinsically attached to any object, information, event, or action (but rather is ascribed by people), the meaning ascribed might vary considerably across individuals. Sensemaking, then, concerns the ways that organization members engage in the creation of meaningful understanding. Thus, we can note that sensemaking *is* meaning construction (Gioia, 1986a). A further issue then evolves: On what basis is meaning ascribed? Put differently, what are the influences on the construction of meaning?

The Influence of Prior Knowledge

What one knows influences what one can know. To every situation a person brings a repertoire of interpretive frameworks developed on the basis of prior learning (Schutz, 1967). Such frameworks for understanding serve to define the interpretation of experience and thus the meaningful explanation of that experience. Because these frameworks are structured in terms of the interpretation of past experience, they tend to *impose* previously ascribed meaning on current experience. For example, the research on framing (Kahneman, Slovic, & Tversky, 1982) shows how the initial evaluative frame an individual uses to interpret a situation influences subsequent thoughts and actions. Thus, meaning often is ascribed to new information simply by relating it to old information. If it can be so related, meaning is available in a de facto manner. Therefore, to some significant degree, prior sensemaking dictates current sensemaking. Knowledge is thus said to reflexively elaborate itself (see Leiter, 1980).

The Influence of Action

Although most lay interpreters of their own experience would conclude that thought precedes action (i.e., that what one thinks influences what one does), it is important to recognize that action often precedes thought (Schutz, 1967; Weick, 1969). Inevitably, thought and action are reciprocally interdependent. Often one makes sense out of a situation by observing what one does in that situation and then reflectively interpreting what one's own action must mean (Weick, 1979). Thus, sensemaking is, in part, a kind of retroactive inference process that involves not only what one knows but what one does. However, inference processes are not limited solely to thinking about past actions, but are also influenced by current and anticipated actions (Gioia, Thomas, Clark & Chittipeddi, 1994; Isabella, 1990; Milliken & Lant, 1991).

The Influence of Emotion

A seriously underrepresented aspect of sensemaking concerns the role that emotions play in the personal and social construction of meaning. Most significant events in a person's experience are imbued with emotion, and as a consequence, people often are given to thinking about how they feel. Emotional experience provides people with a salient means for evaluating and responding to situations that affect their well-being (C. Ford, 1987). The evaluatory nature of emotions provides individuals with additional subjective information that can influence subsequent thoughts and actions (Staw, Sutton & Pelled, 1994). For example, a subjective "feeling" of fear tends to trigger the recall of other fear-related thoughts (Bower, 1981), so that new perceptions tend to be seen as threatening, which, in turn, can cause a person to experience additional fears. In this way, a cognition–emotion cycle can develop that substantially influences the meanings that are ascribed to current perceptions.

The Influence of Context

Meaning is *always* meaning-by-context. Context simply must be supplied for understanding to occur (Leiter, 1980; Mehan & Wood, 1975). The meaning ascribed to a person standing up and screaming during a football game will be different from a similar scream in a mental ward, for instance. In a wider sense the context or setting is "reflexive" with the communication and action that take place within that context (Mehan & Wood, 1975). That is, the setting makes communication and action meaningful, but the communication and action are in fact what define the setting (communication and action explicate settings; settings explicate communication and action). Both are reciprocal and reflexively interdependent; each mutually elaborates the other. Meaning derives from this reflexive interdependence.

Although these features constitute important influences on the products of sensemaking (i.e., the "sense made"), what is important to emphasize at this point is that only a relatively small part of the self-knowledge and social knowledge that result from these influences is available to conscious awareness. The considerable knowledge that a person has developed by cognitively abstracting the understanding of experience is unavailable for direct representation in conscious awareness. This greater part of the store of personal knowledge is retained in tacit form (Polanyi, 1958). As a consequence, an individual is typically in a position of knowing more than he or she can tell (Polanyi, 1966). Why should this be so?

TACIT KNOWLEDGE AND THE STRUCTURE OF CONSCIOUSNESS

Prior to delving into the nature and process of tacit knowledge, it is first necessary to discuss some of the cognitive foundations of such knowledge, as well as the organization of consciousness.

Schemas: The Structures of Knowledge

The sublimation of knowledge to a tacit level is, in great part, a consequence of the necessity to reduce the information processing complexity of the social world to manageable proportions. This daunting task is facilitated by the use of cognitive structures of information called schemas. A schema is a network of related knowledge constructed on the basis of experiential or vicarious learning and held in memory (see Bartlett, 1932; Lord, 1985; Taylor & Crocker, 1981; Walsh, in press). Schemas are used to impose structure and meaning on potentially ambiguous organizational information, events, and situations, and thus to aid sensemaking and action taking (Gioia & Poole, 1984). Indeed, schemas are arguably *the* primary foundations on which sensemaking and action taking are accomplished and communicated (Gioia, 1986a; Gioia & Manz, 1985).

People are held to possess a repertoire of schemas in many different forms (Lord & Foti, 1986), ranging from *self-schemas* that organize information about self-perceptions (Markus, 1977), to *person-schemas* that contain knowledge of various personality types (Cantor & Mischel, 1979), to *role schemas* that retain a sense of behaviors expected of people holding various roles (Taylor & Crocker, 1981), to *script schemas* that maintain webs of structured procedural knowledge about appropriate behaviors in various situations (Abelson, 1981; Gioia & Poole, 1984; see also D. Ford, 1987). Each of these types of schemas is hypothesized to be represented in memory by a "prototype," an abstracted representation that captures the central features of the generalized knowledge that is subsumed in the schema. Understanding, then, is typically accomplished by a process of "prototype matching," wherein current information is implicitly compared to the prototype representing the relevant category of information or schema.[3] If a reasonable match is obtained, no further active cognition is required. The (tacit) information in the schema enables understanding.

Cognitive theorists usually recognize two major modes of information processing: "controlled," which is active, conscious processing of current information, and "automatic," which is passive, essentially unconscious processing (Feldman, 1981). Schema-based processing is typically held to occur automatically, out of conscious awareness. Schematic processing can thus be seen as a means whereby tacit structures of knowledge are accessed, and understanding is accomplished, without conscious recognition of the underlying structures and processes involved.

---

[3] Cicourel (1973) posits a similar process called "searching for the normal form" for the social, rather than individual, setting. Here interactants compare what is being said to what is expected, given the situation, and strive to be able to interpret the communication in terms of what is typical (i.e., "prototypical").

Research in organizational social cognition supports the schematic conception of cognitive structure (Gioia, 1986b; Lord, 1985; Taylor & Crocker, 1981; Walsh, in press). Individuals appear to make sense out of experience by using schemas to organize their *perceptions* into meaningful *conceptions* (D. Ford, 1987; Gioia, 1986a). Given the evidence that knowledge is organized in this fashion, why then is it typically unavailable to active consciousness, thus complicating self-understanding and both inter- and intrapersonal communication? In other words, why is it so difficult to represent tacit knowledge directly in consciousness and thus have it be available for easy manipulation? Much of the following section dealing with this issue is based on a literature review by D. Ford (1987).

The Organization of Consciousness

Human information processing capacity has developed in a way that permits incoming information perceived by the senses to be monitored in a person's consciousness. Remembrance of this "perceptual" information is cognitively coded in the same form as the original incoming information, and therefore can be easily recalled and manipulated in that form in active consciousness. These "perceptible" memories are labeled *perceptual representations*.

Human information processing ability, however, has evolved beyond the capability of simply representing direct perceptual events. We also have developed the ability to extract patterns and consistencies from specific events and to represent them in generalized forms (i.e., schemas). Because such schematic information is generalized information, it is coded in memory in abstract, rather than perceptual form. As a consequence, it cannot enter active consciousness directly (because active consciousness can deal only with *perceptually coded* information). The abstractly coded information is "there;" we use it to interpret and enact organizational life; we merely do not have conscious awareness of it because it is in the "wrong form." It is for this reason that we refer to such information as *tacit knowledge*. This abstracted knowledge can only be *represented* in consciousness by perceptual forms of memory. To enable the representation of abstractions in active consciousness, subsets of "surrogate" perceptual representations develop that are called *linguistic representations*. These are symbols (words, for instance) that become meaningful only when they are associated with other meaningful knowledge.

Although tacit knowledge cannot enter active consciousness directly, it can nonetheless guide action even when out of awareness if the schema containing that knowledge is currently active. Moreover, once activated, tacit knowledge can be modified because it is part of a coherently organized schema. If part of the perceptible content of a schema is altered, then the rest of that schema, including any tacit portions, also changes to maintain a coherent organization

(D. Ford, 1987). One might think of the conscious elements of schema-based knowledge as the tip of an iceberg, with the greater part of the knowledge residing below the surface on a tacit level. If ideas, attitudes, or beliefs in the conscious part of the schema are modified, the other elements of the schema also will be modified outside of active consciousness so that the abstract representations are consistent with the resultant changes.

We should also note that another reason why conscious awareness of tacit knowledge is so difficult derives from the tendency of the representational process to generate higher-order abstractions from simpler abstractions (resulting in more elaborate schemas). Because higher-order abstractions are in a sense farther removed from perceptual representations, they become yet more difficult to translate into active consciousness. As a result, the accessibility of abstract, tacit knowledge might be conceived along a continuum of difficulty. Lower-order abstractions are relatively easier to transform into perceptual form; as the level of abstraction and complexity becomes progressively higher, accessibility becomes progressively more difficult.

COMMUNICATION AND SELF-COMMUNICATION

As a consequence of the nature and operation of tacit knowledge, organization members appear to become "cognitive misers" (Taylor, 1981), effectively reserving conscious capacity and energy for handling current demands and novel situations. Hence, people are often "cruising on automatic" (Gioia, 1986a), depending on tacit, implicit understanding and well-developed action routines to attend to normal events. Given that most situations usually conform to expectation, most people operate on tacit knowledge most of the time. For that reason alone, an understanding of the tacit dimension (Polanyi, 1966) is important to comprehending the construction of individual and social reality and to understanding communication on all levels.

Tacit Communication

In any communicative sensemaking endeavor there are two standpoints to consider: those of both the sender and the receiver. Each is involved in the sensemaking process, and each adopts both standpoints simultaneously when communicating (Handel, 1982). At the elemental level of an interpersonal exchange, both parties are using their simultaneous standpoints to negotiate a sense of their interactive situation, using communication as a medium of exchange (Nonaka, 1994). Each must use tacit understanding to figure out what the other (and the self) cannot, will not, or simply does not say. There is usually enough social knowledge and current information available that both parties can interactively negotiate a sensible construction of the situation. Furthermore, they can interrupt the exchange by asking for clarifications and more detail if not enough is available on the tacit social level.

Consider now the yet more elemental case of communication-with-self, wherein a single individual in effect adopts the roles of both sender and receiver. He or she also conducts this internally communicative sensemaking process within the milieu of tacit personal knowledge (cf. Polanyi, 1958). Given the relative inaccessibility of tacit knowledge, the person is thus in the position of knowing more than he or she can tell (even to self). Still, it is apparent that any personal construction must draw upon more than current information to render experience sensible, and therefore, must access tacit knowledge — typically without the individual knowing *how* it is done or even *that* it is done. By what means do such tacit processes operate?

Tacit Process

Polanyi's (1966) discourse on this issue is instructive here as a point of departure. He notes that "all thought contains components of which we are subsidiarily aware in the focal content of our thinking, and that all thought dwells in its subsidiaries" (p. x). He further argues that we "know" many things explicitly only by relying on a tacit awareness of underlying relationships or background knowledge (without which we could not understand a given observation or experience). In his terms, attention is focused away *from* tacit, internal knowledge structures and processes so that we might attend *to* the more explicit aspects of experience.

For example, effective, experienced managers typically focus attention on the gestalt, global nature of a problem to be solved, rather than the specific details of the problem. (Indeed, if their attention is forced to the details, the problem becomes much more difficult to render as sensible, because it cannot be related to other structured knowledge about similar situations). When asked how they approached the solution to the problem, they often cannot bring forth commentary on the specific features of the problem that cued their solution.

Polanyi's long-standing analysis of this phenomenon suggests that we use tacit knowledge as a fundamental basis for knowing explicit experience. Although that knowledge resides out of active (perceptual) awareness, however, *it is not out of consciousness* in the wider sense. Although people attend explicitly to a problem, they still retain a tacit, implicit knowledge of the features, patterns, and relationships that allow them to deal with the problem in a gestalt manner.

Assuming that the difficulty of representing schema-based knowledge varies according to the degree of development or generalization of the schema (Gioia & Poole, 1984), schemas that are less generalized should be more easily represented than schemas that are more generalized. The upshot of this assumption is that tacit knowledge that is "representable" could then be made available to active awareness, *if appropriately accessed.* One implication of this view is that individuals would be able to improve self-understanding (and social interaction) if they could somehow gain insight into the structure and process of their own tacit understanding. In our view, such insight derives mainly from processes involving self-communication. *Self-communication,* in this sense, *concerns the processes by which an individual might represent his or her own abstract, tacit knowledge in a form that allows articulation of personal knowledge to self.*

SELF-COMMUNICATION PROCESSES

To recapitulate briefly, our fundamental focus is on sensemaking as process and product of the individual and social construction of meaning and on the role of tacit knowledge in such sensemaking. We turn now to some specific processes whereby a person might consciously tap into his or her own schemas that retain the synthesized networks of personal, contextual, and procedural knowledge.

Intuition

Most of us have experienced the phenomenon labeled as intuition—a form of knowing something without knowing how we know. Where might intuition fit into our framework for conceptualization? Intuition historically has been noted as the transmission of perceptions in a way that is out of consciousness (cf. Jung, 1923); knowing thus results without any awareness of "rational" thinking. It is typically seen as a wholistic sort of understanding stemming from feelings, dream-like states, personal images, and symbolic apprehension that occurs in an unexpected fashion (Fisher, 1981). Often, intuition is construed as a mysterious process, inexplicable via usual conceptions of cognition.

We view intuition instead as a legitimate form of internal self-communication. On a metaphorical level, intuition might be viewed as a kind of "leakage" of tacit understanding (retained in schematic form) into explicit awareness of that understanding. It is perhaps most clearly seen, then, as a process wherein schema-based, tacit knowledge is involuntarily rendered into perceptible form, and then into consciousness. When one has an "intuitive feeling," one is drawing on the content of tacit, schematic knowledge. Intuition results, however, only when the schema or repertoire of schemas containing the relevant knowledge is activated (which implies that, to some greater or lesser degree, cognition has been previously focused on a problem or issue). The implication here is that the products of intuition are the result of legitimate, goal-oriented cognition.[4]

Intuition is a revealing example of one-way self-communication from the inside out. What we know tacitly surfaces consciously. Its linkage to tacit knowledge is evidenced because it cannot usually or easily be produced at will and often occurs in the apparent absence of objective "facts" that might justify it (Isaack, 1978). Furthermore, the wellspring of intuition is not logic, but experience. Experience, of course, is a basis on which knowledge becomes schematized. Intuition would thus seem to be an outcome of the often inadvertent accessing of tacit, structured knowledge. Such knowledge, via this one-way communication-to-self, enables an individual to make his or her implicit knowledge explicit.

Intra-active Communication with Self

Conceptualizing intuition as a process and product of tacit internal communication can be instructive; yet it becomes clear that the one-way nature of the process limits its potential. It is not enough simply to tap into tacit knowledge. For the purposes of understanding the self ("knowing thyself" in Socratic terms), making sense of the self in social interaction, and *changing* the self, it becomes necessary not merely to *access,* but to *influence* one's own tacit knowledge. Such a purpose requires an ability, in a sense, to engage in internal two-way communication.

This recognition raises an old question: How can a person know what she or he knows? We have argued that understanding is structured in schematic form. However, we again emphasize that the essential features of such schemas are retained in a form that an individual cannot bring directly into consciousness, but must be represented in some perceptible form. Although this can be done with visual (e.g., dreams) or aural (e.g., music) images, it is predominantly accomplished with language. Language allows one to represent thoughts (that could not otherwise be brought into consciousness) in a perceptible form. Thus, to tap the store of knowledge held in one's repertoire of schemas, one must attach symbolic labels to the content of the schemas. The process of labeling serves as a means whereby one "discovers" (constructs) or "rediscovers" (reconstructs) the meaning of one's experiences. Personal sensemaking for the purpose of learning about the self then becomes, to some significant degree, the process of coming to "know" the structure and process of one's own knowledge.

---

[4] As Dean Gioia, a professional artist, has pointed out to us, however, a barrier to intuition can be created by being *too* goal-oriented—when one becomes so involved in expectations associated with a goal that one ignores or suppresses intuitive knowledge.

Given this depiction and the prior recognition that one's purpose is not simply to learn about the nature of one's own tacit knowledge, but to influence it to useful effect, it becomes obvious that self-communication is the main means available for the modification of tacit knowledge structures—that is, for intentional self-schema change. One can view this process as a special case of schema modification (i.e., learning). In the general case, an individual must first activate a schema and then use controlled processing to integrate new information with the schematized information currently in active consciousness. However, in the processes with which we are concerned, one is attempting to work from the inside out by representing tacit knowledge in a perceptible form so that it can be integrated with other information in active consciousness. Facilitation of schema change through intentional self-communication thus transforms a person into an activist who is personally influencing his or her own internal learning and knowledge. By what overt means, then, can an individual actively begin to understand and alter personal tacit knowledge?

Introspection

To know one's own knowledge obviously requires some form of introspection—a looking inward for the purpose of understanding and changing one's thinking and feeling processes. As in any other knowledge-seeking endeavor, one must become immersed in the procedures whereby knowledge is produced. In the case of personal tacit knowledge, this observation implies that one must become immersed in one's own processes. The prime means of accomplishing that task is to engage oneself in introspective conversation.

The objection to introspection historically has been that there exists no objective means to verify the accuracy of one's own impressions (see Huttenlocher, 1973). In the constructionist view adopted here, where personal sensemaking and meaning construction are at issue, however, accuracy and verifiability of personal impressions are less relevant criteria for assessing the usefulness of introspection. What matters for the purposes given is one's own interpretation. The sense one makes is one's own sense. It is upon that sense that one bases one's understanding and chooses one's course of action. As an initial step toward understanding and action concerning tacit knowledge, it is the *personal* account of experience that matters.[5] Thus, for understanding personal experience, and the tacit rendering of the interpretation of that experience, introspection is a basic technique. The more subtle

---

[5] Subsequent social negotiation and construction clearly might influence the personal interpretation, however. Accuracy of tacit knowledge then becomes a different kind of social construction.

problems concern the "representability," accessibility, and influence-ability of the knowledge that is available.[6]

Advocating the use of introspection, of course, carries the stamp of anathema in many quarters of academia and scholarship, perhaps especially in the study of organizational processes. We believe that the role of introspection should be reconsidered in social and organizational study. Given recent findings about cognitive processing and the organization of consciousness, it would certainly seem appropriate (both theoretically and pragmatically) to further explore the usefulness of introspection, instead of indicting it on historical grounds. Organization members obviously have much more knowledge than is available to ready access. Just as obviously, it behooves us to know the nature and influence of that knowledge. In a modern organizational world centrally defined by frequent change, it is apparent that effective change by people (and therefore organizations) cannot be accomplished without the alteration of the internal structures of knowledge. That alteration can be much more effectively accomplished if an individual engages in a conscious and intentional strategy of understanding and changing personal knowledge.

Affective Reflection

Another technique for probing tacit knowledge entails an assessment of one's affective responses to various situations and events—which we term "affective reflection." By engaging in this process of self-reflection (which is another form of self-communication), one often is able to discern the possible causes of different affective responses. Then, an individual can consider the situational attributes and the underlying tacit knowledge that might be likely sources of the feeling (Ford & Ford, 1986). Subjective feelings are always triggered originally by evaluative thoughts. Because many of these thoughts can be tacit, so one is unaware of the original thoughts that triggered an emotion, one might be able to use emotions to understand these thoughts better.

An example drawn from the data supporting the research reported in C. Ford (1987) is instructive: An executive was aware that he was angry about something, but he did not know quite what it was. As a consequence he began to engage a process of affective self-reflection: "Why am I angry? . . . I must be frustrated from making progress toward some personally meaningful goal . . . What goal? . . . That damn _____ project! . . . How am I blocked? . . . What must that mean about my negative feelings?" In this

---

[6] Epstein (1983) has used the term "preconscious" to characterize cognition that is beyond the level of active, thinking consciousness, yet still accessible through introspective techniques.

fashion, the executive is beginning a process that can lead to insight into tacitly held knowledge of self. Thus, one of the more direct pipelines to personal knowledge via self-communication is to attempt to read one's own feelings. This technique can be useful in sensemaking because it allows one to assign additional meaning to emotional experience. Affective reflection also can provide the initial cues about possible ways to alter the *affective* (and cognitive) components of such knowledge.

Making Tacit Knowledge Explicit

Whether by means of introspection, affective reflection, or other self-communicative procedure, the crux of the issue here is to identify ways in which organization members can better represent their tacit knowledge to themselves so that they can more effectively use it (or change it). Therefore, a pragmatic concern becomes that of finding techniques for tapping the abstracted, tacit knowledge contained in a currently activated schema and representing it in perceptible form. Although space does not permit an in-depth treatment, it might be useful to note some practical techniques. Appendix A summarizes several selected approaches.

As unusual, awkward, or self-conscious as some of these techniques first appear, they have the potential for providing the raw material (conscious representations) for gaining insight into the structure and process of tacit knowledge. If that process can be accomplished, action based on tacit knowledge can be better understood, and conscious alteration of that knowledge can be undertaken.

THE SENSEMAKING CYCLE

To this point we have dealt with many elements concerning sensemaking in organizations. It seems appropriate now to review the relationships among these elements in a descriptive summary portrayal of the individual organizational sensemaking cycle.[7]

Figure 3.1 suggests (beginning at top left) that individuals attend to

---

[7] We can note here that the process that we as authors used to transform the abstarct concepts in this paper into some perceptible form (Figure 3.1) was instrumental in helping *us* articulate our own knowledge of the topic of the chapter to ourselves. We have used techniques of self-communication (as well as interpersonal communication) to develop and make sense of the line of argument put forth in this chapter.

FIG. 3.1   The Sensemaking Cycle.

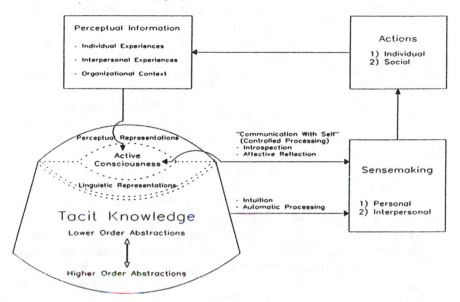

perceptual information, guided mainly by goals they are pursuing. These perceptions can come from a variety of personal, interpersonal, and organizational sources. This information then interacts with the perceptual and linguistic representations currently activated in consciousness (represented by the unidirectional arrow from "perceptual information" to "active consciousness"). Thus, cognitive processing in active consciousness comprises an interaction between what is perceived and what is known. A great part of "what is known," however, is in tacit form. This schematic knowledge is retained in varying degrees of abstraction, with higher level (more generalized) abstractions being more difficult to transform into perceptible forms than can be processed in active consciousness. (The double dotted line indicates the relative difficulty in permeating the boundary between tacit knowledge and other perceptible forms of information and memory). Tacit knowledge, despite its great influence on thought and action, can only be *represented* in active awareness in surrogate forms such as linguistic representations.[8]

The process of representing tactit knowledge in perceptible form is what we are labeling "self-communication" (identified by the bidirectional arrow from

---

[8] We should note that linguistic representations are not absolutely necessary for a person to manipulate ideas in consciousness. See Furth's (1966) work with the congenitally deaf, who obviously think without ever having acquired "language" in the usual fashion.

"active consciousness" to "sensemaking"). Self-communication involves controlled processes such as introspection and affective reflection, which are used in the attempt to represent thoughts and feelings in perceptible form. These products of sensemaking (e.g., linguistic labels, metaphors, images, specific examples, etc.) can then be manipulated actively in consciousness and can thus be used to guide further learning and action (the arrow from "sensemaking" to "action").

On the other hand, intuition and automatic processing (represented by the unidirectional arrow directly from "tacit knowledge" to "sensemaking") are processes wherein cognition and action are produced without awareness of thinking. Cognition is occurring, of course, yet these processes are not represented in active consciousness, but rather at the level of abstract representation. Nonetheless, they also influence action.

Thus, both the "articulated" knowledge in active consciousness and the direct influence of tacit knowledge affect the "sense made," which in turn influences actions in both personal and social contexts and settings. These actions then provide additional direct perceptions to further guide and influence sensemaking. We might also note another benefit to this depiction of organizational sensemaking as a cycle. The question of whether thought precedes action or vice versa (Gioia, 1986a; Schutz, 1967; Thomas, Clark, & Gioia, 1993; Weick, 1979) is shown to depend simply on where one begins the cycle. All are feasible beginning and ending points, and all are cyclically dependent and interactively influential.

RECAPITULATION AND CONCLUSION

Understanding how people understand is a fundamentally important issue in organizational life. This chapter has sought to sketch out a framework for considering and understanding *individual* aspects of organizational sensemaking. From one perspective, ours is a rather narrow view simply *because* it is concerned mainly with individual sensemaking, and does not deal in depth with interpersonal aspects. We maintain, however, that organizational sensemaking does not occur solely through social interaction as the current idiom would seem to have it, but depends to some significant degree on internal communication processes. From another perspective, ours is an arguably wide-ranging view in that it attempts to address such apparently nebulous cognitive structures and processes as tacit knowledge, schemas, and self-communication (including intuition, introspection, and affective reflection). The focus on individual sensemaking and its attendant internal communicative processes, however, suggests that all these aspects of cognition constitute legitimate and useful knowledge, once the structure of consciousness is taken into account.

In this chapter we have adopted a number of specific positions and made several observations and conclusions that are perhaps best summarized in succinct form, as follows:

1. Organizational sensemaking is best understood as both an *individual* (personal) and a *social* (interpersonal) phenomenon. It thus involves *intra*personal, as well as *inter*personal communication processes.

2. Sensemaking is also usefully viewed as both the *process* and the *product* of meaning construction in organizations.

3. An important component of tacit knowledge is emotion, a recognition that broadens the conceptualization of sensemaking activity. Emotion is noted as a salient input to, and outcome of, meaning construction.

4. The individual sensemaking process entails the use of both *explicit* and *tacit* knowledge (involving mainly controlled and automatic information processing, respectively). Of these, tacit knowledge represents by far the greater knowledge base.

5. Tacit knowledge is abstracted knowledge that cannot be brought directly into active consciousness. Such knowledge serves to facilitate comprehension and to guide action, and is retained in the form of cognitive structures called schemas.

6. Tacit knowledge can be made available to active awareness, if properly accessed. Despite the abstract, schema-based nature of tacit knowledge, it can, to various degrees, be represented in perceptible forms that can be manipulated in active consciousness.

7. The means of articulating tacit knowledge revolve around processes of self-communication. Specific methods include intuition, introspection, and affective reflection, among others.

In an overarching sense, we have argued the conceptual grounds for making the study of sensemaking, tacit knowledge, and self-communication an emerging concern for organizational study (cf. Thayer, 1986). We also emphasize the practical concern involved in accounting for these nebulous structures and processes, especially in attempting consciously to tap tacit knowledge. The ultimate goal is to learn to manage the structure and process of one's own tacit knowledge so that one might change it to facilitate more effective organizational action. Thus, the purpose of self-articulation of one's own tacit knowledge is not merely self-understanding, but also self-influence.

APPENDIX A

Selected techniques for representing tacit knowledge in perceptual form so that it can be used in active consciousness:

1. *Symbolic Representation:* Trying to represent ideas using metaphors, analogies, examples, or even illustrations. The power of these forms of language (or pictures) is that they often are able to represent extremely complex ideas in perceptible forms. We have tried to use this technique in this chapter by representing our ideas in pictures (Figure 3.1). Of course, the usefulness of any of these symbolic forms lies in its ability to accurately represent complex tacit knowledge.

2. *Developing Descriptions of Problems on Audio Tape.* By listening to these descriptions as if one were listening to somebody else, one can make inferences about the underlying tacit knowledge supporting these ideas. Paying particular attention to the use of symbols, metaphors, and analogies can be particularly helpful because they are capable of representing abstract ideas.

3. *Diaries:* Keeping diaries can serve as a chronicle not only for problems to be solved but also for reactions to those problems. This method can be helpful for two reasons. First, it allows one to "put ideas down on paper," which is a perceptible form so that one can react to one's own ideas. Second, by reading back in one's diary, one may be able to infer the tacit knowledge underlying the descriptions and reactions to a problem.

4. *Talking with Trusted Colleagues.* Conversation might enable one to see underlying (i.e., tacit) assumptions that one is using when analyzing a problem. Dialogue with others who might have similar tacit knowledge structures may be useful for finding ways of articulating ideas.

5. *Meditation:* Using meditation can be useful for pursuing the "mental sidetracks" that the mind follows as one allows the mind to wander. Following these seemingly random associations can provide one with insight into the structure of tacit knowledge.

REFERENCES

Abelson, R. P. (1981). Psychological status of the script concept. *American Psychologist, 36,* 715–729.

Bartlett, F. C. (1932). *Remembering: An experimental and social study.* Cambridge: Cambridge University Press.

Blumer, H. (1969). *Symbolic interactionism.* Englewood Cliffs, NJ: Prentice-Hall.

Bower, G. H. (1981). Mood and memory. *American Psychologist, 36,* 129–148.

Cantor, N., & Mischel, W. (1979). Prototypes in personal perception. In L. Berkowitz (Ed.), *Advances in experimental social psychology,* Vol. 12. Orlando, FL: Academic Press.

Cicourel, A. V. (1973). *Cognitive sociology: Language and meaning in social interaction.* Baltimore, MD: Penguin.

Decker, P. J. (1980). Effects of symbolic coding and rehearsal in behavior-modeling training. *Journal of Applied Psychology, 65,* 627–634.

Donnellon, A., Gray, B., & Bougon, M. G. (1986). Communication, meaning, and organized action. *Administrative Science Quarterly, 31,* 43–55.

Epstein, S. (1983). The unconscious, the preconscious and the self-concept. In J. Suls & A. Greenwald (Eds.), *Psychological perspectives on the self, Vol. 2: The role of unconscious in an individual's self-system.* Hillsdale, NJ: Erlbaum.

Feldman, J. M. (1981). Beyond attribution theory: Cognitive processes in performance evaluation. *Journal of Applied Psychology, 66,* 127–148.

Fisher, M. (1981). *Intuition.* New York: Dutton.

Fiske, S. T. (1982). Schema-triggered affect: Applications to social perceptions. In M. S. Clarke & S. T. Fiske (Eds.), *Cognition and emotion: The Carnegie-Mellon Symposium* (pp. 57–78). Hillsdale, NJ: Erlbaum.

Ford, C. M. (1987). The role of emotions in an executive's workday. In M. E. Ford & D. H. Ford (Eds.), *Humans as self-constructing living systems: Putting the framework to work* (pp. 235–260). Hillsdale, NJ: Erlbaum.

Ford, C. M., & Ford, D. H. (1986). A method for measuring situational variation and changes in emotions. Paper presented at the 94th American Psychological Association Convention, Washington, DC.

Ford, C. M., & Gioia, D. A. (Eds.). (1995). *Creative action in organizations: Ivory Tower Visions and Real World Voices.* Thousand Oaks, CA: Sage.

Ford, D. H. (1987). *Humans as self-constructing living systems: A developmental perspective on behavior and personality.* Hillsdale, NJ: Erlbaum.

Furth, H. G. (1966). *Thinking without language.* New York: Free Press.

Garfinkel, H. (1967). *Studies in ethnomethodology.* Englewood Cliffs, NJ: Prentice-Hall.

Gioia, D. A. (1986a). Symbols, scripts, and sensemaking: Creating meaning in the organizational experience. In H. P. Sims & D. A. Gioia (Eds.), *The thinking organization* (pp. 49–74). San Francisco, CA: Jossey–Bass.

Gioia, D. A. (1986b). Conclusion: The state of the art in organizational social cognition. In H. P. Sims & D. A. Gioia (Eds.), *The thinking organization* (pp. 336–356). San Francisco: Jossey–Bass.

Gioia, D. A., & Manz, C. C. (1985). Linking cognition and behavior: A script processing interpretation of vicarious learning. *Academy of Management Review, 10,* 527–539.

Gioia, D. A., & Poole, P. P. (1984). Scripts in organizational behavior. *Academy of Management Review, 9,* 449–459.

Gioia, D. A., Donnellon, A., & Sims, H. P., Jr. (1989). Communication and cognition in appraisal: A tale of two paradigms. *Organization Studies, 10,* 503–530.

Gioia, D. A., Thomas, J. B., Clark, S. M., & Chittipeddi, K. (1994). Symbolism and strategic change in academia: The dynamics of sensemaking and influence. *Organization Science, 5,* 363–383.

Goffman, E. (1967). *Interaction ritual.* New York: Pantheon Books.

Handel, W. (1982). *Ethnomethodology: How people make sense.* Englewood Cliffs, NJ: Prentice-Hall.

Huttenlocher, J. (1973). Language and thought. In G. A. Miller (Ed.), *Communication, language, and meaning* (pp. 172–184). New York: Basic Books.

Isaack, T. S. (1978). Intuition: An ignored dimension of management. *Academy of Management Review, 2,* 917–921.

Isabella, L. A. (1990). Evolving interpretations as a change unfolds: How managers construe key organizational events. *Academy of Management Journal, 33,* 7–41.

Jung, C. G. (1923). *Psychological types.* New York: Harcourt, Brace.

Kahneman, D., Slovic, P., & Tversky, A. (Eds.). (1982). *Judgment under uncertainty: Hueristics and biases.* Cambridge: Cambridge University Press.

Leiter, K. (1980). *A primer on ethnomethodology.* New York: Oxford University Press.

Lord, R. G. (1985). An information processing approach to social perceptions, leadership, and behavioral measurement in organizations. In L. L. Cummings & B. M. Staw (Eds.), *Research in organizational behavior,* Vol. 7. Greenwich, CT: JAI Press.

Lord, R. G., & Foti, R. J. (1986). Schema theories, information processing, and organizational behavior. In H. P. Sims & D. A. Gioia (Eds.), *The thinking organization* (pp. 20–48). San Francisco: Jossey–Bass.

Markus, H. (1977). Self-schemata and processing information about the self. *Journal of Personality and Social Psychology, 35,* 63–78.

Mehan, H., & Wood, H. (1975). *The reality of ethnomethodology.* Malabar, FL: Robert E. Krieger.

Milliken, F. J., & Lant, T. K. (1991). The effects of an organization's recent performance history on strategic persistence and change: The role of managerial interpretations. In P. Shrivastava, A. Huff, & J. Dutton (Eds.), *Advances in strategic management* (Vol. 7, pp. 129–156).

Nonaka, I. (1994). A dynamic theory of organizational knowledge creation. *Organization Science, 5,* 14–37.

Polanyi, M. (1958). *Personal knowledge.* Chicago: University of Chicago Press.

Polanyi, M. (1966). *The tacit dimension.* Garden City, NJ: Doubleday.

Putnam, L. L., & Pacanowsky, M. (1983). *Communication and organizations: An interpretive approach.* Beverly Hills, CA: Sage.

Ritti, R. R. (1986). The social bases of organizational knowledge. In L. Thayer (Ed.), *Organization ↔ communication: Emerging perspectives I* (pp. 102–132). Norwood, NJ: Ablex.

Schutz, A. (1967). *The phenomenology of the social world.* Evanston, IL: Northwestern University Press.

Sims, H. P., Jr., & Gioia, D. A. (1986). *The thinking organization.* San Francisco: Jossey–Bass.

Staw, B. M., Sutton, R. I., & Pelled, L. H. (1994). Employee positive emotion and favorable outcomes at the workplace. *Organization Science, 5,* 51–71.

Sternberg, R. J., & Wagner, R. K. (1986). *Practical intelligence: Nature and origins of competence in the everyday world.* New York: Cambridge University Press.

Taylor, S. E. (1981). The interface of cognitive and social psychology. In J. Harvey (Ed.), *Cognition, social behavior, and the environment* (pp. 189–211). Hillsdale, NJ: Erlbaum.

Taylor, S. E., & Crocker, J. (1981). Schematic bases of social information processing. In E. T. Higgins, C. A. Herman, & M. P. Zanna (Eds.), *Social cognition: The Ontario Symposium.* Vol. 1 (pp. 89–134). Hillsdale, NJ: Erlbaum.

Thayer, L. (Ed.). (1986). *Organization ↔ communication: Emerging perspectives I.* Norwood, NJ: Ablex.

Thomas, J. B., Clark, S. M., & Gioia, D. A. (1993). Strategic sensemaking and organizational performance: Linkages among scanning, interpretation, action, and outcomes. *Academy of Management Journal, 36,* 239–270.

Walsh, J. P. (in press). Managerial and organizational cognition: Notes from a trip down memory lane. *Organization Science.*

Weick, K. E. (1969). *The social psychology of organizing.* Reading, MA: Addison–Wesley.

Weick, K. E. (1979). *The social psychology of organizing* (2nd ed.). Reading, MA: Addison–Wesley.

Weick, K. E. (1995). *Sensemaking in organizations.* Thousand Oaks, CA: Sage.

4

The Process of Organizational Sense Making: A Semiotic Phenomenological Model*

Peter M. Kellett

INTRODUCTION: SEMIOTIC PHENOMENOLOGY AND ORGANIZATIONAL RESEARCH

Semiotic phenomenology, as a methodology, entails both phenomenological *method* (Merleau-Ponty, 1962)—that is, the rigorous examination of human conscious experience—and a semiotic *theory* of human communication (Lanigan, 1988). Hence, semiotic phenomenological *methodology* is the combination of semiotic theory and phenomenological method, particularly as it applies to the study of human communication. Within the disciplinary context of human communication research, semiotic phenomenology has proven fruitful in explicating the conscious experience of various communication media, such as interpersonal communication (Ablamiwicz, 1984; Gemin, 1986), and mass communication (Lanigan, 1988; Nelson, 1986; Presnell, 1983). However, the communication medium of the organization (Luhmann, 1982) remains largely untapped in terms of semiotic phenomenological approaches, despite the fact that such an approach may be a useful addition to, and extension of, current approaches to the analysis of the constitution and experience of organizational meaning systems. Semiotic phenomenology provides "both a theory and a method for the valid, scientific study of human communication" (Lanigan, 1988, p. 183). A direct result of the development of semiotic phenomenology is the actualization of communication theoretic models in organizational communication research (Kellett, 1987; Pilotta, Widman, & Jasko, 1988) that entail rather than are entailed by information theory (Lanigan, 1988). This innovation has provided the distinctive feature, or necessary condition, of human communication as "human conscious experi-

---

*A revised version of a paper first presented at the International Communication Association Annual Conference, New Orleans, 1988.

ence that entails a binary analogue logic" (p. 182) (communication theory) that systematically entails a digital logic (information theory).

In this chapter, I take up this thematic of the opposition between information-theoretic and communication-theoretic models of human communication with respect to the problematic of providing a "meaningfully adequate" account of the process of organizational sense making. Thus, my purpose in this chapter is to account for the adequacy of a semiotic phenomenological model of the sense-making process as experienced by new members engaged in organizational entry. The adequacy of this project relies on demonstrating the entailment, and thus extension, of information-theoretic models of sense making by the communication theoretic model I develop. I choose the particular concept of "organizational entry" simply because it implies the eidetic point of empirical transition from "outsider" to "insider" for people (Wanous, 1977). Also, it is the point at which a person, as a "newcomer," is most open to a relationship with the unfamiliar organization (Hughes, 1958; Louis, 1980; Van Maanen, 1977).

I develop the discussion through a number of stages. First, I critically explicate the information-theoretic approach to sense making, illustrated by the "sense making" approach attributed to Dervin (1976, 1980, 1984) and others (Atwood & Dervin, 1982). Second, from this description, I thematize the necessary conditions for a communication-theoretic sense-making model. Third, my interpretation results in a semiotic phenomenological organizational sense-making model that takes consciousness to be the activity of making sense, that is grounded in communication theory. That is, sense making is presented as a communication phenomena that focuses on the directionality of the addressee within a communication relationship with others. To develop the model, I provide a synthesis of Schutz & Luckmann's (1974) discussion of the social stock of knowledge, and Lanigan's (1988) extension of Merleau-Ponty's phenomenology of communication as a semiotic phenomenology of discourse framed within Jakobson's communication theory model of communication (Holenstein, 1976).

THE INFORMATION THEORY APPROACH TO SENSE MAKING

Functionalist approaches to organizations assume that organizational reality can be characterized as a set of causative relations between phenomena (Burrel & Morgan, 1979). This assumption results in the characterization of the process of organizational entry as involving a number of causally related and linear phases. This causality implies that a person is primarily "acted upon" in the process. First, an individual comes into contact with the "new" information environment of the organization (Louis, 1980; Porter, 1974; Van Maanen, 1977; Wanous, 1977) with its attendant norms, values, and roles as a context *for* choice. Second, the individual adapts to (Fiol & Lyles, 1985) and adopts (Feldman, 1981); through information from management and peers, organizationally conventional (functional) behaviors and perceptual schemata as choices *in* context. Hence, the "sense making" act is functional and information-theoretic in that it involves merely the perceptual input, or output, of predefined organizational information. Individuals make either/or choices as to what information is functional for them in their anticipated particular role development. Third, the end point, though a floating boundary condition (Schein, 1971), is the "target role" of an "insider." This is a person who is transformed into an "effective member" (Feldman, 1976). Effective entry and transformation is evidence by behavior that accords with the original norms and values transmitted to the new member (choice *as* context). This model is information-theoretic in the assumption of a linear information context entailing an expressive sender (organizational peers) transmitting messages (organizational instructions), which are received and adopted by the receiver (the new organizational member). This reception function is sense making. To illustrate the sense-making process from an information theory perspective I explicate the so-called "sense-making approach" as it has been applied to the organizational context.

THE INFORMATION THEORETIC SENSE-MAKING MODEL

The sense-making approach centers on the work of Dervin, Jacobson, & Nilan (1982). According to Dervin's approach, sense making comes from an aim to study how people construct meaningful worlds. Sense making is viewed as a *behavior* that enables individuals to progress through "time" and "space" (the organizational discursive context) by engaging in a process of seeking and using information that is sense making. The approach is tied intimately to the process of socialization in that sense making involves the acquisition of "information" not already experienced (Dervin, 1976). Ironically enough, the implicit notion of constructivism in the sense-making act, drawing on Kelly's (1955) work, is offered by Dervin (1980) as a critique of the basic information-processing model. However, this sense-making model, as it has been applied to organizational communication processes (Troester, 1987), remains information-theoretic. The sense-making model involves a three-part process of "situations," "gaps," and "uses" (Figure 4.1) Situations are given as the time/space context where sense is constructed. This primacy of the situation is based on the notion that sense making is situational. Second, "gaps" involve the perception of information needs by individuals in their quest for conceptual closure as a coherent re-presentation of organizational reality. Third, "uses" involve the newly created sense that allows the

FIG. 4.1.   Information Theory Model of Organizational Sense Making.

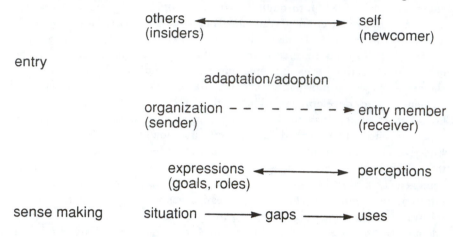

bridging of gaps and the spatial/temporal movement of the new organizational member.

Within an organizational context, the new member naturally encounters certain blocks in movement where understanding is limited. These blocks are perceived as gaps requiring filling or "bridging," illustrated by requests for particular information. For example, he or she might ask a peer or supervisor how a procedure works, or what an event signals within the broader organizational context. The individual makes either/or choices about information needed ("do I need facts about this task?"), and information received ("do the facts give me an either/or choice in behavior?").

Dervin's information theory model of sense making relates precisely to the stages of the functionalist approach to organizational entry. "Situations," the context of sense making, relates to the initial stage of organizational entry where the context is constituted in organizational expression; for example, in the sending of instructions or information about goals, norms, roles, and skills relevant to the new member. "Gaps," the perception of information needs and the seeking of information to fill gaps through questions, forms a feedback loop in the sequence where the process of adopting the organizational constructs being transmitted takes place. A new member may need the clarification of an instruction. By questioning the source of information the need is fulfilled (or not fulfilled) and the adoption/adaptation process of entry continues or returns to the situation stage. The "Uses" stage creates sense through information. It makes use of a relation with the perception stage of the functional process. Here, the organizational information and instruction are received and used in new member's perceptions and expressions. They have lessened the uncertainty of the organizational context through this sense-making process.

The information-theoretic model of sense making provides a relatively adequate account of the conceptual closure provided by direct informative instruction and, to be fair to the proponents of this model, that is what they are mainly concerned with. However, an information-theoretic model is incapable of providing a full account of sense making in an organizational context where sense is made of discourse and cultural systems of meaning outside the realm of direct instruction — that is, where sense is abduced from organizational discourse as a communication event. The information-theoretic model relies on the notion of an information need which is either met, or not met, by the information that is either provided or not provided and, in turn, either lessens or does not lessen uncertainty for the entering organizational member. The digital logic of the information-theoretic approach provides an appealingly simple account of the sense-making approach: Digital decisions provide a sense of the whole from the continuous build-up of knowledge of the parts. Clearly, organizational sense making does involve contexts where digital decisions about information are made.

My purpose is not to refute information theory; rather, it is to show that it is entailed within communication theory and, thus, alone cannot provide a full account of sense making. The task, therefore, is to develop a model that accounts for the digital decisions characteristic of some organizational sense-making acts and that also realizes the analog logic of human communication (communication theory) as primary to any digital operation (information theory). This is, in essence, the necessary condition of an adequate model of organizational sense making. The information-theoretic model accounts for what is directly spoken to the new member: There is either speech or silence, instruction with information value or no instruction with no information value. The task is to develop a model that is sensitive to the nature of meaning as involving an analogue relationship between the spoken and the unspoken that is primary to the digital conditions of either instruction or noninstruction. Also, the model should focus on the meaning construction of new members as an embodied logic that is inescapably communicative, as it always involves meaningful relations with the conduct of others.

SEMIOTIC PHENOMENOLOGICAL MODEL OF SENSE MAKING

The model that I move on to develop (Figure 4.2) insists on a resolution of the limitations of the information-theoretic model as it explicitly integrates the reflexive process of description, reduction, and interpretation as the systemic process of consciousness experiencing the meaning systems of the organizations. This model accounts for (a) the communication situatedness of the process of taking up the meanings of others (phenomenological description), (b) the meanings that are given as thematic in organizational discourse

FIG. 4.2.   Semiotic Phenomenological Model of Organizational Sense Making.

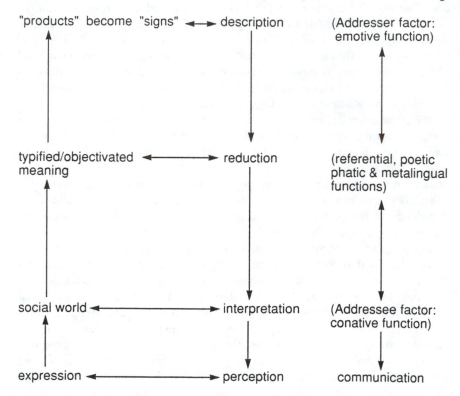

"products" become "signs" ◄──► description   (Addresser factor:
                                                     emotive function)

typified/objectivated ◄──────► reduction   (referential, poetic
meaning   phatic & metalingual
                                                     functions)

social world ◄──────────────► interpretation   (Addressee factor:
                                                     conative function)

expression ◄──────────────► perception   communication

(phenomenological reduction), and (c) the meanings that are taken up as possibilities for the entering member in the organizational World of Others.

Schutz provides a useful framework for describing the constitution of organizational discourse as it is made present to the entering member by giving the combined centripetal functions of *typification* and *objectivation* as the primary means by which the subjective experiences of others (present and/or absent) become sedimented and embodied in discourse as available acts. These are two of what Luhmann (1982) would call process characteristics of the organization. Typification involves the sedimentation of experience around certain central discursive categories that organizational discourse gives as a way of representing others and their experience. Organizations represent others as an interrelated and coherent system in this way. "Boss," "co-workers," and "teamleader" are examples of such typicalities. Objectivation involves the embodiment of subjective experiences in organizational objects and practices. Organizational rituals, myths, and stories are examples of objectivations. The combined processes of typification and objectivation create a temporal dimension of organizational discourse, giving past expressed experience as possibilities for "now." Typification and objectivation determine the selected and disregarded aspects of organizational reality. That is, such discursive systems define the experiences (choices) that count or do not count as "real" in the organization.

Communication is involved when the "products" of typification and objectivation are taken up as meaningful, that is, when they become "signs" of others' conscious experience. This process of "products" becoming "signs" gives the first level of sense making, that is, phenomenological description (of expression); where a failure of the typification occurs, the "other" emerges as a consciousness that presents the entering member with an addresser (emotive function). For example, the way individuals in the organization take up what the entering member realizes is a typification and adapts that to their own style of comportment, which gives the new member a sense of the range of possible expression (the field) in which the self may emerge through choices. This is the first level of sense making and is actualized in the entry process as the point at which the characteristic gestures of other members are meaningful as centrifugal uses of organizational discourse.

The second level of sense making includes the realization that subjective experiences of others, given as signs, relate in specific ways (actualizations) to the organizational system of typifications and objectivations. That is, the signs of others are reduced to their systemic and systematic relation to other signs in the system that give them situated meaning. In communication theoretic terms, the signs of others take on referential, poetic, phatic, or metalingual function depending on their typical relationship within organizational discourse. The entering member begins to realize that the typical function of particular organizational expressions as paradigmatic and syntagmatic categories in the discourse system, although a message may perform a combination of functions. An expression that typically takes on a referential function is one that designates, as a nonarbitrary relationship, an organizational object or practice. For example, the term "flex-time" refers to the relative autonomy of the start and end of the work day. Of course, instruction may provide a sense of this concept, as in the information-theoretic model, although it is only by "living" such a process that the subject "makes sense" of the concept. Expressions that perform the poetic function make use of the principle of equivalence, in that the paradigmatic axis is projected onto the syntagmatic axis—for example, in organizational "folklore" the use of wise sayings that employ poetic structures or patterns are uses of the poetic function. Messages that typically take on the phatic function in organizations are those that serve to establish, prolong, check out, confirm, or discontinue some aspect of communication (Holenstein, 1976). An example is the typification of the formal or informal work group meeting where issues are raised, discussed, or excluded from discussion. There are many forms of the metalinguistic function in organizational discourse. Messages that facilitate reference to organizational discourse or reality serve this metalinguistic function and are central to the constitution of organizational cultures. Organizational humor that functions to comment on some aspect of the organization or an organizational member allows the expression of opinion and values about the organization. This is the metalinguistic function in action.

The third level of sense making (interpretation) involves the actualizations that the new members' own choices of expression and perception create, in particular, organizational contexts (choice of context: communication theory); these are valued and function in particular ways as "real" experienced "worlds." The new member's *capability* to take up signs as meaningful for others is met by an *ability* to express subjective experience through the thematic categories given in others' expressions. For example, the new organizational member knows that his or her work group embodies a certain gestural style, and that this guides the possible expressive choices available, those marked as organizationally appropriate and inappropriate. There is the realization, by the entering member, that her communication acts take on (actualize) particular organizational meanings as they are mediated for others by organizational discourse.

For Schutz, this realization of actualization is the point at which an aspect of the social stock of knowledge becomes meaningful and is acquired. This development gives us the addressee factor (conative function) in communication theory. The addressee factor takes on a reflexive relationship to the addresser in that, as communication, the point at which the addressee "interprets" the addresser's meaning (perception of expression), the addressee simultaneously becomes an addresser (expression of perception). This is the point of conscious experience of organizational membership.

CONCLUSION AND IMPLICATIONS FOR SENSE-MAKING RESEARCH

It is now appropriate to discuss the specific developments in organizational sense-making research that the semiotic phenomenological model offers over the information-theoretic model. The most obvious development is the change in the conceptualizing of sense making as a *communication process*. Sense making, from the viewpoint of the semiotic phenomenological model, is not the linear information internalization of the information-theoretic model; rather, sense making is a communication process that situates the entering member in a dialectical relationship of expression *and* perception with others as they situate themselves within, and negotiate a relationship with, organizational discourse. It is not merely a psychological function but a communication process that centers on the *conscious experience of meaning* by the addressee, here the entering member of the organization.

Second, since sense making has been reformulated as a communication process, this means that prior to the digital decisions entailed within the sense-making process is an analogue logic that is definitional of communication theory. Thus, in the first stage of sense making, where the meanings of others emerge as signs in organizational discourse, the meaning of the signs that are taken up as signaling others emerges from the simultaneous presence, for the entering member, of the typification (possibility) *and* the failure of the typification (actualization) as communication. In other words, prior to the digital decision of the information value of the message (combination by differentiation) is the analog relationship of both typification and failure of typification (differentiation by combination) that is present to the newcomer. The newcomer makes sense of the distinction by "living" the meaning of the relationship between both. Here is a paradigm case of the entailment of information theory by communication theory.

Similarly, at the second stage of sense making, the information value of the distinction between typical functions of organizational discursive categories is derived from the relationship of the particular category, or expression of the category, in its systemic relationship to other categories or expressions in the organizational discursive system. Thus, an act that typically performs a metalingual function has meaning as such because it normally does not perform other typical functions within the organization. It is the combination of the present and absent that gives meaning, and thus information value. It is precisely this semiotic (communication) fact with which the information theoretic model cannot cope. The information value of an organizational expression is not given entirely as a definitional instruction that clarifies a part of the system as in the information-theoretic model; rather, the meaning is taken up in terms of gaining a sense of the whole and how particular parts function in relation to each other within that discursive whole.

The third level of sense making also exemplifies the entailment of information theory within communication theory. The focus at this stage on the taking up of meaningful gestures as *possibilities for the self* relies on the phenomenological concept of *capability.* The focus at this stage is on the choosing process engaged by the new member. Through stage one and two the acts of others have become meaningful as possibilities for the self. Stage three reveals the new member's choice from among those possibilities as a style of expression and perception within the organization. Here again there is the combination of the present (choices of inclusion) and the absent (choices of exclusion) that gives the meaning of the new member's choices. It is this preoccupation with the choosing process that signals a communication theoretic approach in that the process is characterized as the new member's coming to realize that his or her choices constitute organizational contexts in the same way that other member's choices constitute contexts of choice for others. The context of choice is constituted by communication. The information-theoretic model merely focuses on how entering members adapt to predefined information contexts. The choosing process by the new member is secondary to the contextual characteristics (gaps) that guide choices (uses).

With the reformulation of sense making as a communication process rather than a psychological function, organizational sense-making research must develop models that take up the viewpoint of communication theory rather than merely that of information theory. Further research may explore the relationship between the three levels of sense making that I posit. The questions of whether level one may occur without progress to level two and three, whether levels may be bypassed in certain organizational contexts, and the results that such permutations may have, for the sense making of new or established members, a need to be addressed in future research. Detailed empirical organizational studies of sense making that make use of semiotic phenomenological methodology may help to answer such questions as these, and offer sense making research-specific examples of the relationship between information- and communication-theoretic models.

REFERENCES

Ablamiwicz, H. (1984). *An empirical phenomenological study of shame.* Unpublished doctoral dissertation, Department of Speech Communication, Southern Illinois University, Carbondale, IL.

Atwood, R., & Dervin, B. (1982). Challenges to sociocultural predictors of information seeking a test of race versus situation movement state. In M. Burgoon (Ed.), *Communication Yearbook 5* (pp. 549–571). New Brunswick, NJ: Transaction Books.

Burrel, G., & Morgan, G. (1979). *Sociological paradigms and organizational analysis.* London: Heinmann.

Dervin, B. (1976). Strategies for dealing with human information needs: Information or communication. *Journal of Broadcasting, 20,* 323–333.

Dervin, B. (1980). Communication gaps and inequities: Moving toward a reconceptualization. In B. Dervin & M. Voigt (Eds.), *Progress in Communication Sciences 2.* Norwood, NJ: Ablex.

Dervin, B., Jacobson, T., & Nilan, M. (1982). Measuring aspects of information seeking: A test of the quantitative/qualitative methodology. In M. Burgoon (Ed.), *Communication yearbook 6* (pp. 419–445). Beverly Hills, CA: Sage.

Dervin, B. (1984). *The human side of information perspectives for communicating.* Norwood, NJ: Ablex.

Feldman, C. (1976). A contingency theory of socialization. *Administrative Science Quarterly, 21,* 433–452.

Feldman, C. (1981). The multiple socialization of organizational members. *Academy of Management Review, 6,* 309–319.

Fiol, M. C., & Lyles, M. H. (1985). Organizational learning. *Academy of Management Review, 10,* 803–814.

Gemin, J. V. (1986). An archaology of therapeutic discourse: Semiotic phenomenology as a method for discourse analysis. *Belfast Working Papers in Language and Linguistics, 8,* 145–189.

Holenstein, E. (1976). *Roman Jakobson's approach to language: Phenomenological structuralism.* Bloomington: Indiana University Press. (Original work published 1974).

Hughes, E. C. (1958). *Men and their work*. Glencoe, IL: Free Press.

Kellett, P. M. (1987). *The development of a semiotic approach to organizational culture and socialization*. Paper presented at Western States Communication Association Annual Conference, Salt Lake City, UT.

Kelly, G. A. (1955). *A theory of personality: The psychology of personal constructs*. New York: W. W. Norton.

Lanigan, R. L. (1988). *Phenomenology of communication: Merleau-Ponty's thematics in communicology and semiology*. Pittsburgh: Duquesne University Press.

Louis, M. R. (1980). Surprise and sense making: What newcomers experience in entering unfamiliar organizational settings. *Administrative Science Quarterly, 25*, 226–252.

Luhmann, N. (1982). *The differentiation of society*. (S. Holmes & C. Larmore, Trans.). New York: Columbia University Press.

Merleau-Ponty, M. (1962). *Phenomenology of perception* (C. Smith, Trans.). New York: Humanities Press. (Reprinted with translation corrections 1981).

Nelson, J. L. (1986). *The other side of signification: A semiotic phenomenology of televisual experience*. Unpublished doctoral dissertation, Department of Speech Communication, Southern Illinois University, Carbondale, IL.

Pilotta, J. J., Widman, T., & Jasko, S. A. (1988). Meaning and action in the organizational setting: An interpretive approach. In J. A. Anderson (Ed.), *Communication yearbook 11* 1(pp. 310–334). Newbury Park: Sage Publications.

Porter, L. W. (1974). *Behavior in organizations*. New York: McGraw-Hill.

Presnell, M. L. (1983). *Sign, image and desire: Semiotic phenomenology and the film image*. Unpublished doctoral dissertation, Department of Speech Communication, Southern Illinois University, Carbondale, IL.

Schein, E. H. (1971). The individual, the organization, and the career: A conceptual schema. *Journal of Applied Behavioral Science, 7*, 401–427.

Schutz, A., & Luckmann, T. (1974). *Structure of the life world*. London: Heinmann.

Troester, R. L. (1987). Examining the individual's experience with technological change in organizations: A cognitive sense-making approach. Paper presented at the Speech Communication Association Annual Conference, Boston, MA.

Van Mannen, J. (1977). *Organizational careers: Some new perspectives*. New York: Wiley.

Wanous, J. P. (1977). Organizational entry: Newcomers moving from outside to inside. *Psychological Bulletin, 84*, 601–619.

PART III

Consulting Organizations: Where Theory and Practice Meet

5

The Cybernetics of Cybernetics and the Organization of Organization*

Frederick Steier and Kenwyn K. Smith

INTRODUCTION

In this chapter we offer a way of seeing organizations, organizational communication, organizational change, and a basis for interventions with organizations that fits with ideas of the cybernetics of cybernetics, or what has come to be called second-order cybernetics. The chapter has two parts, which should be seen as complementary, each serving as the ground from which the figure of the other may be drawn.

In the first part of this chapter, we have the dual intention of using a dialogue about an organization to illustrate second-order cybernetic principles, while at the same time having those cybernetic principles provide a basis for seeing organizations. This section is a revised version of an article that we were invited to write for, and was published in, a family therapy journal.

The second part is a dialogue with various others, in the form of a "generalized other," who have engaged us with ideas, from the first part, that they have felt motivated to discuss further. These "others" were notable to us in that many of them could be counted among those whose ideas had informed the writing of the article in the first place. This dialogue is a vehicle through which we have reflected upon our own ideas as they were heard in various communities of communication scholars, and through which we have gained a better view of the ground on which the original paper rested.

Thus, as we had hoped, the article itself initiated a conversation from

*This chapter, as the text explains, is a vastly expanded and revised version of a paper published in the *Journal of Strategic and Systemic Therapies*, 1985, Vol. 4, No. 4, 53–65. The authors would like to thank especially, among many others, Rodney Donaldson, Heinz von Foerster, Ernst von Glasersfeld, David Herbst, Jane Jorgenson, Klaus Krippendorff, Per Helmersen, Ib Ravn, Thomas Söderqvist, Lee Thayer, and Eric Trist for the correspondence and conversations about earlier drafts that allowed the other in our dialogue to take shape and substance.

which the development of our own ideas proceeded in a way that could not have been predicted in the initial writing. The conversations with others could, of course, be understood as perturbations to our own conversation, linking the cybernetics of cybernetics to organizations, in a process that reflected the very content we were attempting to understand and describe.

We must point out clearly the context in which the first part of this chapter, the article entitled "Organizations and second order cybernetics," was created. It was written for a family therapy journal that was producing a special issue on organizations. There is a tradition, since the work of Bateson, Jackson, Haley, & Weakland (1956), connecting cybernetics to family therapy. This connection has been realized by family therapists recognizing the importance of seeing what had previously been seen as individual problems as better understood from the perspective of a larger system (i.e., the family). More recently, some inside the family field (e.g., Blount, 1985) and others, including the present authors, have begun to note that family therapy itself is better understood as located within a relevant "context" as a larger system — namely, its own organizations and institutions. This concern is, of course, a mutual one as, for example, the organizational communication world has also come to recognize the descriptive power and prevalence of family metaphors within organizations (cf., Smith & Eisenberg, 1987) — a recognition that, from a cybernetic perspective, might allow us to ask "what, or perhaps where, is this system of relationships called a family to which the family metaphor refers?"

Although the community of scholars to which this article was addressed was "officially" a family systems/family therapy audience, we felt the issues to be relevant to a much wider audience. We endeavored to broaden the circle of readers to include others in both the organizational and cybernetic communities, in part to initiate conversations that would allow the process alluded to above to take place. Those conversations, which allow for a deeper understanding of our own position as it evolves into "our position," are perhaps better understood in dialogic form. The dialogues revolve around discussions from questions and comments by others.

One important point to bear in mind throughout the reading of the chapter is the different senses in which the term organization is employed in the everyday discourse of both organizational members and organizational theorists. That is, "organization" can refer to the organizing process, a result of that organizing process (as in a set of relationships), or an instantiation of that process and result in the form of a particular "organization," such as the Alpha Organization. The different senses of "organization" are of course related to each other, and all three senses are used throughout the text. We hope that the context will provide enough background for the reader to hear us in the way we have intended.

Further, throughout the chapter, we are electing to show how cybernetic thinking can become incorporated into a conversation while talking about cybernetic thinking and organizations. For this we ask the reader to be aware of both levels of discourse throughout the chapter.

ORGANIZATIONS AND SECOND ORDER CYBERNETICS

> Anything said is said by an observer.
> —Maturana, 1970

> Anything said is said to an observer.
> —von Foerster, 1979

Setting the Frame

We recently met Joe Collins, the ombudsperson for the Alpha Organization. He was excited about meeting some cyberneticians because he had just returned from a cybernetics workshop and had been reading copiously in the field. He wanted to describe his job to us in cybernetic terms.

I can now see that my job is to help manage the relationship between the inside and the outside of the organization, to encourage conflicts to be dealt with where they arise, to get people to give feedback to unclog communication channels when they get blocked, and, in general, to help fix things up when internal imbalances cause problems for either members of the organization or important people in the environment.

We asked him what kind of issues he became embroiled in as he did his work. His reply was filled with statements such as the following:

Sometimes our formal evaluation system causes an individual to get a raw deal and when that happens I must bring it to the attention of the relevant people in order to get it corrected.

When management wants to implement a new plan, there are always some workers who have valid reasons for why it won't work—but management usually can't hear what the workers are saying, so it's my job to ensure that their voices are heard.

It doesn't matter how good a change program is in this organization, there are always some people who will resist it. It's my job to make sense oiut of the resistance to change because the power figures here don't have very good ways of thinking about this.

My job is to help people see the systemic implications of their actions—in a way, I'm a cybernetic educator trying to help people interpret what they do in cybernetic terms.

This last statement prompted us to ask him whether he could describe his own actions in cybernetic terms. He looked at us blankly and then said, "I just did."

In this moment we were confronted with the core of second-order cybernetics, or what von Foerster (1974, 1979) first labeled the cybernetics of cybernetics. Joe had clearly learned a lot about cybernetics at this workshop, and his understanding of his role and how his organization operated had certainly been enriched, but there was a larger question we were eager to explore.

"Joe, before you learned about cybernetics you had a set of principles that guided your understanding of your job. What were they?"

"Well, they've changed. I once was very involved with the labor movement and saw things in terms of conflict and the importance of coalition building, confrontation, and negotiation. Then, a few years ago, I started learning about what I'd describe as a managerial perspective—delineation of tasks, allocation of responsibility, coordination, etc."

"And now you're into cybernetics?"

"Well, I wouldn't say it like that. It sounds faddish. But, OK! What's your point?"

"The question is twofold. First, can you see, understand, and describe the changes in your own thinking in cybernetic terms? Here you've moved through three fairly different views of the world—labor supporter to managerial mindset to cybernetician. You've made these shifts swiftly and some callous person might wonder if this is the early onset of a midlife crisis. So perhaps we could see these changes in terms of your own individual development. Or, another possibility is that your different roles in the organization, from shop steward to supervisor to ombudsperson, might simply demand different ways of thinking. Or, perhaps the recent changes in your organization's structure have created tensions that can no longer be understood merely within a labor or managerial framework. Or, perhaps it's just the changing times. The explosion of computers might be making a difference. After all, there's more than a casual link between computing and cybernetics. So, the first issue is how to understand your newfound interest in cybernetics in cybernetic terms. The second one is . . ."

"Wait a minute . . . you guys are too . . ."

At this moment, we faced a choice point. The exchange was already getting defined in teacher–student terms, based upon the didactic principle of us explaining our ideas to Joe. If we'd stayed in a first-order frame, we'd have proceeded, responding to Joe's framing of that moment. However, we also could enter a second-order frame by engaging the *process* operative in this moment, instead of just the content. The outcome of this approach would be unknowable in advance. What was clear, however, was that whatever insight was to emerge would have Joe as copartner in its creation. We moved to the second of these options.

"No, *you* wait a minute. I was talking and I want to make my second point."

"Well, I was feeling overwhelmed and felt the need to grasp your first point before going on to the next one. Is that so unreasonable? After all, you guys are experts. I'm a novice in this stuff and. . ."

"If you're such a novice, it might make sense to just listen to us. If you'd let us explain the second point, the lingering questions you have about the first issues might be cleared up."

"But I don't understand the first point yet . . . anyway, if the second point would help illuminate the first point, why didn't you present that first?"

From a first-order perspective, this conversation was getting out of hand, caught in a spiral of what should be first or second, who was going to control this exchange, whose responsibility it was to create insight, and so on. Suddenly Joe started laughing hysterically.

"I suddenly feel like I'm back in school. You're the teacher and I'm the student feeling dumb . . . and I'm angry at you because I can't understand, and you're not being helpful. Yet I'm trying desperately to be your equal. Here we are trying to define our relationship with each other and describe our way of seeing, while talking about cybernetics."

"Joe, *that's* the second point."

"And that's what second-order cybernetics is?"

"Yes. Developing a description of the observer at the same time that the observer describes the observed. Then the artificial distinction between observed and observer disappears. That's the base of second order cybernetics."

What Is Cybernetics?

Cybernetics had its birth in the work of Norbert Wiener (1948) who studied communication and control in man and machine. In its early formulation the focus was on describing properties of systems that could be observed, with an emphasis upon processes of homeostasis, self-regulation, self-organization, etc. Included within this cybernetics of observed systems was a distinction between deviation-counteracting processes (emphasizing stability) and those of deviation amplification (emphasizing change), a distinction termed as a difference between first (counteracting) and second (amplifying) cybernetics by Maruyama (1963). This distinction must not be confused with that between first- and second-*order* cybernetics as we are describing here.

Process and change were central to cybernetic thinking. Hence, when cybernetic thinkers such as Mead (1968) and von Foerster (1974, 1979) began to apply the principles of cybernetics to itself, the whole field started to go through transformations and changes as profound as those it was attempting to understanding. The shift was one from a cybernetics of *observed* systems to a cybernetics of *observing* systems, which have now come to be called, respectively, first- and second-order cybernetics. This shift, which is fundamentally epistemological in nature, means that the observer must be included in any system of observation or description. As this applies to the study of human organizations, the shift is away from describing the parts, properties, and processes of an organization to issues such as *how* people create relations among the parts, and relations among the relations, that define the identity of the organization.

For example, ombudsperson Joe was tending to treat his organization as something that existed in objective form. He experienced himself as someone who was outside or separate from the system he was attempting to describe. With this level of dissociation from the cybernetic patterns he was explicating, Joe was not attuned to the ideological and political forces helping to shape an ombudsperson's view of the world, nor to the maps and models he was creating and using as ways of explaining the behavior of his organization.

When Joe presented the maps he found useful for understanding his organization, he treated them as objective statements, overlooking the idea that the role he was in and his actions in that role all played a part in the shaping of the maps he was "objectifying." Joe appealed to objectivity and presented his role as though it were something that he had no responsibility in creating. By moving to a second-order perspective and including the observer in the system, it was possible for Joe to see that he and *his* organization, in recursive interaction, were "responsible" for the roles, rules, meanings, and so on that made up his organization as a whole and his role in it.

Hence, cybernetics is at once social, and social cybernetics must be a second order cybernetics—a *cybernetics of cybernetics*—in order that the stipulated purposes of the observer be made part of the system that is observed, and the *autonomy*, and the consequent responsibility of the observer be recognized (von Foerster, 1979). The questions asked from a second-order perspective are themselves of a different order. We might ask now what is "the organization" of which Joe is ombudsperson, but how is it that Joe constructs (and consequently acts with) that organization in his particular way?

Radical Constructivism

To adequately understand second-order cybernetics, it is necessary to appreciate the centrality of the ideas of constructivism. By constructivism we mean that the world, as we know it, is a product of our construction. Hence, the building blocks of our systems of knowing cannot be separated from the phenomena we might be attempting to know. In fact, von Glasersfeld (1984) has called this approach one of *radical* constructivism for, as he notes, radical constructivism "breaks with convention and develops a theory of knowledge in which knowledge does not reflect an 'objective' ontological reality, but *exclusively* an ordering and organization of a world constituted by our experience" (1984, p. 24, our underlining).

Radical constructivism is both a natural outgrowth of, and instrumental in the development of, the cybernetics of observing systems. Epistemologically oriented, radical constructivism, as developed by von Glasersfeld (1984), points out the poverty of a correspondence principle of knowledge, and instead argues that there is a variety of constructions of knowing that will fit a given set of experiences (as well as make them "those experiences"). It focuses on a recognition that we inevitably create the lenses through which we view the world and the criteria that we use as standards for measuring that which we would hope to understand in "objective" terms. It treats the very notion of objectivity as an element of our socially constructed world.

In our social world, we create measuring devices (foot rulers, G.N.P., performance criteria, etc.) as standards to which our experience can be compared. However, we often ignore or choose to forget the arbitrariness (in the sense that they are based on one particular set of assumptions that fit one particular set of experiences—i.e., they are discretionary) of the constructed standards. When we seek to understand phenomena we experience by comparing "data" to these standards, we usually attribute differences between our observed or experienced data and our standards as problems or properties of the data rather than questioning the standards we have created as the basis of our comparison. We often impose our "standards" on "data" that we have created, whether they fit or not.

As we made this point to Joe, he wondered aloud what relevance this idea had to his role in making sure that individuals who were treated unfairly by his organization's formal evaluation system had adequate redress for their concerns. It was hard for him to see that the very notion of an evaluation process as it is often enacted sets in concrete something that is essentially discretionary. That one individual doesn't fit the evaluation system is as much a comment about the evaluation system (including its creators and interpreters) as it is about the individual in question.

We asked whether his observation of the "raw deals" that individuals got ever led to a change in the original criteria, or was it always incumbent upon the individual to work out a way to fit his or her experience into the system. Joe seemed to be "getting the point" until he raised a particular problem with which he had been dealing. The problem was that of an excellent engineer who had been promoted to a management position and had begun to perform "poorly."

> I just couldn't get this guy to see that in order to become a good manager in our organization, he had to change certain of his behaviors. He seemed to want the organization to adapt to his style and he couldn't see how it was his responsibility to learn how to fit in with the prevailing managerial culture. It seems a shame since he is very creative and could become a competent management specialist. But he just doesn't do well on the evaluation performance chart with which managers get rated. If only he could see that there's a best way of behaving as a manager, and behave accordingly . . . Do you know any good management training programs to which we could send him?

At this moment we told Joe that he could think about changing his way of thinking about adapation and fit if he wanted to fit in with a second-order cybernetics perspective. We had our tongues in our cheeks, and Joe laughed.

Adaptation and Fit

Organizational adaptation has been conceived of in two broad ways. The first is to treat adaptation as a reaction to circumstances that demand an alteration in the behavior of the organization in order for it to continue surviving or thriving within the environment in which it is located. Framed this way, the environment is seen as stimulating the reactions of the organization. Changes in the environment become "inputs" for the organization that then "outputs" altered behaviors that are "acceptable" to the prevailing forces external to it. Such a view treats the "adapting" organization as a rather passive entity. A variant on the above theme which accords the adapting organization a little less passivity, while remaining just as reactive, is when the organization, not liking the demands for change it receives from its environment, seeks out an alternative environment in which to relocate.

A second perspective, elaborated by Bateson (1979), highlighted the limitations of this "adjust to the environment" interpretation of adaptation. He noted that what seemed to be an adaptation often might well be counteradaptive in the long run, in that "adaptations" are often not accompanied by shifts in the entire distribution of options, and do not retain the needed variety. That is, some adaptations usually "eat up" or reduce the degree of flexibility or variety in a system, variety and flexibility that might be critical for adjusting to later events that systems may encounter. This can be seen clearly where organizations attempt to create a best adaptation (such as maximizing profits) and in the process become vastly overspecialized, reducing their capability to change at a later date. The experience of Chrysler illustrates the above. The whole of their physical plant was so calibrated for the manufacture of large cars that when the 1973 oil crisis struck they faced a choice: rebuilt their plants to produce small, more fuel-efficient cars as an adaptation to the changed environment, or stay with their present production systems, save the money the conversion process would cost, and wait it out until the environment returned to a condition where they could thrive. They chose the latter path only to be enormously threatened when the environment refused to change in the desired direction.

One point Bateson highlighted was the link between adaptation and addiction. The central issue is that as an organizationd becomes more tightly defined (in an adaptive way more tightly linked to its ecological niche) the options for its actions become narrower. At the extreme they become reduced to the level at which fundamentally there are no options for the organization other than to continue doing what it's doing. At this point, all behavior is repetitive and the organization comes to depend upon these repetitions to survive. This can be thought of as an addition to that particular adaptive option. As such, Bateson argues, the adaptation is counteradaptive. Or an adaptation which appeared so sophisticated at one time can end up becoming the foundation of maladaption at another time. This is perhaps a cybernetic reformulation, in social relations, of the Marxist proposition that all entities create the seeds of their own destruction.

If adaptation, viewed in this limiting way, can be problematic for a social entity, for the reasons discussed above, how then are organizational actors to think about the phenomenon the concept of adaptation was designed to address?

Von Glasersfeld (1984), building on the foundations that Bateson's critique offered, elaborated an epistemologically enriching way out. He points out that many of the key misconceptions about adaptation arose because of how Darwin's famous dictum, "the survival of the *fit*," became interpreted. This has, over the years, been translated into "the survival of the fittest," implying that it is the strong who survive. Von Glasersfeld discusses the inappropriateness of this view and adds to Bateson's notion that adaptation, without a concomitant shift in an entire distribution of options, can be a process through which variety becomes "eaten up" or reduced and thereby a process in which flexibility is lost.

Von Glasersfeld argues that a fruitful way to think about "fits" is in the metaphor of a key *fitting* into a lock. He notes that any particular lock may be opened by numerous keys, a dubious awareness we have due to the contribution of the professional burglar. If we discover a particular key opens the lock, we don't describe it as the fittest; we merely say it fits. In fact, no key that opens the door is any more or less fit than any other. What we do discover is that some keys will not open the lock no matter how much we pull and twist. In this sense, Darwin's dictum might better be expressed as "the elimination of the *non-fitting* (or un-fit)." This switch in understanding makes the whole subject of adaptation into one where evolution is primarily one of elimination rather than survival. The mere fact that an organization has not yet had its contours so constrained that it doesn't "fit into the lock" is no guarantee that this possibility is not just around the corner. Hence, a more modest slogan for those surviving entities and one that is congruent with this evolutionary perspective might even be "not yet extinguished" rather than "survival of the fit(test)." It is the *viability* of the system, rather then its adaptability, that is critical (von Glasersfeld, 1980).

There are clear parallels between theories of evolution and theories of knowledge. We invent theories of the world that fit into our experiences. This fit is not isomorphic in the sense of how we traditionally think of a map as representing a territory. Rather, it is a fit more of the kind of the key in the lock. The theories may be then thought of as a "constructed nature" rather than representational form. They fit, not because they mirror a particular reality, but because they sustain a particular version (or set of versions) of the constructed "realities" to which the theories are linked. The self-referential nature of this relationship between our theories and our realities needs to be appreciated. That is, our theories refer not to a reality which is "out there" but to a model (of "reality") we have also constructed.

We noticed that, as we were making these last points, Joe had been nodding his head in affirmation rather vigorously, and now his face broke into an eager smile.

"I think I'm beginning to see. By choosing a particular set of evaluation standards, I am constructing an idea of what an acceptable manager is, and by using this standard in a particular way, such as a metric, I define the idea that there is a best manager. I wonder how it is that supervisors, upper managers, or ombudspersons, for that matter, see things in such a way as to create such an evaluative device?"

"That, Joe, is a wonderfully phrased question of a second-order cybernetic nature."

"Something you said earlier is becoming clearer now. It's that bit about the observer and autonomy. But do we all mean the same thing when we speak of autonomy?"

Autonomy

The business ownership of *The New Yorker* may change hands, but the idea of *The New Yorker* — the tradition of *The New Yorker*, the spirit of *The New Yorker* —

has never been owned by anyone and never will be owned by anyone. It cannot be bought or sold. It exists in the minds of a group of writers, artists, editors, and editorial assistants who have been drawn together by literary, journalistic, aesthetic, and ethical principles they share, and by a shared outlook on the world. (*The New Yorker,* 22 April, 1985)

One concept that has been made central in cybernetics is that of the autonomy of a system. Understanding how cyberneticians think about autonomy is important because they treat this subject differently than do organizational theoriests and some open systems thinkers, who link autonomy to the concept of hierarchy and to an organization's set of interdependent relationships between activities inside and activities outside the organization. That is, the authority for that autonomy is seen as residing outside or above the particular organization, system, or subsystem in question. A summary of some of the fine early work with autonomy as understood by organizational theorists, with specific reference to autonomous work groups, is provided in Herbst (1962).

Maturana and Varela (1980) have brought into focus the idea that the relations that constitute the organization of a system can be understood entirely in terms of that system's internal processes. In these regards the system may be seen as *organizationally closed.* One consequence of using the term organizational closure is that traditional systems theoreticians may hear this as a challenge to the very principles of open systems thinking. When cyberneticians speak of a system as being organizatioinally closed, they do not mean that the system has no relations with its environment. What they are saying is that the internal relations with which that systems constitutes itself have a coherence that does not involve any reference to the system's environment. *When the term "closed" is used it must be tied to a particular domain.* For example, both living and social systems are generally open with respect to energy, such as food, although they are organizationally closed with respect to their modes of digesting that food. You could say that a digestive system brings in food in order to maintain itself through such activity. It actively seeks out food that, by digesting it, keeps that digestive system a coherent internal organization. (It chooses food over rocks, for example.) Thus, when a system is described as autonomous, this means that it is closed in terms of the *organizational* relations with which it constitutes itself as a system.

In this view, interdependence and autonomy are not opposites; rather, they can be seen as complementary concepts. Referring to our earlier metaphor of fit, we can say that autonomy is to interdependence as the key fits in the lock. That is, *it is precisely through its external interdependencies in certain domains that a system can be autonomous in its organizational domain.* Organizations must be seen as autonomous systems within their ecological niche that we call the context.

Maturana and Varela (1980) elaborate on these ideas based upon their concerns as biologists. The operations and relations that interested them initially were relations of production. The phenomenon they described, autopoiesis, is, literally, the process of self-production. However, as Varela (1981) neatly points out, autopoiesis, or self-production, is but one member of a class of phenomena, or a class of processes of organizational closure. What is of interest to us in the study of organizations is not a one-to-one correspondence of the principles of autopoiesis to organizations, but rather an attempt to capture the essence of the process of organizational closure in a social domain. To do this, we must focus not only on relations of production, but also on the production of relations; relations that are more clearly specified in a social domain, such as those of communication, language, and so on.

Thus, when we speak of the autonomy of a system, we speak of its organizational closure, and are interested in the processes by which a social system defines its own boundaries and maintains its own identity. Its internal coherence is key. What is of special value in focusing on the issue of autonomy is that it allows us to move away from the dominant belief in many systems-theoretic perspectives, that all issues related to the internal life of a system can be understood only in terms of the interaction between inside and outside.

At this point Joe commented on how exciting this new concept of autonomy is. We responded by indicating that autonomy has been significantly addressed in the literature of group processes. The work of Freud, Redl, and Bion illustrates a version of what can be meant by autonomy. Freud (1922) focused on the relationship between the followers and the leader of a group and argued that leadership results from a number of individuals choosing the same person to put in place of their own ego ideal; in other words, the leader is made into a reference point through which individuals can connect with each other. Redl (1942), building on Freud's foundation, indicated that group formation occurred whenever a central person was made (a) an object of identification, or (b) an object to whom strong emotions were directed, or (c) an ego support. In other words, group life could be explained by referring only to the internal life of this social entity.

Bion (1961) took the work of Freud and Redl many steps further, noting three key dynamics that he labeled fight/flight, pairing, and dependency. In short, he described the process of members feeling dependent on the group and then feeling fearful that the group would not be a reliable entity to take care of their dependency needs. This fear evokes in the members the desire to fight with that which might deprive them or overwhelm them in the group. Yet the fear of what could be evoked in the fight triggers the response of wanting to take flight. In the process, the very flight from the fight that is triggered by the fear of what to do about one's dependency makes the group a "fragile" and undependable setting to give expression to one's dependency needs. The resultant fragmentation sets the stage for the emergence of pairing where individuals search for others with whom they can link. Bion suggests that the *inner life* of a group can be understood in terms of the interplay among these three processes, which he refers to as "basic assumptions."

What is crucial for our purpose here is to highlight that the descriptions offered by Freud, Redl, and Bion provide a way of seeing a group strictly in terms of relationships that are internal to the group. These relationships, whether labeled identification with the ego ideal, or fight/flight, or whatever from some other discourse are thus organizationally closed in that in order to understand the *organizing* process of the group, there is no need to refer to anything outside of it.

While expressions of autonomy in organizational settings can be seen to have a rich history, of which we have provided a mere glimpse, current thinking in cybernetics creates both a systematization and a general paradigm of autonomous systems that transcends distinctions about the type of system (i.e., biological or social) of interest. This paradigm has been proposed by Varela (1984, 1987), building on his own work and the work of Maturana, and labeled the autonomous systems paradigm.

Varela (1984) describes his autonomous systems paradigm as a shift from the earlier input/output paradigm (which he refers to as the Turing paradigm). The input/output framework is a circular, cybernetic description of a system with the emphasis on the way the organization reacts (passively) to external inputs. In order to understand this process, reference must be made to something outside the system; it is other referential. The focus in this input/output model can be seen to be on control, for while from one view the system can be said to be adapting to changes in the environment, from another view one can understand an "adaptation" as being governed by the kind of input. Thus, an intervener, helper, or consultant will try to predict the kind of "adaptation" the organization will make to a particular input, and, by such an understanding, control the organization by dictating the input. While this view is consistent with the circularity of cybernetic systems, it emphasizes this circularity through its understanding of an organization as a passive entity reacting to an input in terms of a control orientation. Thus, the view is one of: "If we understand how a system will adapt, we, as interveners, have the opportunity to control that system; that is, place it in an environment in which it will 'adapt' in a particular way."

Varela's thoughts shifts us from the passive model of an organization that reacts to inputs to an active one that can best be understood in terms of the mutual interconnections within that organization. In this autonomous systems way of thinking, the idea of inputs and outputs can be replaced by concepts of perturbations and compensations. Perturbations can be thought of as triggers or catalysts for organizational change, but which themselves do not determine the direction of that change. While these newer terms may at one

level may have been understood merely as a shift in labels, a change in the
language used is necessary to convey a different way of thinking; that is, input
and output as metaphors of process carry with them baggage that needs to be
transcended.

Just as we explained this last point, we noticed a troubled look on Joe's
face. We asked what was disturbing him.

"I'm confused. I was thinking that I understood second-order cybernetics as
the cybernetics of observing systems. Now, this way of seeing organizations
as autonomous systems is appealing, but weren't the descriptions of the
autonomy of group processes about observed systems and first order cybernetics. What did I miss?"

Joe was indeed allowing us to see ourselves and our descriptions better. He
was focusing on the idea that the cybernetics of autonomy as the study of
organizational closure in systems is not identical with the cybernetics of
observing systems. Autonomy can arise in a first-order cybernetic description
(i.e., in describing an observed system), and be consistent with the principles
of cybernetics. There are, however, some very important links between ideas
of autonomy and princples of second-order cybernetics.

First-order cybernetics, from the perspective of autonomy, can be thought
of as interested in the closed loop that defines that system's organization, and
hence, creates its identity. Second-order cybernetics allows the observer that
specifies the description that, in turn, creates the closed loop to be included in
a larger loop. This larger loop can also be seen as organizationally closed, and
thus autonomous, but it is a loop that characterizes the observing system, and
that is a key difference.

It is interesting to note that, as described above, an input/output systems
paradigm focuses on processes of control, even when we are interested in the
process of adaptation (in the von Glasersfeld sense of viability). Once you
admit the *responsibility* of an (autonomous) observer into any system of
description — which you must do from a second-order cybernetics perspective — the paradigm of control no longer fits. It does not fit because it seeks to
place responsibility for the constructions or observations in a system external
to itself. However, the paradigm of autonomy, even as a first-order cybernetics description, does fit with second-order notions. If we admit the
autonomy of the distinctions that *we* draw as the basis of our descriptions, we
must also admit the autonomy of *others'* describing. That is what was meant
earlier by objectivity being an element of a socially constructed world.

First-order ideas of autonomy, as they describe an observed system, are
thus only a part of the loop with which we are concerned in second-order
cybernetics, but a useful part. We objectify things so as to get on with our
daily activities, such as preparing meals, etc. That is, we try not to live

exclusively in a second-order world, seeing ourselves through our constructions, but we must visit it often.

A consequence of second-order cybernetics is that it allows us to see first-order concepts, such as autonomy, in a new light. That is, it is useful to talk of the autonomy of an observed system, bearing in mind that it is we who are choosing to see it that way. However, we must also realize that the particular set(s) of relations that constitute the system's autonomy are constructed in a very special way by the participants (who are also observers) in that system. *There is an integrity to the coherence of the system of meanings that the participants (and we as observers) interactively create.* It is the observer's responsibility to respect this. Thus, second-order cybernetics is very much concerned not only with espistemology, but with *ethics.*

Implications

Taking a second-order cybernetic perspective brings many implications for organizational members, managers, researchers, and interveners. We identify a few here.

1. If we acknowledge reality as a socially constructed process, then any attempt to map what is going on in organization is at the same time both a very impressionistic activity and an act that alters (and creates) the "landscape" by the very process of mapping it.

2. Radical constructivism puts squarely in front of us the recognition that our theories about what transpires in organizations are vehicles for creating and sustaining the very things our theories are designed to comprehend. For example, the massive research on performance appraisal and the tools that have been elaborated to conduct it have made performance appraisal into an activity that leaves hidden or unexplored both the epistemological foundation on which it is predicated, and the agenda of those whose interests are served by these systems.

3. The second-order cybernetic thinking highlights that social reality is constructed such that all experience can be framed in ways that generate multiple meanings. Hence, disagreement about what is transpiring within an organization is as much a statement about the nature of reality creation and the multiple frames that can be generated as it is about the "phenomena" over which the disagreements exist.

4. The various strands of multiple realities that are constructed in organizations are the fabric from which the texture of organizational life is created. Organizations have activities and tangible facets, but it is mostly the coherence of their multiple meaning systems that give them their particular character.

5. For a researcher who wants to understand an organization, there is an epistemological task of bringing together one's preformulated theories with the indigenous symbol systems within the organization to cocreate, with its members, pictures, metaphors and theories that are focused primarily on fitting the local scene. The critical issue is to avoid imposing one's theories on the organization without denying that we all bring such theories to our attempts to understand. This is the basis of a methodology that is particularly needed in intervention research (Steier, 1985).

6. As interveners operating within a second order cybernetic framework, our actions may be viewed as perturbations. It is necessary for us to respect the organization's internal integrity and to accept whatever the organization elects to make out of the perturbations we generate. That is, organizations are never changed by the actions of the intervener. The most we can do is to catalyze conditions within which change may occur.

7. *Organizational members, managers, researchers, and interventionists are all actors in observing systems.*

SECOND ORDER CYBERNETICS AND ORGANIZATIONS

Observers ultimately observe themselves.
Krippendorff, 1984

The authors reflect through conversations with relevant others and become their own metaobservers

—*I am not so sure that the concept of closure deals with the problems that made the open-systems advocates in the 1950s such eager advocates of a new holistic approach.*

—I do not see us as trying to refute the earlier open systems work that spawned such enthusiasm in both its proponents as well as in a generation of followers (including both of us).

—*I do not follow you. I heard your argument as one advocating organizations as better understood as closed systems. Did I miss something?*

—Perhaps we did not explain ourselves quite clearly. And perhaps the confusion arises from a type of logic through which most people look at systems in general, and organizations in particular. That is, most people understand choices, such as the closed/open systems perspective distinction, as being an either/or choice (systems must be either open or closed) rather than one that can be understood from a both/and logic. Systems are both open and closed, and we tried to point out that this openness or closedness must be tied to a particular domain of operations. For example, we tried to argue that human organizations are systems that are open with respect to energy, while being closed to organization. In fact, it is precisely because they are open with respect to energy exchanges with an environment that they can retain their particular character of autonomy or organizational closure. The interdependency is key. (We hope that we are answering your concern rather than just repeating ourselves here.___

— *Well, no matter about the repetition. I'm beginning to see what you are saying. But if you thought that people would hear your argument from an either/or perspective, which would make a lot of sense given our traditional western training in Aristotelian logic types, why didn't you understand that this is how you might reasonably be heard, and proceed accordingly? You are asking people to see organizations differently and see how they see organizations differently at the same time, and that is no small request.*

—You are right about our need to recognize how we might be heard as part of what it is that we are trying to say. Again we have the issue of context entering into a system of description, and a conversation.

— *I can see that the open systems movement was a response and a challenge to most previous work in organizations (and in systems in general) that sought to understand an organization by, as in most physical experiments, closing that system off from any environmental disturbances so that the nature of disturbances to which the system could respond could be controlled. This created a closed systems view of any organization. The strength of the ecology movement in part derived from a readiness on the part of the scientific community to refute this closed systems approach and to see the relevance of the mutual feedback (an idea coming from cybernetics) between a system and its natural environment, as well as to see the folly (or better, future disastrous consequences) of any system that ignored its natural environment. This ecological movement had a strong parallel statement in the organizational field with, for example, the organizational ecology work of Emery and Trist (1972; Trist, 1976). You are now saything that we must go back, or perhaps it is forward, to a closed-systems thinking, but it seems clear to me now that this is a closure of a very different kind than that of which we usually think. Perhaps you can elaborate more.*

—Perhaps it is a bit like a point from Zen. I think that we had to see that systems were not closed, in order to see in which way they are closed, and this could only have been done through the recognition of the contributions of open systems theory. We have traditionally relied on thinking that has banished ideas of self-reference and paradox (which allow for a closure of any kind) to noperson's land. And yet, the understanding of paradox is central to understanding group life (Smith & Berg, 1987). Further, once we recognize that a dictionary, for example, is a closed system of referents (words being defined in terms of other words, etc.), and that there is no way "out of this dilemma," we begin to appreciate how we are always tied to a system of communication that grows out of self-reference (cf, Luhmann, 1990). This is not a trivial example, because it is through processes of language and communication that a social system such as "an organization" may attain the particular kind of organizational closure that it does.

—Forgive me for thinking this a bit abstract. Can you explain it a bit more simply.

—We'll try. Perhaps it is important to see that there are different kinds of organizational closure. That is, the relations that define an identity of a system as that particular kind of system may, in a sense, occupy different kinds of "spaces." The idea that living systems are autopoietic (Maturana & Varela, 1980), or that they literally produce themselves (cells produce cells that are identical to their producers) is an example of organizational closure in the physical/biological space. But that is not what interests us most in the understanding of social organizations. Here the organizational closure is better understood as one in the semantic/descriptive, or better, relational/ cognitive space. That is, the relations that create a system as an organization are relations of language and communication, specified through symbolic acts. Perhaps we should go back even a bit further. *The organization attains the status "organization" by its members' intersubjectively constructing the idea of what the organization "is" through their recursive interaction.* They quite literally distinguish the organization from its environment (or background) by their own inter-acts of drawing distinctions in their language.

—So the organizational closure in which I would be interested is one of a cognitive kind.

—Yes, but what is most interesting is that it is a cognition that is at once social. Maturana (1985) notes that "the mind is not in the head," and here he is no doubt indicating that, following Bateson (1972, 1979), mind exists in a social and hence ecological space. Such a recognition forms a basis for the social constructionism of Gergen (1985), and an extension into an ecological constructionism (Steier, 1991).

—But you pointed out that we are not interested in the physical space. And yet are not many organizations concerned with the production of things physical, like automobiles, computers, or books?

—There is a wonderful essay by Herbst (1974) entitled "The Product of Work is People," in which he argues for an understanding of organizations as producing *human relations,* no matter what physical units may be involved in the organization's daily life. It is precisely through the (processes of production) of the physical entities that the particular form of human relations will evolve. Thus, their manner of languaging is tied to, but not determined by, their activities. We must not take lightly that in this age of rapidly changing technological forms, organizations must be understood as sociotechnical systems (c.f., Emery & Trist, 1960; Herbst, 1985). But it is through the sense-making operations of the people involved that the organization can be understood as autonomous. It is the members who determine, through their activities, what relationships will constitute "the organization" for them. And this is done through the recurrent interactions of the members. It cannot be done for them, although you certainly have many organizations where what constitutes the relevant relationships designed to create that organization's "image" are attempted to be dictated "from the top." If this were indeed possible, it would imply that the sense-making and experiencing apparatus that are developed as a history of the interaction of that group could be legislated from outside that group. The organizer could then be separated from the organized in the relevant organization (which does indeed happen in the physical space of most organizations), and the organization, as a system of relationships, would not be spread out throughout the system, as it must. A self-organizing system is precisely one that can *not* be separated into a part that "does the organizing" and a part that "gets organized."

— *You seem to be getting at an important distinction here with regard to language and communication. Earlier you made reference to a dictionary as being self-referential. And of course a dictionary can be understood as providing a basis for a shared understanding in a situation. But "it" does this (I say "it" here because it is the dictionary's human creators to whom the appeal for reference is made) by, in a sense, defining from outside the system. The group, or organization, members, must however interpret "the literal definition" in their own way based upon their assumed shared experiences. And I would guess that it is the latter in which you are interested — how the system defines itself for itself.*

—Right. One way of describing that distinction is between definition as an external reference, and a constitutive definition — one created in the domain of interactions of the group about itself. It is a bit like Geertz's (1973) description of the Balinese cockfight — a story that a system tells itself about itself. Here, we might refer to such a description as a *narrative of self-reference*. In our case the narrative takes the form of how the organization members define the organization as well as its environment(s). This can be seen as a constitutive definition, and, further, as including the very stories that the members tell that make that organization become "real" to them. Jorgenson (1989, 1991) has looked at such questions with families, where she became concerned with how families defined themselves (a constitutive definition) rather than just how sociologists, psychologists, family therapists, etc., defined "the family."

— *Of course, the family members may indeed be informed by those "formal" external definitions of family, and they will certainly be aware of them, but these definitions get re-understood in light of a family's own experiences of "family" through which they constitute their own definition. And how these self-definitions are constituted would seem to be inextricably linked to the system's autonomy. However, that would seem to bring up a rather thorny issue. You make a strong point for recognizing that most earlier, noncybernetic approaches to autonomy in organizations were not really about "autonomy" in that the permission for a group to be autonomous, with respect to the carrying out of a production process, for example, had to be granted by upper management to the work groups. And then you make a strong argument, with which I agree, for recognizing that autonomy, understood as how a system creates its own identity by its own internal interactions and transactions, separating itself from its background with regard to the organizing dimensions that are important to its identity, is not something that can be legislated, or granted. And yet, if I understand you correctly with regard to your ideas of second-order cybernetics and your focus on the observing system, do you still not need the observer to specify whether or not a social system is indeed autonomous. Do you want, as an observer, to give "linguistic permission" by virtue of your own idea of autonomy?*

—Of course, a nonreflective work team, for example, is not necessarily, in their terms, behaving as an autonomous system. They are simply behaving. Their behavior as a system becomes autonomous for an observer when that observer says that this is so and this observation is accepted in the observer's community. So we agree with you in some sense. And yet, we do feel that there is a difference between legislating the constraints, as a manager, within which a group may "make autonomous decisions," etc., and *understanding* and then describing a group's autonomy with regard to its "shared" experiences through its own local language connected to its own local activities. This autonomy, as it is so described, is not an exclusive property of the group, or even of the group-in-a-context, but rather constructed as such by an observer. However, if this construction is done in a manner in keeping with second-order cybernetic principles, it simultaneously recognizes the integrity of the constructions of the group members, in "their own terms," and that whatever is sought to be known "in their own terms" must always be translated into the observer's terms (so as to be heard by the observer's community), in a process that will closely resemble Gadamer's (1976) hermeneutic "merging of horizons." This is no doubt why Jorgenson (1989, 1991) refers to her "findings" as *co-constructions*. (This is also a point that we tried to emphasize in points one and five in our earlier (first part) implications). An important distinction for communication researchers, interested in social systems, then, is that between systems where the members are cognizing organisms, capable of specifying their own autonomy in their social/cognitive space, and systems that would interest a physicist, or a microbiologist, for example, where the elements of those systems are not social/cognitive entities capable of defining their own system. In social systems, the observer is also a participant, and, more importantly, the participants are also observers. In nonsocial systems, the observer, although always a participant in the system observed, is not observing a system that has members who will also act as observers.

— You seem to have a great deal of difficulty here in that you want to tie the observer to the observed, much as Yeats asked how we can know the dancer from the dance, and yet you seem, in your descriptions, still to separate them.

—That is a good point for which we have no easy answer. The difficulty would seem to lie in our language, which is a decidedly linear one (and one that may predispose us to linear thinking). I think we need to, as a basis for our communicative acts, develop a more clearly *relational* language, a language that of course involves "us" reflexively using "it." Then we might begin to take seriously observing (and languaging) as relational processes.

— There is something else that you said that I found a bit difficult to swallow, if you will be so bold as to allow me to continue with your "food and digestion" metaphor from earlier. It is, in fact, one of your concluding remarks — now, how can an organization

be an observing system? *More specifically, members, managers, and researchers are indeed all observers, but in what sense could they be said to be "actors in an observing system?"*

—This is actually a key point of our argument. And your question, we think, reflects a bias in our culture toward thinking of cognition as something contained within an individual, and further, an individual person whose boundaries are demarcated by "a bag of skin." Personhood need not be confined to such physical boundaries as, for example, Gergen (1977, 1991) and Shweder and Miller (1985) have argued.

—So this would connect to your earlier mention of Maturana's point that "the mind is not in the head"—it, being constructed in language, is in a "social space," and is culture bound.

—And yet, we have the dilemma that we feel experience to be individually generated, in the sense that I cannot experience what you experience, and yet this experience becomes "this experience" through a language that is at once social, and in some sense "shared." So, again, we must use a circular, both/and logic here to recognize the circular relationship between individual experience and shared language. Of course, our languages, being tied to our experiences, are not perfectly shared (how could we ever know this if it were) but merely fit, as our key in our lock. It is an intersubjectivity that is key. As Rommetveit (1979) has pointed out, we must, paradoxically, assume a perfect intersubjectivity in order to achieve a partial intersubjectivity in real discourse.

—But by claiming that an organization should be thought of as an observing system, you would seem to be saying something a bit deeper than that—something at the level of organization as a system.

—Yes, I believe we are. I suppose that the easiest way of explaining this issue is to note that many systems thinkers have taken as a starting point the idea that the system is more than the sum of its parts. Now this may be true in some instances, but misstates the issue. The system can easily also be less than the sum of its parts—have you ever tried to do a crossword puzzle with 10 people? A better way of stating this dictum is simply that the system is different than the sum of its parts—it exists in a different phenomenal domain, made up of relations between its members. In addition, members in an organization will "observe" differently in that organizational context (as their observing will be tied to the activities and languaging in their organization) than they might otherwise. So, in this sense, you have an organization made up of individuals who, even given the culture-bound idea of individual we have alluded to earlier, are observers. Yet, these individuals are in the act of creating "their organization," and their organization will observe in a manner very much understood from the members' symbolic and communicative *relationships*. In fact, Argyris and Schön (1978) faced a similar dilemma when developing the notion of organizational learning, and adopted a similar approach—an approach that provides the systemic basis for "The Learning Organization" (Senge, 1990).

— *Connected to the idea of organizational learning, another point you made was that organizations are never changed by the actions of the intervener. In what sense do you mean this? And why would anyone want to hire you as a consultant if you don't believe that you change them?*

—Again, the key issue is that WE do not "cause" changes to take place in an organization. At the same time, we, by virtue of our relationship to "an organization," help to create or co-construct the very organization we are "helping." Thus, from a traditional perspective, our earlier implications number one and six would seem, paradoxically, to contradict each other. And yet, their juxtaposition is central to a second-order cybernetic perspective. What we intended is that an organization, as constructed by the multiple meaning systems that make it "that organization" as an autonomous entity, change in accordance to their own self-referential processes. We can certainly catalyze, or facilitate change here, but it is the internal coherence of the organization that decides how "it" will change. Or, as Maturana (1987) claims, it is the structure (in his terms, the varying relationships that make that organization realize its particular form) that determine in what way change will occur. But there is a larger issue here that concerns how communities of interveners and helpers have heard this idea. Many seem to feel that if change is not caused by the helper, then it must be caused by the organization. And what this would (wrongly) seem to do is to remove the helper/intervener (and the inquiring researcher, particularly the communication researcher, as well; Steier, 1988b) from any responsibility in the change process. And nothing could be further from the *whole* way of seeing implied by a second-order cybernetic view. What is required is to recognize your role as a helper in the change process, as not causing change (you do not have to claim credit for "it") but yet participating in a change process, although in a different, non-linear–causal way. *It is a view that requires both humility and responsibility.*

The Metaobservers Reflect on the Whole Process and Review Their Grounding

In looking back over this dialogue and conversation, we can perhaps recognize a stronger statement of some ideas that were proposed earlier, in the first part of this chapter. That is, although the idea of control has been central to the description of cybernetics going back to Wiener's (1948) original formulation, it does not seem to fit both the second-order (observing) and first-order (observed) ways of seeing from a systemic perspective. This has been made clearer to us by thinking about the relationship between second-order cybernetics and organizations. The implicit direction requested of us in the earlier article was, first, to develop a description of the key ideas of second-order cybernetics, and then to say what this might mean for thinking about organizational life. However, a result of that exercise and the ensuing conversations has been to rethink what the premises were that made such adevelopment possible. Thus, thinking about organization from a second-order cybernetic perspective has implications for thinking about (second-order) cybernetics (and the circle is redrawn).

Two important consequences arise. The first is that, as appeared in the dialogue, separating a first order (observed) from a second order (observing) has been heard as invoking a distinction that is precisely one to be avoided if one does not wish to, and recognizes that you cannot, separate observing from observed in any system — they are inextricably linked. More importantly, if we recognize second-order cybernetics as arising by applying (first-order) cybernetics to itself, the inclusion of the observer had to be implicit in the earlier formulations of cybernetics, and it was (cf., Ashby, 1956; McCulloch, 1974). It can be seen that, as early cybernetic work was historically situated in a post World War II technological wave, the engineering applications of cybernetics took hold, and the epistemological aspects (including the importance of observing) were "put on the back burner" for many in the young field. Interestingly, this sole emphasis was not the case for the core group of cyberneticians that was developing the theoretical foundations of the field, as can be seen by the titles of the Macy conferences that fostered the development of cybernetics — "Cybernetics: Circular Causal and Feedback Mechanisms in Biological and Social Systems" (in fact, the fifth of these conferences was devoted to language) (von Foerster, Mead, & Teuber, 1952). So perhaps cybernetics, and the cybernetics of cybernetics, are better terms here. (At the same time, we should still be wary of understanding "second-order" ideas in a "first-order" frame, such as trying to objectively study "other observing systems" apart from our own tools — an approach referred to as one kind of trivial, or naive, constructivism; Steier, 1988b, 1991.)

Second, and most relevant to communication, is that the dominant metaphor of cybernetics can be seen as initially moving from control to one of understanding (Maturana, 1988). As Maturana notes, in describing a steersman (traditionally a dominant figure in cybernetics):

As the skipper acts from his or her metadomain of discourse as an observer, in what we may call his or her understanding of the situation, the shape of the ship (the position of the rudder) will change through the interactions of the skipper with the wheel in a manner contingent to his or her understanding. In our daily discourse, we say that the skipper controls the course of the ship, but the phenomenon that takes place is not that. What the skipper does is to make his or her understanding part of the domain of interactions of the ship, thus making the drift of the ship contingent to it. (1988, p. 7)

He concludes by advocating that cybernetics means "the science and art of understanding."

In reflecting on the conversations that have led to the production of this chapter, such a shift is both consistent with and supported by the view advocated here, with a slight, but rather important, modification. Understanding, as Maturana also notes, must not here be taken as being of something that exists apart from the very process of understanding. However, it must also be seen as linked to action—"the active understander who becomes an understander by participating in a network of understanding in a situation" (Steier, 1988a). Taking seriously the circularity that has been essential to cybernetic thought, cybernetics can then be thought of as "the art and science of *reflexive* understanding" (Steier, 1988a). *Most importantly, such an understanding must be seen as embodying and being embodied by the communication process.* Thus, it is understood that communication research can only be understood by communication research. Communication is spread throughout the system, and is not some thing locatable in any part. It is such a recognition, through taking reflexivity seriously, that cybernetics can be seen to have, as its own root metaphor, the *mutual processes* that allow for what we take as control, or self-organization, to become possible—cybernetics as "mutualling" (Steier, 1992).

Thinking back on the mutual relationship between organization and cybernetics, such a view would seem to allow for the joint processes of *self-reflection and dialogue* that we have tried to present in both form and content, and to also allow for the *responsibility and humility* that should be the guiding ethic for any organization (helper/researcher/member) understander.

REFERENCES

Argyris, C., & Schön, D. A. (1978). *Organizational learning: A theory of action perspective.* Reading, MA: Addison–Wesley.

Ashby, W. R. (1956). *An introduction to cybernetics.* London: Chapman and Hall.

Bateson, G. (1972). *Steps to an ecology of mind.* New York: Ballantine Books.

Bateson, G. (1979). *Mind and nature: A necessary unity.* New York: E. P. Dutton.

Bateson, G., Jackson, D. D., Haley, J., & Weakland, J. H. (1956). Toward a theory of schizophrenia. *Behavioral Science, 1,* 251–264.

Bion, W. R. (1961). *Experience in groups.* London: Tavistock.

Blount, A. (1985). Toward a "systematically" organized mental health center. In D. Campbell & R. Draper (Eds.), *Applications of systemic therapy.* London: Grune and Stratton.

Emery, F. E., & Trist, E. L. (1960). Socio-technical systems. In C. W. Churchman & M. Verhulst (Eds.), *Management sciences: Models and techniques* (pp. 83–97). Oxford: Pergamon.

Emery, F. E., & Trist, E. L. (1972). *Toward a social ecology.* London: Plenum Press.

Freud, S. (1922). *Group psychology and the analysis of the ego.* New York: Liveright.

Gadamer, H. G. (1976). Philosophical hermeneutics (D. E. Lange, Trans. and Ed.). Berkeley: University of California Press.

Geertz, C. (1973). Deep play: Notes on the Balinese cockfight. In C. Geertz, *The interpretation of cultures* (pp. 412–453). New York: Basic Books.

Gergen, K. J. (1977). The social construction of self-knowledge. In T. Mischel (Ed.), *The self: Psychological and philosophical issues* (pp. 139–169). Totowa, NJ: Rowman and Littlefield.

Gergen, K. J. (1985). The social constructionist movement in modern psychology. *American Psychologist, 40,* 266–275.

Gergen, K. J. (1991). *The saturated self.* New York: Basic Books.

Herbst, P. G. (1962). *Autonomous group functioning.* London: Tavistock.

Herbst, P. G. (1974). The product of work is people. In P. G. Herbst (Ed.), *Socio-technical design: Strategies in multidisciplinary research* (pp. 212–217). London: Tavistock.

Herbst, D. P. (1985). *Introduction to socio-technical thinking: A dialogic presentation.* Oslo, Norway: Work Research Institutes Documents 11/85.

Jorgenson, J. (1989). Where is the family in family communicaion: Exploring families' self-definitions. *Journal of Applied Communication Research, 17,* 27–41.

Jorgenson, J. (1991). Co-constructing the interviewer/Co-constructing family. In F. Steier (Ed.), *Research and reflexivity.* London: Sage.

Krippendorff, K. (1984). Poster designed for American Society for Cybernetics Annual Meeting, Philadelphia, PA.

Luhmann, N. (1990). *Essays on self-reference.* New York: Columbia University Press.

Maruyama, M. (1963). The second cybernetics: Deviation amplifying mutual causal processes. *American Scientist, 51,* 164–179.

Maturana, H. R. (1970). Neurophysiology of cognition. In P. L. Garvin (Ed.), *Cognition: A multiple view* (pp. 3–23). New York: Spartan Books.

Maturana, H. R. (1985). The mind is not in the head. *Journal of Social and Biological Structures, 8,* 308–311.

Maturana, H. R. (1987). Everything is said by an observer. In W. I. Thompson (Ed.), *Gaia: A way of knowing* (pp. 65–82). Great Barrington, MA: Lindisfarne Press.

Maturana, H. R. (1988, Spring). The notions of cybernetics. *Continuing the Conversation, 12,* 7.

Maturana, H. R., & Varela, F. J. (1980). *Autopoiesis and cognition: The realization of the living.* Boston: Reidel.

McCulloch, W. S. (1974). Recollections of the many sources of cybernetics. *ASC Forum, 6,* 5–16.

Mead, M. (1968). Cybernetics of cybernetics. In H. von Foerster, J. D. White, L. J. Peterson, & J. K. Russell (Eds.), *Purposive systems: The first annual symposium of the American Society for Cybernetics.* New York: Spartan.

Redl, F. (1942). Group emotion and leadership. *Psychiatry, 5,* 573–596.

Rommetveit, R. (1979). On negative rationalism in scholarly studies of verbal communication and dynamic residuals in the construction of human intersubjectivity. In R. Rommetveit & R. M. Blakar (Eds.), *Studies of language, thought and verbal communication* (pp. 147–161). London: Academic Press.

Senge, P. (1990). *The fifth discipline: The art and practice of the learning organization.* New York: Doubleday.

Shweder, R. A., & Miller, J. G. (1985). The social construction of the person: How is it possible? In K. J. Gergen & K. E. Davis (Eds.), *The social construction of the person* (pp. 41–69). New York: Springer–Verlag.

Smith, K. K., & Berg, D. N. (1987). *Paradoxes of group life.* San Francisco: Jossey-Bass.

Smith, R. C., & Eisenberg, E. M. (1987). Conflict at Disneyland: A root-metaphor analysis. *Communication Monographs, 54,* 367–380.

Steier, F. (1985). Toward a cybernetic methodology of family therapy research: Fitting research methods to family practice. In L. L. Andreozzi (Ed.), *Integrating research and clinical practice.* Rockville, MD: Aspen Systems.

Steier, F. (1988a, Spring). On cybernetics as reflexive understanding. *Continuing the Conversation, 12,* 7–8.

Steier, F. (1988b). Om a reise til et sted for forste gang og se det som der du kom fra: Refleksjoner om krysskulturelle refleksjoner. [On going to a place for a first time and seeing it as where you are coming from: Reflections on cross-cultural reflections]. In H. Hartveit (Ed.), *Gjennom speilet og tilbake* [Through the mirror and back]. Oslo, Norway: Tano.

Steier, F. (1991). Reflexivity and methodology: An ecological constructionism. In F. Steier (Ed.), *Research and reflexivity.* London: Sage.

Steier, F. (1992). Cybernetics as . . . mutualling. *Cybernetics and Human Knowing, 1,* 3–10.

Talk of the Town. April 22, 1985. *The New Yorker,* p. 36.

Trist, E. L. (1976). A concept of organizational ecology. *Australian Journal of Management, 2,* 33–58.

Varela, F. (1981). Describing the logic of the living: The adequacy and limitations of the idea of autopoiesis. In M. Zeleny (Ed.), *Autopoiesis: A theory of living organization* (pp. 36–48). New York: North Holland.

Varela, F. (1984, November). The cybernetics of autonomy. Address given at the annual meeting, American Society for Cybernetics, Philadelphia, PA.

Varela, F. (1987). Laying down a path in walking. In W. I. Thompson (Ed.), *Gaia: A way of knowing* (pp. 48–64). Great Barrington, MA: Lindisfarne Press.

von Foerster, H. (1974). *Cybernetics of cybernetics.* Urbana: University of Illinois, Biological Computer Laboratory.

von Foerster, H. (1979). Cybernetics of cybernetics. In K. Krippendorff (Ed.), *Communication and control in society* (pp. 5–8). New York: Gordon and Breach.

von Foerster, H., Mead, M., & Teuber, H. L. (1952). A note by the editors. In H. von Foerster, M. Mead, & H. L. Teuber (Eds.), *Cybernetics: Circular causal and feedback mechanisms in biological and social systems. Transactions of the Eighth Conference, 1951* (pp. xi–xx). New York: Josiah Macy, Jr. Foundation.

von Glasersfeld, E. (1980). The concepts of adaptation and viability in a radical constructivist theory of knowledge. In I. Sigel, R. Golinkoff, and D. Brodzinsky (Eds.), *New directions in Piagetian theory and their application to education* (pp. 87–95). Hillsdale, NJ: Erlbaum.

von Glasersfeld, E. (1984). An introduction to radical constructivism. In P. Watzlawick (Ed.), *The invented reality* (pp. 17–40). New York: Norton.

Wiener, N. (1948). *Cybernetics: Or control and communication in the animal and the machine.* Cambridge: MIT Press.

6

Communication and Organization: Reconsiderations::Speculations

Lee Thayer

History may be regarded as a record of the struggle of man to realize his aspirations through organization. . . .

C. H. Cooley, in *Social Organization*

The "perfectest" organization—whether a small love affair or a huge automobile manufacturing affair—would be one in which self-interests and enterprise interests are indistinguishable.

But there will be, for us, no perfect organization. Nor will there be, for us, the capacity to know one if we saw one.

To exist in a perfect organization would be to be perfectly unconscious of that existence. The example to which we are referred is that of the Biblical Garden of Eden. In wanting to know whether the existence we had there was the only one possible, we were condemned forever to make up our own. To be conscious of the conditions of our lives, the sentence read, was forever to be faced with the necessity of making them up as we go along.

And of trying to explain what we had created.

We could not be imperfect in a perfect world. If we wanted to be imperfect—to be conscious of what our lives are like—then we would have to create whatever imperfect conditions of life seemed consistent with our own imperfections (or what Nietzsche would call "errors").

If this is the case, and it seems altogether likely, then what we are faced with is trying to explain our social organizations and enterprises with the same mentality with which they are created. To be human is to live in a world of our own making; and it is to want to or even to need to explain that world as if it were independent of the mind for which it exists.

The world we know and the mind we "know" it with are two aspects of the same thing. That may seem cruel punishment for wanting merely to be conscious—or, perhaps, self-conscious. But that's the price we must continue to pay. And as absurd as that may seem, it does at least explain why it is that no matter how far or how fast we go, we never arrive. Our theories turn out to be no more perfect than our organizations and social arrangements.

Our designs on the world, practical or theoretical, will continue to be imperfect because *we* are. To be conscious of something is to have to try to figure out why it is the way it is. So we find ourselves ever trying, with our imperfect minds, to figure out why our imperfect organizations are the way they are.

I

There are certainly other ways of explaining this exquisite human dilemma, just as there always are and always will be other ways of explaining anything. To be human is to produce and market, to trade in and live by, explanations. We are who we are in virtue of the explanations we have proferred and consumed about ourselves. And our social worlds are the way they are in virtue of the explanations we have proferred and consumed about them. The catch is that the things we explain are never independent of our explanations of them. ("I regard consciousness as fundamental," said Max Planck; "I regard matter as derivative from consciousness.")

Weber, for example (and indeed Dewey and James and Simmel, as well), took the position that reality — including the reality of organizations — is inexhaustible. Human organizations are too complex to be fully comprehended. And a theory of things human would be no more than one of an indefinite number of vantage points on social phenomena. A theory of organizations, therefore, could be nothing more than an abstraction that distorts, simplifies, and curtails understanding. Not even the smallest aspects of reality can be intellectually subdued, Weber believed. Nor do grand syntheses offer any greater approximations to "truth."

And as Hume concluded, along with Kant, the "laws" of nature or of social process that we devise are *not* aspects of nature or of society. Nor is causality itself an aspect either of nature or of social process. Such "laws" as we may profess to have "discovered" are ultimately features of mind contemplating nature or social enterprise — categories that the mind foists on what it contemplates.

Suffering the hegemony of "scientificality" (as Arendt, 1959, called it), we imagine that our inquiries and our theoretical pronouncements are for the purpose of insight. Not so, James (after Bergson) suggested: The concepts we talk with are for the purpose of construction, or of reconstruction. Our talk, whether as heads of enterprises or as academicians, is primarily for the purpose of lending credence and legitimacy to the concepts and categories by which we "know" the world (cf. von Hayek, 1975). What we see, when we look into the natural or the social world, is some reflection of the categories of mind we look with.

Ashby's (1956) now well-known "Theorem" is another way of "explaining" the dilemma. What he suggested, in effect, was that the thing that is to know something must be at least as complex as the thing which it is attempting to know. In order to comprehend an organization, for example, the human mind that is to do the comprehending must be as large and as complex as that organization — else, as Weber said, that abstract understanding simplifies and distorts. It is intriguing to speculate on the implications. Since one's comprehension or grasp of *any* social process would necessitate one's comprehension of one's self as a part of that social process, how would it be possible for one to be more complex than oneself? Since comprehending some aspect of the world in which we live would necessitate comprehending the mind that comprehends it, how would that be possible? To understand ourselves, we would have to be more complex than we are. To understand the social enterprises of which we are a part, we would have to be more complex than they are. And "they" *are* only as we can know them.

It is, indeed, a knotty problem.

The existentialists and the phenomenologists and the symbolic interactionists put another twist on the dilemma. The only way to "know" the world that another knows is to know it from his or her point of view. The world the sociologist describes is not the world as we people know it. So what I may say of an organization or a social collective may provide *a* way of talking about it — for those who are properly indoctrinated in that way of talking about/ understanding it. But it is not the same organization or the same social process that is known by one of its members. To "really" know it, one would have to be so much a part of it that one could no longer be aware of it in any "objective" way. But no observer's "objective" explanation ever really matches — is never really the same thing *as* — any one member's "subjective" experience of it. So which is the "real" organization?

We might also consider Heschel's (1965) caveat: that the "truth" of any theory about people and their artifacts is "either creative or irrelevant, but never merely descriptive" (p. 8). His reasoning? That whenever and however we "describe" the "nature" of man, we fashion it. We become, he says, what we think of ourselves. The corollary, of course, is that our organizations become what we think of them, that the "nature" of our organizations includes what we think they are.

It is this complicity of our understandings of things in the way things are and the way things will be that the historian Polak (1973) dealt with in detail in his *The Image of the Future,* and the physicist Gabor (1964) in his *Inventing the Future.* Like the religious philosopher Heschel, they ask us to observe how our understandings of the nature of things human become a part of the nature of those things. Neither people nor their social institutions have a nature of their own; we become, in the social institutions in which we have our lives, what we think of ourselves. "They" are not independent of our consciousness of them (cf. Brown, 1978), nor we of the way our nature — "human nature" — is enabled and constrained within them.

What it comes down to is that no way of organizing social or economic or political life is "natural." And no way of explaining or theorizing about social arrangements and social enterprise — about organization — can be "true" in the sense that it is "true" to their "nature," that it merely "describes." An explanation may be irrelevant in the sense that people do not "pick up" on it. A scientific theory may be "true," but it is irrelevant if significant numbers of scientists do not "buy into" it. Or a scientific theory may be "false," but if significant enough numbers of scientists hold it to be "true," then it will be creative, in the sense that there will be consequences for the direction of growth of knowledge in that field of science, and perhaps for human and social life as well.

Since we cannot know whether a theory of man or of man's social arrangements is "true" or not (given the logical constraint of having to use our minds to assess the "truth" of what we can know only with our minds), we may have to be content with some other criterion for assessing the value of our understandings of things human. We may need to shift our focus from the "nature" of things to the "direction" of things. We may need to shift our concerns from that of understanding things to that of understanding the *consequences* of the way we understand things.

Every way of organizing has consequences. And every way of understanding or theorizing *about* one or another way of organizing things has consequences. It may be logically impossible for us ever to know the "nature" of human communication or of human organizations. What we *can* know is that certain ways of talking lead to certain consequences, and that different ways of organizing lead to different consequences.

Any way of talking about either organization or communication may be irrelevant or creative — it may be of no consequence or of *some* consequence. But, if Heschel is "right," no way of talking about communication or about organization can be merely descriptive. The test of a good theory of either is not whether or not it is "true," but what we can *do* with it (Lewin, 1948; Whitehead, 1948).

And thus any way of explaining the world is a way of changing it.[1] So how do we propose to change that part of the world we intend to explain — the role communication plays in the life and the performance of organizations?

---

[1]The more relevant question to be asked about Freudian "theory," for example, is not whether it is true, but where our understanding of it and belief in it have led us. What consequences has that way of explaining the "nature" of human and social life had for us?

II

Weber's conclusions as to the sheer impossibility of ever arriving at a theory which would capture the "truth" of social organization or social process, or Ashby's proposition anent the logical impossibility of doing so, seem neither to have deterred we moderns, for whom all things *must* be possible, or to have dampened our enthusiasm for the "race to truth" about all such matters. Hardly a month goes by without the announcement of some ultimate new theory. Apparently, like those long-forgotten Austrians who coined the expression, we've taken the position that "the situation is hopeless, but not serious" (cf. Watzlawick, 1983).

Perhaps it is merely that we are compelled to justify and legitimate our inextinguishable intellectual expeditions in *some* way — and that's the way that makes sense to us — that we are accumulating "scientific" knowledge that will one day lead us to the ultimate truth about whatever it is we say we are examining. No matter that we already have, as Otto Rank once suggested, more "truth" than we could ever use.

Does this mean we should take Weber seriously? That we should abandon our quest?

Perhaps not. But there are, indeed, certain advantages that fall to those who take Weber seriously.

One advantage, as Blake told us, follows from the understanding that everything that is capable of being believed is an image of the truth. And the advantage is in finally acknowledging that truth is a function of people and not of things. That is, that the "nature" of oranges or of organizations is a mental artifact, and that human and social *consequences* flow not from what "is," but from how we see it, from the meaning and/or the significance or the value or the utility we ascribe to it in our perception of it — in short, from our *beliefs* about it, our imaginations of it. Whether those beliefs are "true" or not must also be decided by humans; no matter what scheme for measuring or inquiring or modeling or theorizing or truth sifting we may agree to, those too are beliefs. That they might be widely or even universally held does not make those ways of "minding" the world the same thing *as* the world.

And how is this an advantage? When we eliminate "truth" as the only or the ultimate criterion of explaining organizations, our eyes are opened to the partial or limited usefulness of *every* perspective on organizations. As the old man says at the end of the film adaptation of Hemingway's *Islands in the Stream,* "It's all true!"

Are organizations political? Yes, they are (Crozier & Friedberg, 1980). Is "information" vital to organizational functioning? Yes, but no more so than even the "petty" politics of everyday life in organizations. Is power an issue in organizations? Yes. But structure is important too, isn't it? Yes, it is. And couldn't we say that everything hinges upon interpersonal relationships in organizations — that they couldn't function without those relationships? Yes, we could say that. Isn't behavior in organizations often not rational (Weick, 1977), but ritualistic — "symbolic" (cf. Morgan, 1983; Pondy, Frost, Morgan, & Dandridge, 1983) and even self-serving at times? Yes. Do people ever cease being "psychological" just because they are "in" organizations? No (de Vries & Miller, 1984). Isn't plain semantics important — that people may use a word that has a different meaning for someone else in or out of the organization? Yes. And isn't the clarity of reports and instructions critical to organizational efficiency? It may be, of course. But if things were perfectly controlled, then there could be no creativity, no innovation? Seems to make sense, doesn't it? How about the current panacea: Isn't organizational *culture* where it's at? Yes. But things do bottom out in certain economic issues, don't they? Yes, that's the case, too. And the way people "communicate" in organizations — that's critical too, isn't it? Yes. But doesn't the presence of unions, or at least of adversarial attitudes, affect *how* people can communicate in organizations? Yes. Certain things can be accomplished "better" by replacing people with automatic or even computer-controlled systems, can't they? Yes. So, is management a science or an art? Yes.

And so on. You get the point: that whether a perspective or a "theory" about organizations is "true" or not depends on whether we believe it or not. There needs to be another measure. There may be many ideas about organizations that could be useful even though there may be no way of assessing their "truth." A quarterback may determine that pivoting on his left foot instead of his right gives him more balance to do what he has to do next. If that way of pivoting improves his performance, we don't have to ask whether it is "true" or not. If *how* meetings are run becomes more important than what is accomplished, we've gained something at the cost of something else. Which is more important? Can there be a "theory" *of* that? Is it "true"?

Consultants and academicians may compete for the "truth of the day" about managing or assessing organizational performance. But are our organizations and institutions that much better and more trouble-free as a consequence of all of the "truth" we have perpetrated about them?

To whose "theory" of organization or of communication in organizations does Iaccoca attribute his "success"?

Another advantage of taking Weber seriously is that we could avoid considerable confusion and frustration. We seem to be confused about what our theories are *for*. And frustrated by the relative indifference to them, not only on the part of those who own and run organizations, but by our colleagues as well. Why is it that the comings and goings of panaceas for running or designing or fixing organizations look so much like patterns of fashion-mongering and fashion-following? Are the scientific/academic and the real/practical enterprises as irreparably distinct as Weber said they are? We seem in general to be about as hotly in pursuit of how Mr. Geneen thinks we should conduct our research as he is of how we think he should run his corporation. That may not be as it "should" be, but it is the way it is. What would we do differently, or how would we do differently what we do, if we were to accept that these are two distinct kinds of enterprises?

Is the underlying logic of these two universes of discourse the same? (And whatever else we may argue they be, they are certainly two different universes of discourse.) In the everyday life of organizations, whatever "works" has thereby a certain validity — a certain, at least expedient, "truth" value. In the world of social science research, the issue of "truth" is quite different: it has to do with what "causes" what, based on our observations of what, in some situation or other, we believe to have "caused" what, from the perspective of the theory or the hypothesis we employed to inform the "facts" of that situation. The practicing manager asks himself (or herself): "What do I need to do — within the realm of my personal and organizational resources to 'cause' that result?" knowing all the time that the outcome will depend on his or her limited perception of the situation, on what kinds of resources he or she can bring to bear, on his or her position of authority or power in the organization, on what somebody else does or does not do, on 67 other exigencies and 13 other *known* contingencies, on all the shoring up he or she does to guard against being wrong, and on luck — among other things. The paradigm of explaining things that the researcher uses is simply not the paradigm of explaining things that is used by the practicing manager. The organization member's performance is not judged on the basis of how much "truth" he has gathered; it is judged on what he or she accomplished given only the standard of what he or she was expected to accomplish. The test of the premises employed is not a "truth" test, but a "workability" test.

If an organization member succeeds at her task, she can say, "I did it." If a social science researcher were to succeed at his task, and were to be consistent, he would have to say, "The theory did it." When he says, "*My* theory is true," he is of course doing the same thing that the practicing manager is doing, even though he would deny it. For where is the theory that led him, unwaveringly, to the "true" one?

If the world is reducible to a theory or a model, then so are we. Yet another advantage of taking Weber seriously is that it would preclude our wading into *that* conceptual quagmire.

III

So what we are talking about when we talk about "organizational communication" (or any of its variants) depends upon what is meant by "organization" and by "communication" (Thayer, 1967). A look at the literature will reveal a remarkable range of meanings.

That may be obvious. But for all its apparent obviousness, there is precious little evidence that we are concerned that we may be talking about different things. What is important about it is that there are no self-evident facts: We select and inform those facts that seem to us to be relevant to our understanding of the thing we are looking at. If I understand organization to be that complex set of social arrangements understood by people that enables and constrains their communication, I will collect different facts, and interpret those facts differently, than will you, if you conceive organization as that which obtains on an organization chart of exclusively for-profit corporations. The communication problems you will "see" will be different from those I will "see." And you will look for their sources or their "causes" in different places than I would. If you think an organization is an entity that exists independently of its "stakeholders" (its members or any others who have a "stake" in what happens in it, or to it, or as a result of it, etc. — cf. Mitroff, 1983), and I think an organization exists *only* in the minds of those stakeholders, and has no existence separate from their ways of minding it, then we are certainly going to "see" the role of communication in the life and the performance of the organization differently.

It isn't so much that we don't know what we're talking about. It's that we don't often realize that we may be talking about different things. And that seems serious enough to justify giving some attention here to the two basic terms of our discourse, and to what appear to me to be some shortfalls and some discrepancies in our conventional understandings of communication and organization.

- Most of those who write about management or about organization, and many (if not most) of those who write about managerial or organizational communication, seem to be predisposed to treat communication as a subset of managerial or of organizational behavior. In the same way that communication is not a subset of psychology, but psychology a subset of communication, isn't it the other way around? To reduce communication to just one more thing that employees or managers or executives *do* when at work is to mutilate and obscure the very phenomena we need to lead from to explain everything else that is going on, and in which we have to find the solution to most other problems. Communication is only in its most trivial aspect something that people "do." In its more profound aspect, it is what people *are,* and what people use to create and maintain the human contexts (including every human organization) in which they have their existence. It is *in* communication (as Dewey said) that people create and maintain reality — which is to say, the only reality they will ever know. Minds are products of communication, as are all other human artifacts. The very *idea* of management (and of organization) has been created in words. People do not live in *the* world of things; they live in *a* world of the *meanings* of things. And those meanings are created and maintained, altered or exploited, only *in* communication.

- To treat communication as merely a way of "conveying" information (cf.

Reddy, 1979) is to leave those who do so with the problem of accounting for organization and behavior in some other way. And those other ways — whatever they may be — always turn out to be blind alleys. To impute a "hierarchy of needs" to people as a basis for motivating or manipulating them may be easy to teach and easy to learn. But it begs the issue that human "needs" are themselves normative — that is, created and maintained *in* communication. They do not exist apart from the way they are created *in* communication. And to "see" organization as something separate from the ways in which "its" stakeholders construct and reconstruct "it" in their everyday conversations about it and allusions to it is to "see" something other than what is known to those people who constitute the organization. This creates a special kind of pseudo-difficulty not only for organization/ management theorists, but for practitioners as well. It is the manager or executive who assumes that the realities of the organization (as he or she sees them) are self-evident who actually creates problems that would not exist if he (or she) recognized that organizational realities are *social* realities (cf. Berger & Luckmann, 1966), created and maintained in communication — and that this is as true for him as it is for others. As Weick (1979) says, people make sense of the world by seeing things upon which they have already imposed what they believe. And belief is a social product — something that has to be produced and reproduced in the way people talk about those things every day.

- For Cooley (1902), "the imaginations which people have of one another are the *solid facts* of society . . . the object of study is primarily an imaginative idea or group of ideas in the mind. . . ." To understand communication as Cooley does is to shift the focus of "solid fact" from those objects and events "out there" to people's imaginations of them. The "solid facts" in a financial statement are not to be found in what is printed on the page, but in the sense or the import which some reader imagines those data to have. This is a shift in perspective, in *empirical* outlook, which very few writers on the subject have been able to make. When it is not made, we end up looking for the right things in the wrong places, and the wrong things in the right places. To say, for example, that a particular decline in market share *means* that we *have to* do this or that may make sense, but it glosses the critical step — that of some*one* taking that report into account in some way. And it is that *interpretation* that constitutes the subject matter of the study of communication in social process (i.e., in organizations), and *not* the thing which was interpreted.[2]

---

[2]One might compare Hugh Duncan's (1962) observation that "the greatest body of observable social 'facts' (is) not derived from what people do but from what they say about what they do" (p. 146).

- To see communication in this way is to depart from our conceptual hegemonies in yet another direction. The reigning "paradigm" in communication study remains $A \to B = X$, which translates "A" "communicates" something to "B" with "X" result. Since the formula is algebraic, you can plug in the "known" "variables," and solve for the remaining one. This has an immediate appeal (it makes immediate "good sense") to us in this culture, because we are in the control business. And this is a control formula. It has long also been a part of our "conventional wisdom," and we have, by applying it where it ought not be applied, created insoluble problems. For example, as soon as the responsibility for learning is shifted from the pupil to the teacher in schools, the ensuing problems of "education" become insoluble. Where the teacher is responsible for "communicating" what is to be learned to the pupil, but where the pupil has little or no responsibility for the acquisition, translation, and digestion of knowledge and ideas that may be indispensable to the quality of civilized life, if not to his or her own, nothing much is going to happen beyond the classroom or beyond those semester-long chunks in which the teacher "teaches" and the pupil is examined, typically not on what he or she has learned of any long-range human value, but on what the teacher "said" — on the data that were presented. This is a perversion not only of the idea of communication, but of the espoused aims of that institution as well.

What happens when one is caught up in that reigning "paradigm" (cf. Morgan, 1980) — and it is difficult if not impossible *not* to be caught up in it since it is part and parcel of our "deep culture" — is that the focus shifts from the receiver (the auditor) to the speaker, and the criterion from efficacy to "effectiveness." In the process, we generate an illusion about what is going on. For example, if a driver runs through a red traffic light and smashes into another car, our "engineering" mentality (if this is what it is) goes immediately to the "need" to have brighter or bigger or better-placed traffic lights. The parallel here is when some individal commits a crime and says he got the idea for it from watching television; in this case, caught up as we are in our conceptual biases, our thoughts may run immediately to a "solution," which usually involves some sort of attempt to constrain or censor television programming. Either way, we miss the point. It is not the red light that "causes" most drivers to stop; it is the way they take it into account — the meaning and the significance they ascribe to it. It is not some television show that "causes" someone to commit a crime. *No* television show is meaningful in and of itself, and certainly there is nothing in "it" that compels one to do anything about it whatsoever.

What we may want to acknowledge here, as difficult as it may be to do so, is that "communication" as "output" is relatively inconsequential. What *is* consequential is how people take the world into account: not, in short, what-is-going-on or even what is "in" the message proferred them, but how they interpret it. God said to Adam, "Don't." Adam did. The lesson is there for all who might be able to learn from it — that all human consequences flow from the way people interpret the world, not from the way the world "is," that all human and social consequences flow from the way people interpret what is said to them and what they read, not from what those messages "say."

It is a largely unlearned lesson that lies at the heart of a great many problems in human relationships of all sorts, and certainly at the heart of a great many unnecessary difficulties and problems in organizations. "We all receive," said Thomas Aquinas, "according to our ability to receive." What is critical in human communication wherever it occurs is not the speaker's eloquence nor even his sincerity; it is the receiver's (or the auditor's) capacity *to acquire and to interpret* that knowledge which may be of value to him or to the institutions whose cause he would further, and his *inclinations* to do so one way rather than another. We may hold the originator responsible to a degree for the clarity or the timeliness or even the relevance of his message (its relevance, that is, to those who have the capacity and the internalized "need" to acquire that message and to interpret it in some beneficial way). But we cannot hold the originator responsible for the auditor's *interpretation* of that message. A healthy and vigorous organization cannot be built on the assumption that communication is solely the originator's responsibility, and that "perfect" communication somehow rests upon the notion of perfect transmission. To do so would be to fly in the face of the wisdom offered us in the story of the Garden of Eden. Or, what shall we say — that God was just a lousy "communicator"?

"Whatever *can* be misunderstood," the apocryphal saying goes, "*will* be misunderstood." And what *can* be misunderstood? Anything, by someone or another.

I'm not talking here about some technique of "listening," or something so prosaic as merely repeating back what the speaker said as evidence that the auditor "understood." I'm talking about *who owns the responsibility for acquiring and interpreting relevant knowledge,* either on behalf of oneself, or on behalf of some organization or institution. And I'm taking about the profound consequences that follow on from the position one takes on this matter.

We live in a culture where considerable "lip service" is given to the notion of "individuality." But if we look carefully what we see is that we lay claim to "individuality" for our rights and freedoms and privileges and entitlements. But responsibility for our failures and shortcomings and inadequacies are much more likely to be laid to our parents, our teachers, our bosses, or to "society" itself. We claim responsibility for our accomplishments, but deny responsibility for our shortfalls. If we succeed in school, we are likely to point to our diligence or our intelligence. If we fail, it was the "teacher's" fault, or the school's fault.

I have dwelt upon this point at some length because it seems to me central to our understanding of communication in general, and of communication in on-purpose organizations in particular. We can't begin to enhance the performance of our organizations in general until we eliminate this perversity in our thinking—in its most basic form the assumption that what the auditor receives and how he understands it and what he does about it is the originator's responsibility. Until the auditor *owns* the responsibility for the consequences of how he or she acquires and interprets and makes use of information or knowledge, we will continue to produce the most implacable of the problems we are trying to solve, *viz.,* how to "organize" people in organizations, or how to make organizations more "intelligent" with respect to their environments, and so on.

One additional example before moving on to other questions about our conventional understandings of "communication" and of "organization." The most crucial decision any organization member ever makes on behalf of that organization is who to admit to membership. If those who are selected into an organization are "perfect" for the role they will play in it, then those persons will function as a part of the solution to any problem the organization faces, and not as a part of the problem—keeping in mind that they cannot be a part of the solution if they are a part of the problem. And perhaps the most telling criterion for selecting people into organizations—although it is one few organizations use—is not that person's technical skills or occupational competencies. It is, rather, how astute that individual has been over time in acquiring and interpreting and making use of the information (or knowledge) that person "needed" in order to carry out his or her own aims in life. If a person has demonstrated the ability to do this for himself (or herself), he or she will be able to do this on behalf of the organization. It is the most generalizable human competence that can be had or offered. In developing this rare and profound competence, the individual comes to see himself or herself as the instrument of his (or her) own destiny. And a person who is the instrument of his (or her) own destiny can make positive and provocative contributions to the destiny of *any* human organization. For this is the person who understands that the quality of life at work, for example, is his (or her) responsibility, not someone else's—just as the quality of one's own life in general is one's own responsibility, ultimately, and not the responsibility of some other person or group or abstraction (e.g., "society"). And this is the person, as well, who understands that anticipating and preventing problems on the job, and of seeing and interpreting them "intelligently" when they do occur, of acquiring and interpreting and making use of organizational "intelligence" on the job, is an undilutable responsibility of one's own.

Every person who "understands" this also understands the underlying issue in communication—that is, that every human organization works best only when each individual assumes responsibility for the consequences of how he or she acquires and interprets and makes use of knowledge in the performance of one's tasks. It is the manager who has not realized what it takes to be the instrument of *his* own destiny who is ready to take on responsibility for another's. And that's how the problem, so merely "psychological" and apparently harmless in the abstract, becomes compounded, and becomes the underlying obstacle to high-level, "intelligent" performance throughout human organizations of every sort.

Every statement about the world, and every observation/interpretation of it is evaluative. If a perception, one is reporting to oneself what-is-going-on *relative to* what *should*-be-going-on. If a statement to others, one is reporting on what-is-going-on *relative to* what-*should*-be-going-on. If an interpretation of that statement, one is reporting to oneself what that other understands is-going-on *relative to* how the receiver understands what *should*-be-going-on, given that statement. And so on.

There are no neutral observations or interpretations. There are no merely descriptive statements (as Heschel told us). When people disagree, or when they "misunderstand" one another, it may be at the level of what-is-going-on. For our interpretations of the events of the world may certainly differ. But it may also be at the level of what-should-be-going-on. And we don't realize that the difficulty may be at this level, simply because we are inclined to assume this level away, or to assume that we are automatically in accord at this level. When we say, for example, "I don't understand why so-and-so didn't see such-and-such a problem," we may be making an observation on his perceptabilities. But we may just as well be making an observation about his (or her) understandings of the way the world is "supposed to" be. Or our own. Which? Which is the "true" or the "right" observation/interpretation? Is the superior's interpretation of what-is-going-on and his (or her) assumption about what-*should*-be-going-on "truer" simply because of his (or her) position? What constitutes superior "vision" or perception or interpretation? If an organizational problem is what obtains in the discrepancy between what-is-going-on and what-should-be-going-on, does it make sense that the superior establishes the parameters for all such problems by being the source of what-should-be-going-on? If it does, then the way we typically organize our organizations makes sense. If it doesn't, then we may want to question one of our fundamental assumptions. For many of the most onerous difficulties in organizing people comes from how we differentially enfranchise those people with respect to whose interpretation takes precedence. It would, of course, be ideal if we could organize people in such a way that the most "intelligent" interpretation (the one that turns out to be most beneficial to the organization and its members) is the one that always takes precedence. But we don't usually organize things with that in mind.

And this is where our understandings of "communication" and of "organization" begin to intersect.

So what ought we to say about some of the inadequacies of our
"conventional wisdoms" about organizations?

Because "organization" is a noun, and because, as we all know, nouns are
words used to categorize *entities* of some sort, it seems no trick at all to conceive
of "organizations" as things—as complex things, perhaps, but as things
nonetheless. What could be more obvious than the fact that General Motors
is some *thing* in our world?

In doing so, we see organizations very differently than did Simmel. For
Simmel (1971), societies and organizations are *ongoing* accomplishments, ever
in a state of continual production (since they are produced and reproduced
every day in communication). They are *events* that are never completed. And
they have no reality outside those accomplishments, no reality outside the
ways in which they are daily reproduced in the conversations of stakeholders
about them, or on behalf of them.

One might compare this vantage point with that of Dewey and of James,
both of whom saw organizations as nothing but the activities and relations of
individuals to one another, a challenge to the conventional wisdom which was
later echoed by Bridgman (1959, esp. Ch. 7). All reality, the reality of human
organizations no less, must be socially reconstructed on a continuous basis,
for we do not live in *the* world of things, but in *a* world of the meanings of
things. And those meanings must not only be created in everyday communication, and in rituals and symbols and signs, but must be recreated and
maintained in communication, else they will fade and eventually be transformed or disappear altogether.

What gives us the *illusion* of the tangibility of organizations is to be found
in the fact that the "stakeholders" of that organization have at least a part of
their identity in the meanings that they attach to the relationships between
themselves and that organization (what Sherif & Cantril, 1947 referred to as
"ego involvement"). And it is in the efforts of those "stakeholders" to
perpetuate *themselves* through perpetuating those relationships that organizations have their apparent and continuing existence for their "stakeholders."
We daily "enact" (to use Weick's term, following Burke) our relationships to
all of those social organizations and institutions in which we have a "stake," in
order to "enact" ourselves. The "solid facts" of social life, Cooley said, are the
meanings of things—our ways of "minding" the world—and it is these that we
must continuously reconfirm through reenactment. And it is therein that
organizations and organizational life have their continuity, and what seems to
us their obvious tangibility (cf. Hawes, 1974).

If that seems difficult, consider for a moment the size and the scope of the
error we otherwise fall prey to. We have long believed ("known" would
probably be a better word), for example, that organizations could be "fixed"
in much the same way that we might "fix" a car or a television set or a broken
bone. For years we developed panacea upon panacea for solving organiza-

tional ills and for maximizing organizational "performance." Early on, it was "scientific management." Later, it was "human relations." Then we had Theory Y, and later even Theory Z. During all of this time when we were busy accumulating the intellectual wherewithal for "fixing" our organizations, individual productivity (held constant for capital investment) was declining, and, more recently, we've been forced to acknowledge that we've been bested in the design and management of organizations for productivity, and, even in some cases, for innovation.

How can we "explain" this fact — that, essentially, the more we "knew" about how to design and "fix" organizations, the worse they got? How, indeed, other than to recognize that "fixing" organizations doesn't really change anything, as long as the same people constitute that organization. What better evidence have we that organizations are "enacted" or reconstructed daily by the conversations and the activities and the thoughts of their "stakeholders"? The "best" motivation or productivity scheme available isn't going to make either a significant or long-lasting difference in organizational or individual performance unless a significant number of significant people in that organization change the ways they relate to each other and to the "organization." The quickest way to change an organization is to change those who sit in the seats of power. This is because the organization that *they* see is not the one that was "seen" and known by those they are replacing. And their different ways of identifying with and relating to the "organization" forces everyone around them to make adjustments; the "organization" is thus changed at the level of the source of the only reality it will ever have, not at some supeerficial level at which some attempt has been made to "fix" it.

"Fixing" organizations requires "fixing" the imaginations that stakeholders have of it, "fixing" the meanings they attribute to it through their imagined relationships with "it." To paraphrase Park (1967), "The (organization) is . . . *a state of mind* [italics added], a body of customs and traditions, and of the organized attitudes and sentiments that inhere in these customs. . . ." And these are a function of the everyday reconstruction of the social reality of that organization by its stakeholders — a focal point for the study of communication and organization.

So the realities that define and channel "organizational behavior" — all of those activities and decisions and observations that comprise the sum total of what people do in and on behalf of organizations every day — are those that obtain in the minds of their stakeholders. But an organization's stakeholders are rarely of one mind — they "see" it and know it and relate to it differently. An organization is different things for different people.

Some part of these differences can be attributed to the individual's "purview" — that is, to the range of vision afforded by one's position in it or role with respect to it. Thus, the receptionist has a different purview of the organization than does the systems analyst; the purchasing clerk has a different purview of the organization than does the person in charge of training; the salesman has a different purview of the organization than does the machine operator; and so on.

Such differences of purview can also be attributed in part to one's "trained incapacity," as Veblen called it. One comes to see the world in and through one's occupational competencies and credentials — whether one has achieved one's own special "trained incapacities" through experience or education (cf. Bensman & Lilienfeld, 1973). There is an old saying: To a man with a hammer in his hand, all the world appears to be a nail. Thus the MIS expert sees the condition of the firm rising or falling on "information," the "helpline" volunteer on sympathy, the bank teller on accuracy, the bureaucrat on following the rules, the financial officer on managing money, the trucker on his virtuosity in traffic and narrow alleys, the market researcher on his or her numbers, the public relations expert on the "image" of the firm, the marketing manager on "market strategy," the old-timer on his "experience," the CEO on his "leadership," the upwardly mobile young executive (yuppie?) on his ability to "politic," and so on. One of "Murphy's Laws" says that "the chief cause of problems in organizations is solutions." There's more here than a chuckle. The problems an organization has are generally those for which there are fashionable "solutions." This, too, is a fundamental aspect of communication and organization.

Differences of purview may also be attributed in part to one's membership — real or ascribed — in various "epistemic communities." An "epistemic community" (cf. Holzner, 1968 or Maanen & Barley, 1984) is a set of people who "share" the same knowledges and the same ways of valuing that knowledge *and* its sources; they "see" the world in similar ways because they have come to "share" certain ideologies on which they stand to look at it. An example is the commonplace observation that the person who is promoted out of a work group to be supervisor very quickly takes on a supervisory "mentality" and drops his (or her) worker "mentality."[3] Where he (or she) was once one of "us," he (or she) now appears to think and act like one of "them." People may hobnob with "liberals" or with "conservatives" because those individuals seem more compatible. These are "epistemic communities." The leisure-time activities that workers engage in may be different from those that managers engage in; these, too, are based in "epistemic communities." Those who believe that there is no substitute for "experience" are likely to trade "war stories" (and thus engage in constructing organizational reality) with "like-minded" people, in the same way that those who believe that extended education is the answer to every organization's problems will have a preference for talking to each other.

---

[3]Geertz's (1983) observation on the correspondence between roles and mentality is both pertinent and provocative: "Those roles we think to occupy turn out to be minds we find ourselves to have" (p. 155).

Such segmenting of the "reality" of organizations through different ways of "networking" or of constructing communication systems within organizations is therefore also a fundamental aspect of the study of communication and organization (cf. Tichy, 1981). We have to ask the question, not "What's true?" but "*Whose* truth?" since there are always competing truths in every human organization. Even husbands and wives sometimes disagree about what was, is, or ought to be the case. Sometimes always.

IV

One must assume *some* vantage points from which to "see" the world. No one "sees" the world directly. We always "see" it with our minds. And our minds are social products. How we understand the world is imposed upon it, not taken from it. The world we know is a function of the ways we have been in — formed to take it into — account. There is no such thing as "objectivity," if by that we mean seeing the world as "it" is rather than as we are; being "objective" is merely another way of being subjective. An outsider's perspective may be *useful,* because of his (or her) unique vantage point — which may come down to nothing more than that person's ignorance of something that to us seems self-evident and inescapable. The consultant's perspective is not necessarily "truer" — just perhaps uniquely useful, since it is not burdened with the local conventional wisdoms about this or that.

So what vantage point shall we take?

Let us assume, for the moment, that Diebold (1985) is "correct," and that the key executive officer of the future will be the Chief Information Officer. Let us call him the Chief Communication Officer, for we are well aware that information is not knowledge, and that the availability of information is not the same thing as the capacity to discern either what needs knowing or what to do about it. And let us assume the vantage point of this powerful new role in organizations.

How ought we to *think about* what we are supposed to do?

First, our task would be anchored in some sense of what constitutes "intelligent" behavior. The purpose of communication is not — or should not be — merely to "communicate." It is not — or should not be — merely to say things or listen to things, or to write things or read things, or even to think about things. It is to make some "intelligent" contribution to our ways of knowing, being, saying, having, or doing in the world. The ultimate test of the value of any information or any bit of knowledge is its usefulness in furthering our aims, whatever those may be. The *relevance* of any information or bit of knowledge, in fact, is its relevance *to* some aim or objective or goal. If you don't care where you're going, then any way of getting "there" is as good as any other.

So, as this hypothetical Chief Communication Officer, we would want to recognize that a central and continuing part of our task would be that of keeping articulated goals for the organization in front of everyone in the organization, and of doing whatever is necessary to integrate the goals of every unit and department with the goals of every individual in those units and departments, *and* those with the goals of "the organization." Now, knowing that to be "real" these understood goals and aims would have to be created and maintained in everyday communication between and among those particular stakeholders of the organization, we would recognize that our task is to orchestrate those conversations in some way. The metaphor we might want to use is that of a jazz group, in which people fulfill themselves both by playing with others in some sort of coordinated way, and also be improving on their own "parts," with the acknowledgement and help of the other "players."

Our central and continuous task would be to figure out how to organize and orchestrate communication patterns and events in such a way that "intelligent" communication behavior on the part of any unit in the organization would facilitate and contribute to "intelligent" performance on the part of the next higher unit of which it is a part, on the part of the next lower units that are parts of it, and on the part of every other unit anywhere in the organization whose past, present, or future performance might be somehow affected by that behavior. All this hinges upon *intelligent* communication behavior everywhere in the organization.

And we would recognize that communication is essentially people taking the world into account in some way. Departments do not "communicate." Neither do "reports" or telephone calls. The *consequential* product of any meeting is to be found only in the interpretations that individuals make of it, whether they were there or not. So we would know that "intelligent" communication behavior would depend either upon hiring people who have a track record as being "intelligent" communicators — or of having to develop this "intelligence" in-house. We would never imagine, however, that any way of taking the world into account, or that any instance of comprehension or of expression, is neutral. Each instance — every communication event and every communication system — is either contributing to the "intelligent" performance of the unit being thereby informed, or is impeding it. There is no "magic" in messages or in information systems. The conditions of individual and of collective performance in organizations are given in the "intelligence" of the communication behavior which informs that performance. We would know that the appropriate "skills" may be critical to "intelligent" communication behavior. And we would know that technics — techniques and technologies — "intelligently" adopted and deployed can make a difference. But we would also know that there is no communication tool which can be better than the person who uses it (cf. Feldman & March, 1981; Hull, Sadek, & Willner, 1982).

We would conceive of the organization as defined in a social space by the nature of its relationships with its stakeholders or constituencies. To know how one is constrained, or to know how one might be enabled, would require knowing at all times the conditions of these relationships—which constitute for the organization its essential environment. Those relationships determine the health of the organization, its state of adaptation, its potential—in short, all of the conditions of its performance.

Who are these "stakeholders"? Every employee is a stakeholder, although there are typically individual and group differences in how that "stake" is seen and valued. Every supplier and every provider of services is a stakeholder. Every stockowner, if there are any, is a stakeholder. That person or those persons who have a claim against the economic value of the organization are stakeholders. Every client or every customer is a stakeholder. Every competitor is a stakeholder, in the sense that, minimally, one's imaginations about one's competitors are an important part of one's perception of the world. There are tax and regulatory or sponsoring or protective government agencies of all sorts that may be stakeholders. Any person or persons who broker or who critique or evaluate some organization's products or services are stakeholders. All of those persons who have something to sell to or to inform an organization of are stakeholders. Every past employee and, in a sense, every prospective employee (or resource) is a stakeholder. Every other organization of the same sort is a stakeholder, in the sense that they are the way they are in part because of the existence of every other organization of that sort. Trade and professional associations are therefore somewhat mutual stakeholders as are those who write about and do research on them. And "the public": Every society has a "stake" in all of those organizations of which it is comprised. First, every member of every organization who talks to someone else makes that other person a stakeholder, if for no other reason than that that organization is now a part of that person's "reality." Second, particularly in a society such as our own, most organizations and institutions of some size have a public image—that is, there is some aggregative "public opinion" about it, if only locally. The larger the organization, the more social concern there may be about it; and, for the very largest organizations and institutions, this is increasingly played out "in" the media. Third, the organizations and institutions which comprise a society embody the legitimate "social forms" (Simmel, 1971) in which human communication and human activity *may* take place. So the society or the civilization is always a stakeholder of a very special sort.[4]

What we would know is that one cannot "know" or control these stakehold-

---

[4]Communication always occurs (can only occur) in some imagined social context (or "social form"—Simmel, 1971), so every communicative individual has a "stake" in those social arrangements within which communication is to occur. It isn't precisely the "society" that has the stake, of course. It is all of those people who have a stake in that (imagined) society.

ers. One must relate to them, very much in the same spirit that one must relate to a lover. No relationship worth having can be "engineered." Each party has an interest in the relationship, and being "intelligent" here means taking account of those interests (cf. Elfrey, 1982; Sawyer, 1985), even though people may not be able to articulate them in any definitive way. One can be who one is only because those to whom one is related are who they are. Thus stakeholding is always mutual. And this is as true for every organization of every size and type as it is for every individual. We can't exist—at least not consciously—without being stakeholders and having stakeholders. Our task: to be better stakeholders, and to help others function as better stakeholders for us. The measure of how well we do this is in how indistinguishable our separate self-interests become. There's a "communication" task of no small proportion.

As this hypothetical new Chief Communication Officer, we would also know that the performance of the organization, at least as far as our own purview is concerned, rests on the communicative competence of every member of the organization (that is, upon how "intelligently" every member of the organization performs communicatively), and on how things are otherwise organized.

The *structure* or the form of every human organization (and of every human institution) is a manifestation of our beliefs about who has the prerogative to explain things to whom—and on whom those explanations are incumbent (Duncan, 1962; Hage, Aiken, & Marrett, 1971). Our organizations are structured the way they are in large part because it makes sense to us that this prerogative should be distributed hierarchically—that is, that the prerogative to explain things to people increases as one moves "up" the organization. "Power" is ultimately a matter of who has the prerogative to explain things to whom. It wouldn't have to be that way. But we are predisposed in our culture to see things in terms of subordinacy–superordinacy, and our social forms reflect and legitimate that way of seeing the world (cf. Rice & Bishoprick, 1971).

This brings us back to an earlier predicament. Suppose the hierarchical superior is not the person who is best equipped to explain something to his "subordinates" and thereby establish the nature of the reality of that which is being explained. If the behavior that ensues is less "intelligent" than it might otherwise have been, haven't we inadvertently given preference to form over function (that is, to the validity of the structure over the "intelligence" of the explanation)? What we may want to conclude is that the intelligence of any organization is not merely the sum of the intelligence of its members. In an organization, the intelligence of any member to acquire and utilize knowledge in the interests of intelligent behavior is always modified by how reality is orchestrated in that organization—by how things are enabled and constrained to happen in that organization: in other words, by its explanatory structure (cf. Westerlund & Sjostrand, 1979). The critical factor in organizing human organizations is its explanatory structure—that is, who gets enfranchised to explain what to whom. We would devise ways of maximizing the *intelligence* of the explanatory structure in the organization by making *these* issues central to the criteria for hiring, placement, promotion, and performance evaluation.

The prerogative to explain things is the power to orchestrate other people's reality. As our hypothetical new Chief Communication Officer, we would therefore devise special training programs for every person in a headship or leadership position in the organization. Our purpose here would be, first, to make it clear that every conversation that these persons have with others is constitutive of the reality of the organization that those others utilize to interpret every observation and experience of it; and, second, that every explanation that they offer has two levels—the level of what-is-going-on (WIGO), and the level of what-should-be-going-on (WSBGO). So the interpretive and explanatory skills of these key people are the most sensitive and influential sources of reality construction in the organization. It is the CEO, in fact, whose understandings of the world are the most influential (Thayer, in press). Unless he or she realizes that every statement and every reply he or she makes—in every conversation held every day—orchestrates both the real and the ideal for those other people in the most profound ways, there is little hope of improving the overall performance of the organization in any significant or long-lasting way.

So what we would do with our fellow "leaders" (for there is no "leadership" more telling than this) is to learn how to talk, and how to listen, in ways that orchestrate the kind of reality that leads to more intelligent performance. Not working harder, but smarter. And the key to this lies in the assumptions that each makes about the nature of human nature (that is, why people are the way they are, why people do what they do, etc.), and about why things happen the way they do. Whatever assumptions about these mundane aspects of organizational life leaders make, those assumptions will be implicit in their every conversation with others. Some assumptions are simply more constitutive of those imagined realities that enable and constrain high performance than others. There is no leadership task or obligation more important than learning what those are, and how to express them and legitimate them in others' thinking and behavior.

We would also know that every problem that the organization "has" originates in someone's explanation of some discrepancy between (WIGO) and (WSBGO). Our conventional wisdom about organizing organizations tells us that only those who have "managerial" positions are enfranchised to "see" and interpret organizational problems. Here is a great opportunity to improve the health and the "intelligence" of the organization. In an organization of 200 people, let us say, instead of having 30 of those people function as the eyes and ears of the organization, and those given precedence according to how high "up" in the organization they are located, why not have 200 sets of eyes and ears on the world? Why not have 200 people at work on the problems of the organization rather than just 30?

When Réne McPherson was CEO of the Dana Corporation, he remarked: "Until we believe (that) the expert in any job is the person performing it, we shall forever limit the potential of that person." And if we limit the potential of just one person in an organization, we have limited the potential, and the performance, of that organization.

What we would want to achieve is the maximum possible *decentralization of the ownership of problems* (cf. Taylor, 1985). In general, we would want the person closest to the problem to be the one to "see" it, to interpret and explain it, to "solve" it, and to live with the consequences. And since every problem is a perceived discrepancy between WIGO and WSBGO, we would have to see to every individual's capacity for taking the world into account (for being communicated with), for acquiring and putting to use the kind of knowledge needed to ingelligently discern WIGO, WSBGO, and the nature of the difference. These are the cardinal communication competencies.

Under these circumstances, those who have the need for certain information or for certain knowledge would demand it—thus creating inductively not only the most efficient and efficacious *information system* possible, but the criteria for its content as well (cf. Christie, 1981). This is the kind of intelligence infrastructure that seems to characterize every healthy, adaptive, high-performance organization.

There is much else that our hypothetical Chief Communication Officer should know and do. But most of that could be generated from the nonconventional way of thinking outlined above.

V

Every conscious act involves communication. We take the world into account as we are enabled and constrained to do so, as it is *possible* for us to do so, given the categories and predispositions available to us in the social construction of our minds. We "see" the world we "see," given the very meanings we have to "see" it with.

Those meanings—those categories and predispositions—the very mind with which we would "grasp" and relate to and adapt to the world in which we live (even the very "me" or "we" that would do so): All of these are created and maintained in communication.

The "consciousness" that informs humans acts must itself be created and maintained in communication. We literally "talk" every infant into consciousness—of self, as we would have it known, and of the world, as we know it.

Whatever distinguishes us as uniquely "human" has had to be built into us, and has had to be maintained in us, *in* communication.

And every human enterprise involving two or more people has had to be constructed and maintained in communication. For there to be an "us," or a "GM," we have to be able to *imagine* it, and we have to be able to imagine it in some sort of mutually relating or mutually involving way—all this requires communication. The past we know, the present we experience, and the future we anticipate: These are all made of words and images and ideas; these are all products of our ways of speaking of the world or of interpreting it in some way, and of our ways of taking the world into account in some way; these are all products of the mind—all human artifacts. And every mind is produced and maintained in communication, just as every human enterprise is produced and maintained in communication (cf. Sederberg, 1984). We literally talk ourselves and our social enterprises into the only existence they will ever have.

Every conscious human act occurs in the context of *some* kind of organization, of *some* social form. That context may be no more than the way one's own mind is structured or organized, the shape and the form it has taken on in the continuous process of its making. Or it may be an imagined social institution (e.g., marriage or the legal system), or social relationship (e.g., a friendship, or kinship, or an economic or cultural partnership). Or that conscious human act may occur in the context of some conscious human organization—as that organization is imagined or "known" by those humans who *constitute* it in the nature of their consciousness of it as stakeholders. Their "stake" in that organization is given *in* the nature of their consciousness of it— in the meaning and the significance and the utility they ascribe to it.

It is in the context of one's image or consciousness of an organization that one speaks to oneself and to others, that one listens to oneself and to others, that one takes the world into account, *on behalf of* that organization. These are, too, ultimately or presciently, all matters of communication.

And every human artifact, whether it be a bridge or an idea, a city or a ballpoint pen or a war, is, necessarily, a product of communication—if for no other reason than that it is a product of mind, graspable or understandable only by a human mind, which is itself both consequence and source of all human communication. Human artifacts may be made of other materials— of steel or plastic or gears or belts or concrete or pistons or fibers, or of hundreds of thousands of combinations of these and many more. But they are also made of words. They must have some meaning for us before they can be imagined or thought about or talked about by us. And they will exist only insofar as they are meaningful to one or more humans, and they will exist only *in* the meaning they have for one or more humans. A natural or a human artifact may indeed exist independently of our conceptions or understandings of it. But if we would be conscious of it, if we would take it into account or speak of it in some way—if we would make of it a *mental* artifact, then we must grasp it according to its meaning for us, and translate it into whatever meaning we can attribute to it.

And meanings, to be "shared" by even one other person, are matters of communication. For to live consciously is to live, not in *the* world of things, but in *a* world of the meanings of things. And meanings are products of communication, not of things.

If all of this is so—and I can see no way empirically to escape either these propositions or the implications of these propositions—we then come face to face with a most extraordinary question: How, then, did it come to pass that communication is seen as the handmaiden of organization and management theory—and thought—and not the other way around?

To speak of communication and organization is to speak of every way in which an organization is constituted to take into account its relevant environment (i.e., the attitudes, orientations, and self-interests of its stake-holders), and itself; every way in which an organization is constituted to enable and constrain the articulation and coordination of its parts and every activity undertaken on behalf of it; and every way in which an organization is constituted to communicate *about* itself and its products, services, or *raisons d'être*. The "every way an organization is constituted" here refers to how every stakeholder takes the world into account and what he or she says or does on behalf of the organization—for that is what "the organization" comes down to—telling oneself and others WIGO and WSBGO, negotiating the differences, and informing all of the artifacts produced therefrom.

So everything that is *vital* about an organization's existence, about its condition, its performance, and its possible futures is given in the nature of the communication within which it is engendered and enacted. How, then, did it happen that communication came to be seen as the handmaiden of management and organization theory—and thought—rather than the other way around?

We can conclude by speculating on some of the reasons for, and consequences of, this remarkable perversion.

1. Boulding (1956) once remarked that academic disciplines seem to have been invented inversely to their correspondence to vital human interests—with cosmology first and psychology but a newcomer. And as a discipline, communication comes on the scene after the establishment of "management" and "organization behavior" as academic disciplines. Not only does it have less status and prestige, but there are the inevitable territorial struggles. Just as those who are prejudiced—against learn their roles before those who are prejudiced against them, those in communication learned to accept their lower-class status and to behave as sycophants, willing to play second fiddle to any and all of the social or behavioral sciences, just to be permitted to play at all.

"Communication" was but grudgingly accepted as the handmaiden of the already-existing academic disciplines at the outset. Notice how, even today, in order to take on the cloak of respectability, communication researchers cite those in their "superior" disciplines, and respectfully.[55] Only infrequently do those in the social and behavioral sciences deign either to read or to cite those who do their work in "communication."

All this has clouded our perception of communication as the integrating concept in the social and behavioral sciences, and continues to inhibit the development of the explanatory concepts on which theories of "management" and of "organization" ultimately depend.

2. To "see" communication as just one more function (and an incidental one at that) of management, or as just one more "aspect" of organizations — that is, as parallel to, and equal to, such activities as planning, controlling, leading, and organizing — mutilates and glosses at a preconceptual level the very phenomena we want to study. If there is a chapter in a management book on "communication," the implication and the inference are likely to be that "communication" is but one more thing that a manager "does." The problem here is that communication is of a different order: All marketing involves communication, but all communication does not involve marketing. All finance involves communication, but all communication does not involve finance. All planning involves communication, but all communication does not involve planning. All manufacturing involves communication — we have been told, for example, that 80 percent of all direct labor costs are costs of "communication" — but all communication does not involve manufacturing, and so on.

Please understand that my argument is not a "territorial" one — not one of academic "politics" (though it has obvious implications for both). My argument is not that communication is of a *superior* order — just a different order. To treat communication as just one more thing that is "done" in organizations and by managers is to gloss over or obscure several of the most important facts *about* communication in organizations — that organizations have their existence only in the way they are constructed and reconstructed in everyday conversation, for example, and that they have no reality apart from the way they come to be imagined by their stakeholders through how they are talked about and imaged *in* communication. Kenneth Burke was wont to say that any way of seeing is a way of not seeing. That is the issue. We are all susceptible to hegemonies of thought, which may preclude our apprehending the very thing we are looking for. It apparently makes sense even to those "in" the field of communication study that "management" or that "ethnography"

---

[5]Redding (1979) points out that we not only import concepts from these "superior" disciplines. In doing so, we also import the ideologies that inform those concepts.

are both of higher status, because the one is understood to be preeminent, the other more "scientific." Every way of lookng at the world brings with it unavoidable tradeoffs. What we miss seeing by assuming that communication is merely a handmaiden of organization and management may be far more important conceptually than what we thereby set ourselves up to see (cf. Ritti, 1985, for an example of what can be done with movement away from the hegemonic perspective).

3. There remains a certain misconception of communication itself. One author recently referred to the "objects in the world that everybody shares." Another to the "capacity of objects, gestures, and spacial relations" in organizations "to speak for. . . ." Ours is a subject–predicate world, a deeply ingrained aspect of the Western episteme. There are causes and there are effects. That bias blindly bulldozes us through mountains of contrary facts when it comes to communication.

For this is the very point of being human: that we do not live in *the* world of objects or events, but in *a* world of the *meanings* of those objects and events. No object or event is intrinsically meaningful. That's what being human is all about, as Wittgenstein said: to be that creature which *must* construe and attribute meaning to every thing of which we would be mindful, or of which we would speak. When it comes to organization and management thought, we suffer greatly from what Whitehead (1948) referred to as "misplaced concreteness": We attribute factuality to the wrong things (cf. Berger, 1967). It is our *concepts* of things, our imaginations (as Cooley said, and Boulding, 1956), which constitute the only reality we will ever know — not the things themselves (whatever or however they may be). It isn't what-is-going-on that is "real": It is what we say about it — for consequences flow not from the way things "are," but from our interpretations of the way things "are."

Even communication scholars falter here and exhibit ambivalences, but the *power* of communication lies not in the "nature" of things, or even in what is said about them. "There is no meaning (even) in a message except what . . . people put into it," Schramm (1971) wrote. And Thurber once quipped, "A word to the wise isn't sufficient if it doesn't make any sense." The reality of any organization lies in how its various sets of stakeholders "mind" it, not in how "it" is, but in how they take it into account (cf. Frost & Moore, in press).

Management, and organization, theory will be written quite differently if we ever come to accept this way of looking at the world (in spite of our longstanding predilections to the contrary). For everything "communicates" in the sense that any person or any epistemic community may take anything whatsoever into account in arriving at an image or an understanding of an organization, or of a manager, or a performance appraisal scheme. There are no "facts," as such: there are only interpreted facts. The question is not, What are the facts? but, What interpretation was put upon what facts, and by whom? For the *nature* of any relationship, or of any organization, is given in those interpretations.

In "science," at least in our popular conception of that human enterprise, what "is" *works*. In social life, which is to say, in communication, what "works" *is*. The direction of understanding is exactly reversed.

4. There is another fundamental difficulty with our conception of communication. Our analytic/reductionist predispositions (cf. Manning, 1979) may lead us to study communication by looking at its parts (or, more accurately, what we have posited to be its parts).

But *communication is global*. People do not "add up" the parts of something when they take it into account. They "see" it as a whole, and they see it immediately. It is the meaningfulness of the whole that informs the parts, and not the other way around.

Communication is historical. Not only is an interpretation of WIGO influenced by imaginations of the future and imaginations about the past, but it is an event which is never finished. Stopping the flow of mental/communicative life may be a bit like stop-action motion on a video. Which is the reality—the continuing motion or the single frame? If it is the continuing motion, where is it occurring—in the past, the present, or the future? Social activity, whether our own or another's, "makes sense" to us only because we can imagine its plausible historical origins *and* its plausible future consequences.

Communication is irreversible. When someone takes something into account in some way, that person is no longer who he or she was before doing so, however slight or significant the difference may be. And we can never "go back" to a prior state. Ask anyone who has fallen "out" of love. Or ask any group of employees when they are faced with a current organizational pronouncement; they are never as "innocent" as they were the time before— or the time before that. This means that the "context" and the elements are ever changing—a circumstance that is not at all amenable to our "scientistic" approaches. David Reynolds, a disciple of the Japanese contemporary of Freud—Shōma Morita—calls it "playing ball on running water" (Reynolds, 1984).

Communication is improvisational. What this means is that we may know the scripts or the themes or the plots that go with the roles we play in organizations and out, but our version of those roles is always more or less an improvisation, just as our ways of taking the world into account and expressing ourselves in that world are "variations" on certain understood and normative themes. But this is no trivial matter. Things are organized the way they are, and things "are" the way they are, and things are done the way they are done because, and only because, we can provide one another with "explanations" that justify or legitimate those ways of doing or of being (cf. Martin, 1982; Starbuck, 1982)—or of having or of saying or of knowing.

We're making it all up, as Simmel suggested, as we go along. Like people,

organizations are ever in the process of *becoming* whatever the imaginations of
their stakeholders make necessary—and/or possible.

5. Many historical accidents have also led to a fragmentation of thought
about, and activities related to, organizational communication. There is
consumer research and there is "employee communication"; there is industrial
espionage (Bottom & Gallati, 1984) and there is corporate advocacy; there is
public relations and there is organizational intelligence; there is public
opinion research and there is corporate communications; there is advertising
and there is internal communications; and so on.

Metaphors abound. If we "are what we eat," then organizations are some
function of that information they have ingested, or, more accurately, of how
their stakeholders have taken the world into account on behalf of those
organizations. We get confused; we sometimes overlook the difference, even,
between data and information—even though we know that "information" is
information only to some person. There is not an ounce of information in a
ton of data, unless someone says so, in which case it is possible that there may
be a ton of information in an ounce of data.

The difficulty, of course, is that people who work in "management
information systems" may use the term differently than do those who work in
training. The former may believe there is "information" on the sheets that
come off the printer. The latter may be convinced that there are certain
people who couldn't be informed that the building was falling on them even
if those trainers deployed a multimedia presentation to "tell" them so.

The problem is not the fragmentation as such. It is that people who take up
different occupations or professions also take up different argots—different
ways of talking about the world. And these constitute different world views.
So the public relations people not only don't, but very often *can't*, talk to the
employee relations people. And those who do consumer research rarely speak
the language of the boardroom.

The modern organization is thus figuratively, if not literally, a kind of
Tower of Babel. People talk, but they don't talk the same "language."
Communicatively, it would be a bit like a person's having one mind with
which to perceive the world, and quite a different one to guide his or her
actions in it. It is small wonder that the various stakeholders of an
organization are rarely of "one mind" about it.

Is it possible that this continued fragmentation of communicative activities
and thought—justified, perhaps, as "specialization of function"—may have
the effect of leaving the central and vital function untended? Doesn't the label
on a can of soup represent the company as much as does its "logo"? Don't a
waitress's mannerisms give face and voice to the restaurant as much as (or
more than) does its advertising? Aren't employee attitudes about a company's
products at least as important as consumer attitudes? If so, who would mount
the ad campaign directed at *them*? Where *is* the integrative mechanism—the

one that would attend and integrate the vital aspects of the organization's communicative existence?

For what is vital to the condition and the evolution of the organization is how its stakeholders imagine the past, the present, and the future of "their" organization in its imagined environment, given their own self-interests, as they imagine those to be. Which of the various specialized agencies of organizational communication address *those* issues? And where is the agency that would *intelligently* integrate all of an organization's communicative activities — internal and external, operational, strategic, regulatory, whatever — into a coherent system informed by those issues?

VI

The fundamental issues in the study of communication and organization are not to be found *in* communication, or *in* organizations, or *in* the relationship between them. They are to be found where every fundamental human issue is to be found — in how we construe or imagine communication, in how we conceive of or imagine organization, and in how we construct in our imagination a relationship between the one and the other — if, indeed, we wish to see them as one and other.

What I have tried to do here is to raise some questions about how we have done this in the past, and about the conditions we may have made and missed in the process. If nothing else, they may be the kinds of questions that could enhance and inspirit our intellectual adventure.

Hopefully, they might thereby improve the performance of that enterprise in which we are all stakeholders. If it is through organization that we have to realize our aspirations, as Cooley suggested, we may need to ask whether the shortfall for our civilization is in our aspirations or in how we have come to think about the coincidence of communication and organization.

REFERENCES

Arendt, H. (1959). *The human condition.* Garden City, New York: Doubleday.

Ashby, W. R. (1956). *An introduction to cybernetics.* New York: John Wiley & Sons.

Bensman, J., & Lilienfeld, R. (1973). *Craft and consciousness: Occupational technique and the development of world images.* New York: John Wiley & Sons.

Berger, P. L. (1967). *The sacred canopy.* Garden City, New York: Doubleday.

Berger, P. L., & Luckmann, T. (1966). *The social construction of reality.* Garden City, New York: Doubleday.

Bottom, N. R., & Gallati, R. R. J. (1984). *Industrial espionage: Intelligence techniques and countermeasures.* Boston: Butterworth.

Boulding, K. (1956). *The image: Knowledge in life and society.* Ann Arbor: University of Michigan Press.

Bridgman, P. W. (1959). *The way things are.* Cambridge, MA: Harvard University Press.

Brown, R. H. (1978). Bureaucracy as praxis: Toward a political phenomenology of formal organizations. *Administrative Science Quarterly, 23,* 365-382.

Christie, B. (1981). *Face-to-file communication: A psychological approach to information systems.* New York: John Wiley & Sons.

Cooley, C. H. (1902). *Human nature and the social order.* New York: Scribner's.

Crozier, M., & Friedberg, E. (1980). *Actors and systems: The politics of collective action.* Chicago: University of Chicago Press.

Diebold, J. (1985). *Managing information.* New York: Amacom.

Duncan, H. D. (1962). *Communication and social order.* New York: Bedminster.

Elfrey, P. (1982). *The hidden agenda: Recognizing what really matters at work.* New York: John Wiley & Sons.

Feldman, M. S., & March, J. G. (1981). Information in organizations as signal and symbol. *Administrative Science Quarterly, 26,* 171-186.

Frost, P. J., & Moore, L. F. (Eds.) (in press). *Organizational culture and the meaning of life in the workplace.*

Gabor, D. (1964). *Inventing the future.* New York: Knopf.

Geertz, C. (1983). *Local knowledge.* New York: Basic Books.

Hage, J., Aiken, M., & Marrett, C. B. (1971). Organizational structure and communications. *American Sociological Review, 36,* 860-871.

Hawes, L. C. (1974). Social collectives as communication: Perspective on organizational communication. *Quarterly Journal of Speech, 60,* 497-502.

Heschel, A. J. (1965). *Who is man?* Stanford, CA: Stanford University Press.

Holzner, B. (1968). *Reality construction in society.* Cambridge, MA: Schenkman.

Kets de Vries, M. F. R., & Miller, D. (1984). *The neurotic organization.* San Francisco: Jossey-Bass.

Lewin, K. (1948). *Resolving social conflicts.* New York: Harper.

Maanen, J. V., & Barley, S. R. (1984). Occupational communities: Culture and control in organizations. *Research in Organizational Behavior, 6,* 287-365.

Manning, P. K. (1979). Metaphors of the field: Varieties of organizational discourse. *Administrative Science Quarterly, 24,* 660-671.

Martin, J. (1982). Stories and scripts in organizational settings. In A. H. Hastorf & A. M. Isen (Eds.), *Cognitive Social Psychology* (pp. 255-305). New York: Elsevier/North-Holland.

Mitroff, I. I. (1983). *Stakeholders of the organizational mind.* San Francisco: Jossey-Bass.

Morgan, G. (1980). Paradigms, metaphors, and puzzle-solving in organization theory. *Administrative Science Quarterly, 25,* 605-622.

Morgan, G. (Ed.) (1983). *Beyond method: Strategies for social research.* Beverly Hills, CA: Sage.

Park, R. E. (1967). *The city.* Chicago: University of Chicago Press.

Polak, F. (1973). *The image of the future.* (E. Boulding, Trans.). San Francisco: Jossey-Bass.

Pondy, L. R., Frost, P., Morgan, G., & Dandridge, T. (Eds.). (1983). *Organizational symbolism.* Greenwich, CT: JAI Press.

Redding, W. C. (1979). Organizational communication theory and research: An overview. In B. D. Ruben (Ed.), *Communication yearbook 3* (pp. 309-341). New Brunswick, NJ: Transaction Books.

Reddy, M. J. (1979). The conduit metaphor—A case of frame conflict in our language about language. In A. Ortony (Ed.), *Metaphor and thought* (pp. 186-201). Cambridge: Cambridge University Press.

Reynolds, D. K. (1984). *Playing ball on running water.* New York: Quill.

Rice, G. H., Jr., & Bishoprick, D. W. (1971). *Conceptual models of organization.* New York: Appleton-Century-Crofts.

Ritti, R. R. (1985). The Social Bases of Organizational Knowledge. In L. Thayer (Ed.), *Organization ↔ communication: Emerging perspectives I* (pp. 102-132). Norwood, NJ: Ablex.

Sawyer, G. C. (1985). *Business and its environment: Managing social impact.* Englewood Cliffs, NJ: Prentice-Hall.

Schramm, W. (1971). The Nature of Communication between Humans. In W. Schramm & D. F. Roberts (Eds.), *The process and effects of mass communication.* Urbana: University of Illinois Press.

Sherif, M., & Cantril, H. (1947). *The psychology of ego-involvements.* New York: John Wiley & Sons.

Simmel, G. (1971). *On individuality and social forms.* D. N. Levine (Ed.). Chicago: University of Chicago Press.

Starbuck, W. H. (1982). Congealing oil: Inventing ideologies to justify acting ideologies out. *Journal of Management Studies, 19,* 3–27.

Taylor, J. R. (1985). New communication technologies and the emergence of distributed organizations: Looking beyond 1984. In L. Thayer (Ed.), *Organization ↔ communication: Emerging perspectives I* (pp. 231–273). Norwood, NJ: Ablex.

Thayer, L. (1967). Communication and Organization. In F. E. X. Dance (Ed.), *Human communication theory: Original essays* (pp. 70–115). New York: Holt, Rinehart and Winston.

Thayer, L. (1985). *Organization ↔ communication: Emerging perspectives I.* Norwood, NJ: Ablex.

Thayer, L. (in press). *Making high-performance organizations: The logic of virtuosity.*

Tichy, N. M. (1981). Networks in organizations. In P. C. Nystrom & W. H. Starbuck (Eds.), *Handbook of organizational design,* Vol. 2. New York: Oxford University Press.

von Hayek, F. A. (1975). The pretence of knowledge. *Swedish Journal of Economics, 77,* 433–442.

Watzlawick, P. (1983). *The situation is hopeless, but not serious: The pursuit of unhappiness.* New York: Norton.

Weick, K. E. (1977). Re-punctuating the problem. In P. S. Goodman & Associates (Eds.), *New perspectives on organizational effectiveness* (pp. 37–53). San Francisco: Jossey-Bass.

Weick, K. E. (1979). *The social psychology of organizing.* (2nd ed.). Reading, MA: Addison-Wesley.

Westerlund, G., & Sjostrand, S. E. (1979). *Organizational myths.* London: Harper & Row.

Whitehead, A. N. (1948). *Science and the modern world.* New York: Macmillan. (Original work published 1925)

PART IV

The Internal Environment (Culture, Ecology) and Some of Its Implications

7

Toward a Cultural Ecology of Organizing*

James L. Everett

This chapter develops a framework for the description and analysis of organizations based on Weick's (1979a) "sociocultural evolution model" of organizing. The framework integrates theoretical and methodological developments in organizational theory and anthropological ecology to inform and extend Weick's model in a domain proposed as organizational cultural ecology. This approach is built from conceptual refinements to Weick's model that focus on integrating a concept of culture with the model while maintaining its emphasis on the significance of environmental enactment to organizing. Toward these ends, organizational cultural ecology is proposed as the analysis of relationships between the culture of an organization and the organizational environment. Within the terms of Weick's model, organizational cultural ecology is the analysis of the mediation of environmental enactment by organizational culture.

I propose that ethnoecology (i.e., actor-based models of organization/ environment relationships) be adopted as a principal research strategy within the domain of organizational culture ecology to inform analysis at two levels:

1. At the individual level, ethnoecology can provide a means of identifying cognitive material of organizational actors such as cause maps specified in Weick's model.

2. At the organizational level, ethnoecology can serve as a means of identifying cultural influences on the organizing processes.

Thus, organizational cultural ecology, by adopting the methods and goals of ethnoecology, supports Weick's (1979a) view that analytical strategies for organizational research proceed from a recognition that "problems within

*An earlier version of this chapter was presented at the International Communication Association Conference, New Orleans, May 1988. I am grateful to Charles Bantz for several important criticisms made to that version of this chapter.

organizations must be approached at both the psychological and sociological level" (p. 33).

This chapter begins with a brief review of Weick's model of organizing. The model is assessed and found to require refinements in three specific areas: (a) integration of a concept of culture within the theoretical elements of the model, (b) integration of a distinction between ecological change and environmental change which are confused in the model, and (c) following from use of the goals and methods of ethnoecology to identify actor-based ecological models to compensate for the intractability of interlocked behavior cycles. Finally, I argue that organizational cultural ecology is essential to the effort to understand organizational adaptation given the view that environmental enactment is the fundamental drive to organizing.

WEICK'S MODEL OF ORGANIZNG

Weick (1979a) provides a sociocultural evolution model of organizing.[1] Organizing refers to those processes that constitute organizations. In an argument derived from Campbell's (1965) discussion of biological evolution, Weick proposes that the concepts of sociocultural evolution be used to explicate the processes of organizing. Weick's model is based on the components of biological evolution — variation, selection, and retention. Campbell (1965) writes that "for an evolutionary process to take place there needs to be variations (as by mutation, trial, etc.), stable aspects of the environment differentially selecting among such variations, and a retention–propagation system rigidly holding on to the selected variations" (pp. 306–307). Theorists of evolutionary social change who followed Campbell also posit these elements. For example, Durham (1976) argues that any theory of cultural evolution must incorporate sources of variation, selection criteria, and mechanisms for retention of positively selected variants.

Weick argues for several "amendments" to Campbell's discussion in order to make it applicable to organizational theory. The most important of these amendments is a substitution of the concept of "enactment" for the process of variation in biological evolution. Weick argues that enactment, that is, the process by which what is acted upon by organizing is created, should be used instead of variation when referring to organizing. He argues that "enactment is to organizing as variation is to natural selection" (p. 130). In Weick's view,

---

[1] All references to "Weick's model" refer to Weick (1979a) except where indicated. An important revision that took place in the 1979 version of the organizing model is the removal of the subprocesses of "Assembly Rules" and "Behavior Cycles Selected" in the enactment process. The 1979 version substitutes "Ecological Change" and "Enacted Equivocality" as the major subprocesses within the enactment process.

variation is introduced into organizing processes within the process of enactment. Therefore, in organizational sociocultural evolution, enactment subsumes the processes by which variations are produced.[22]

Weick's model is an information-processing model in which selection and retention reduce equivocality inherent to environmental enactment. Weick argues that ecological change (resulting from environmental conditions) is the essential drive to organizing processes. He asserts that "ecological changes provide the enactable environment, the raw materials for sense-making" (p. 130). However, in order to emphasize the significance of enactment to organizing, Weick proposes that "the external environment literally bends around the enactments of people. . ."(p. 130). The centrality of environmental enactment within the model puts this activity at the heart of its utility and significance. Consequently, Bougon, Weick, and Binkhorst (1977) content that "this interactive, creative, and continuous constructing of the mind and the environment is central to cognitive organizational theory because the individual processes involved select and control organizational activities, development, and evolution" (p. 606).

The selection process is the means by which the raw data of individuals is transformed via retrospective sense-making into useful information. Weick (1977) contends that:

> taken in reverse order, there is the enactment process of saying, which is followed by the selection process of transforming the saying into information. . . . Once the enacted stream of talk [raw data] has been parsed [in the selection process], an enacted environment exists. The enacted environment is something that organizational members momentarily "know" and "feel they understand." (p. 280)

The final process of organizing — retention — is a process in which the output from selection is retained (stored), and further reduced in equivocality. Weick (1979a) asserts that "retention is a reservoir of beliefs" (p. 187).

Influences on Enactment

Given the significance of enactment to organizing, there is an imperative to examine the influences and constraints to enactment. There are two primary sets of influences on enactment in Weick's model. The first set of influences are those associated with the individual psychology of "cause maps." Weick (1979b) defines cause maps as the perceived patterns and cause–effect relationships among raw data elements identified during enactment processes. These maps shape enactment by constraining the amount of material

---

[2]This assertion does not imply that variations require progress or direction.

available for sense-making. Weick considers this constraint to be analogous to variation in the evolution of biological systems.

The second set of influences on environmental enactment operate at the organizational level. Within the selection process, cause maps and enacted environments of individuals are transformed into information through interlocked behavior cycles among the organizational actors. Weick (1979a) proposes that "the raw material fed into selection consists of equivocal enactments and cause maps of varying equivocality" (p. 179). At the organizational level, an enacted environment is the product of a negotiated consensus as to what constitutes the environment. Weick asserts that "the crucial collective act in organizations may consist of members trying to negotiate a consensus on which portions of the enacted display are figure and which are ground" (Weick, 1977, p. 290). Negotiation takes place around differences in the "causal maps" of individuals. These differences constitute the equivocality on which the selection process operates. Interlocked behavior cycles among group members reduce variations among any set of individual causal maps held by organizational members. Weick (1979a) contends that "[interlocked behavior cycles within organizations] are assembled into larger subassemblies in the interest of stabilizing equivocal displays and transforming them into information, enacted environments, and cause maps" (p. 113). Once differences among the cause maps of individuals are reduced, a consensus develops concerning what might be termed a collective causal map. At the organizational level of analysis, an enacted environment is generally agreed to and shared among group members, and is stored in retention. Thus, while individual psychology is clearly significant to the initial phase of environmental enactment, the process that has the greatest significance at the organizational level of analysis is selection.[33]

ASSESSMENT OF WEICK'S MODEL

In order to build a truly sociocultural–evolution model of organizing, there are three primary areas of Weick's model that need to be addressed. First, his model does not specify a concept of culture. Second, it confuses the concepts

---

[3]Weick (1969) argues: "Up until the information reaches the selection process, it is pragmatically conditioned by the interests of the individual actor. But when this information is passed along to the selection process, collective rather than individual pragmatics control the establishment of meaning . . . [The selection process] consists of criteria built up from collective action, criteria that maintain collective action . . . The selection process is analogous to a decision center in organizations. . . . Selection is the hub into which inputs are fed from diverse sets of actors (p. 70) . . . It is the function of the selection process to sort out [the equivocal inputs from the enactment process] and make them less equivocal (p. 71).

of ecology and environment. Third, the component of interlocked behavior cycles that is essential to both versions of the model (1969; 1979a) is largely invisible to retrospective analysis.

The Culture Concept in Organizing

Weick specifies a model of organizing based on socio*cultural* evolution. Such a model, by definition, presents an imperative to explore the relationship of organizational culture to organizing. The omission of a concept of culture also reduces the significance of the model to similar models in the anthropological literature, and, conversely, inhibits the degree to which anthropological approaches and ethnographies can inform Weick's model.

There are two challenges for studies that attempt to move Weick's model in a truly socio*cultural* direction. First, one must isolate the substance of cultural influences in the processes of organizing to integrate a concept of culture with the model. Second, there is an imperative to explore the consequences of this integration to organizing and adaptation as these concepts are described by Weick. These two challenges represent the theoretical and research imperatives for organizational cultural ecology.

In keeping with the cognitive elements and requirements of Weick's model, and in association with a view of culture consistent with its use in the recent cognitive tradition of cultural anthropology, I propose that organizational culture be viewed as a system of learned and socially transmitted knowledge (Holland & Quinn, 1980; Hutchins, 1980; Spiro, 1984). Variations of this approach have been used successfully by such organizational theorists as Van Maanen and Barley (1985), Morey Schein (1985), Luthans (1984), Gregory (1983), and Harris and Cronen (1979). Weick (1985) also suggests the utility of such a perspective on culture with the statement that, "Culture is not defined by what I do but by what I presume *others* know, believe, and mean when *they* do what *they* do" (p. 387). This view of organizational culture suggests that comprehension (and therefore enactment—what the environment is understood to be) cannot proceed independently from influences of the organizational culture. Because of the significance of enactment to the model, the inclusion of a concept of culture as social knowledge is particularly important to understanding how organizing is articulated with ecological change.

An essential element within organizational cultural ecology is the view of organizations as sociocultural systems-in-environments. This perspective is based on a distinction between the cultural realm and the social realm in organizations. The cultural realm of organizations is constituted as social knowledge, that is, the ideational aspects of organizational life. The behavioral patterns of organizational members constitute the social realm of organizational life. The most important theoretical consequence to this sociocultural perspective is rejection of the notion that organizations can be justifiably viewed as cultures (e.g., O'Donnell-Trujillo & Pacanowky, 1982). Such a view unnecessarily limits the significance of the culture concept to organizational studies by obscuring the relationships between collective action, the social knowledge of organizational members, and the processes that shape the organization and organizational life. As Keesing (1974) notes, "To understand culture and diversity, we must see cultures as complex cybernetic systems of humans-in-environments. An ideational model of culture in isolation prevents our understanding of change and adaptation" (p. 91). The view of organizations as sociocultural systems-in-environments posits that relationships between the social and cultural realms within the organization, when placed in the context of features of the organizational environment, illuminate the nature of organization and organizational life. This perspective has been articulated by Bee (1974) who proposes that "a group's way of life is considered a social and cultural system whose components influence each other in such a way that a change in one may have some effect on the others" (p. 13).

Culture and Organizational Communication

Pacanowsky and O'Donnell-Trujillo (1982) argue that "organizational culture study reaffirms the centrality of communicative behaviors in organizational inquiry" (p. 129). Within this general perspective, the proposed domain of organizational cultural ecology posits organizational communication as central to the coupling of the cultural and the social in organizations. Organizational communication, as the device that couples the cultural and the social in organizations, mediates the effects of the organizational environment on the organization as well as organizational action toward the environment. Environmental effects on the organizational sociocultural system are linked directly with the processes of organizational communication. In terms of environmental effects on the organization, organizational communication (in Weick's model via interlocked behavior cycles) interprets the consequences of organizational action toward the environment. This sense-making can take place through planned and directed action of the organization (e.g., internal employee communication and training programs), or through tacit consensus on the part of organizational members, or both. Organizational culture mediates organizational action toward the environment through its role as a normative and perceptual constraint to collective action. The normative component of an organizational culture acts to sanction and warrant some forms of behavior out of the universe of behaviors that are possible with respect to some situation. This sanctioning or warranting is accomplished communicatively. That is, the organizational culture, constituted as a cognitive system, is manifest as organizational action (collective behavior) via communicative processes within the organization. Organizational action is predicated on the transformation of cultural elements into social action via organizational communication.

The Concepts of Ecology and Environment

The second problem within Weick's model is the confusion of the terms *environment* and *ecology*. The model stipulates that "ecological change" is primary in the process of organizing. This usage is inconsistent with ecological theory. Ecology is the study of the *relationships* between organisms and their environments, and is not conceptually equivalent to "the environment" (Hawley, 1986). Ecology is the study of process and relation, not static entities. Thus, ecological change in Weick's model should be refined to refer specifically to change in the relationship of organizing and environment. These changes constitute inputs to organizing processes. This refinement does not alter Weick's formulation of the significance of enactment to organizing processes. Weick's model is based on the view that the environment is not sufficient to explain organizing (that is, the model does not posit environmental determinism), but it is a necessary component to discuss the processes by which organizing is accomplished.

The concepts of evolution and ecology are essential to the analysis of organizations within organizational cultural ecology. Following Smith (1981), "Evolutionary ecology combines the basic elements of Darwinian (natural selection) theory with an emphasis on adaptive responses to various kinds of ecological problems and opportunities" (p. 29). Ecological concepts are essential in macrolevel sociocultural analysis because the system is placed within the context of particular features of the environment. Evolutionary concepts are essential because the organization is viewed as derived from selective processes operating on the interaction of environmental features and behavioral outcomes of the organizational culture over time. Keesing (1976) argues:

> [The ideational designs-for-living characteristic of a particular people—i.e., culture] are only one set of elements shaping the behavior of a population in an ecosystem; it is on these behavior patterns that evolutionary processes operate. We are not asking then how cultures evolve, but how sociocultural systems-in-environments evolve. (p. 206)

Interlocked Behavior Cycles

The third problem inherent to the use of Weick's model is the description and analysis of interlocked behavior cycles. Weick's argument is derived from the perspective that interpersonal networks (the social context for interlocked behavior cycles) are essential to the reduction of equivocality in organizing. The processes of selection and retention are "composed of two elements: assembly rules and interlocked behavior cycles" (Weick, 1979a, p. 113). Interlocked behavior cycles move the level of analysis in the organizing model from the individual to the collective. However, systematic documentation of these components of organizing is a virtual impossibility in any complex organizational setting. While Bantz and Smith (1977) offer the most rigorous empirical test that operationalizes the concept of behavior cycles, of the existing studies that utilize or test Weick's model only Kreps (1980) examines interlocked behavior cycles in a complex organizational setting. However, the cycles remain theoretically significant to the operation of the model. The problem is a methodological one. Any sort of retrospective organizational analysis makes the identification and description of interlocked behavior cycles difficult. It is unlikely that such interactions would ever be documented in a manner appropriate to the needs of Weick's model. Such documentation might be possible when analysis of organizing includes analysis of interactions of individuals over the period of time necessary for reduction of equivocality. These studies would be limited to those organizing sequences in which long-term analysis of the interactions in certain interpersonal networks were possible to monitor. Such conditions are likely to be very infrequent for most organizational analysis.

The problem of documenting interlocked behavior cycles is analogous to the attempt to study reproductive sequences in biological speciation. Such sequences result from a multitude of reproductive events among individuals. It is through differential reproductive success that species evolve. However, such individual events are largely invisible to analysis that generalizes at the level of the evolutionary ecology of a species. In the same fashion, Weick's model suffers not from a theoretical failure, but from an analytical requirement (interlocked behavior cycles) that is methodologically intractable. The main components of Weick's model of sociocultural evolution — enactment, selection, and retention — can be used to examine organizing, but the component of interlocked behavior cycles in the selection and retention processes will be unavailable to most analysis.

ETHNOECOLOGY AND THE IDENTIFICATION OF CULTURAL MATERIAL IN ORGANIZING

Weick's sociocultural evolution model of organizing is a significant effort to adopt the concepts and propositions of evolutionary biology and ecology to organizational theory and analysis. While there exists a history of anthropological approaches that utilize bioecological models to study cultures (e.g., Durham, 1982; Steward's [1977] cultural ecology, and Sahlins & Service,

1960, on the evolution of social systems), Weick's work is the first to call for such an approach for organizations. However, as noted above, the use of a truly sociocultural evolution model of organizing requires researchers to be able to empirically capture the cultural in organizing.

Ecological Anthropology

Recent work in the area of anthropological ecology can be used as a paradigm case for the development of theory on cultural influences on organizing. Ecological anthropology studies the relation of culture to environment. According to Jochim (1981), "The ecological approach in anthropology tries to widen the viewpoint of the discipline (and by contrast, often to emphasize) the human interaction with the environment" (p. 3). He adds that "ecological anthropology is clearly separate from older theories of environmental determinism. The importance of aspects of the natural environment is recognized, but by no means are these aspects seen as prime movers in determining human behavior" (p. 4). Recent work in human ecology proceeds from the view that "it is because we see nature in terms of cultural images, and because it is to these that we respond, that a proper understanding of indigenous knowledge and cognitive structures is theoretically crucial to the analysis of ecological relations" (Ellen, 1982, p. 206).

Orlove's (1980) review of the theoretical history of the study of ecology in anthropology provides insight as to why this subject area serves as a paradigm for work on the relationship of organizational environments and organizational cultures.

Initially, work in ecological anthropology was characterized by attempts to depict universal stages through which cultures were said to have passed. This work was subsequently grouped under the label of unilineal cultural evolutionism. Orlove describes more recent work in ecological anthropology as derived from a theoretical perspective that moves the analytical locus from individual social groups to the population (groups of social units within an ecosystem). This trend is mirrored in organizational sociology where the analytical trend has been from the study of focal (individual) organizations to populations of organizations (e.g., McKelevy & Aldrich, 1983).

Orlove describes "processual ecology" as the most recent trend in studies within ecological anthropology. This approach links several essential factors in the culture/environment relationship:

1. an emphasis on diachronic views of culture change
2. the formation of adaptive strategies within cultures
3. the incorporation of actor-based models of the environment for examining proximate factors that influence the cultural behavior of individuals and aggregates.

The incorporation of actor-based models into explanatory and descriptive frameworks is an important trend in human ecological and cultural studies (Ellen, 1982). The impetus to incorporate actor-based models of local ecology is derived from the assumption that examination of the meaning and significance of cultural phenomena proceeds from a focus on individuals of the group (Durham, 1976; Vayda & McCay, 1975). Orlove (1980) suggests that this development in anthropological ecology was a response to the deterministic emphasis accorded environmental variables in early ecological studies of culture in anthropology (e.g., Harris, 1980). According to Orlove (1980):

> a major influence on the processual ecological anthropology is the actor-based models which have received general interest in social anthropology. . . . The actor-based models have several advantages: they account for a wider range of social organization than previous models do; they permit a more precise analysis of the parameters of behavior and the variation of behavior within populations; they admit more readily of an examination of conflict and competition; they offer the potential of examining change through an analysis of the processes which generate economic, political, and social relations. (p. 246)

Organizational cultural ecology proceeds from the view that integrating a concept of culture with Weick's ecologically based model of organizing enhances exploration of what Weick deems as essential to organizing—enact ed environments. In keeping with Weick's model, the primary concern for such a focus is to explore "the way in which the cognitive organization of recognized environmental phenomena affects (consciously or unconsciously) ecological interactions" (Ellen, 1982, p. 210). From this perspective, actor-based models are particularly important for understanding the organizing processes identified by Weick. Pondy and Mitroff (1979) argue for a similar direction in organizational studies with their contention that "one of an organization's most crucial design decisions concerns how it attempts to design its own environment" (p. 13).

Within organizational cultural ecology, ethnoecology can serve as a means of identifying cultural material present in the selection and retention processes. Ethnoecology is the study of a group's conceptualization of relationships of the group to its environment from the actor's point of view (Fowler, 1977; Johnson, 1974). Integration of cognitive materials like cause maps and individual-enacted environments within Weick's model is based on the working hypothesis that there is an interplay between the organizing process of selection and the organizational culture. That an organization's culture is a critical selective process which operates in association with others identified by Weick follows from the view of culture as a system of social knowledge (Spiro, 1984). This system constrains environmental enactment by influencing or constituting selection criteria within the selection process. The organizational culture subsumes or specifies the nature of many of the other selective systems identified by Weick (1979a), including "diffusion," "imitation," and "selective perpetuation of temporal variations." Weick argues that "the selection process contains one or more of these six mechanisms. They are the media through which selection criteria operate" (p. 125).

ORGANIZATIONAL CULTURAL ECOLOGY: UNITING CULTURE AND ECOLOGY IN THE ANALYSIS OF ORGANIZING

The contingency perspective that dominates organizational theory (Duncan & Weiss, 1979) holds that "organizations are treated as open systems which engage in exchanges with their environments. The internal structures and processes which comprise an organization are argued to reflect the characteristics of those environments" (p. 76). As these authors note, this perspective presents an analytical imperative to understand the "fit" of the organization to the environment. The concept of culture presented in this study in conjunction with Weick's model has very specific implications for this theoretical approach. Weick's model is based on the notion that what contingency theory holds as givens in its analytic framework (organization and environment) may be more reasonable to treat as problematic conceptual devices than as empirical entities.

From the perspective of Weick's sociocultural model, the pivotal concept of "fit" in the contingency perspective is best understood in terms of the minds of organizational members rather than features of organizations and environments taken as analytical givens. At the same time, Weick and other cognitive theorists acknowledge the presence of "grains of truth" in the accounts of actors with respect to the organizations and environments they enact. Weick (1979b) argues:

> in any situation where people enact their environment there usually are grains of truth that invite elaboration. Enactment isn't a hallucination. Typically it meets the environment halfway. But what happens is that the actor in the organization plays a major role in unrandomizing and giving order to the bewildering number of variables that constitute those grains. (p. 45)

The concept of culture as argued in this chapter is essential to efforts to understand the minds of actors in order to explore the fit between the organization and its environment. Weick's approach requires that this fit be examined largely in terms of the cognition of organizational actors. Within the perspective of organizational cultural ecology, the emphasis for analysis of the degree of fit between organization and environment is shifted to a view of the relationship as a cultural construct. There is substantial precedence for this shift in the area of cultural ecology where culture is viewed both as a mediator of fit (e.g., in human ecological studies), and in cognitive approaches to culture where it is viewed as a source of the fit. This argument is also made in interpretive organizational studies (e.g., Smircich, 1983). Pondy and Mitroff (1979) also argue for this direction in their call for organizational theorists to reformulate open system models of organizations. They contend that "by redefining the unit of analysis as the organization plus the environment, we would be forced to define the bounds of rationality to be broader, to invoke a concept of *ecological* or *systematic* rationality" (p. 16).

Organizational Cultural Ecology and Organizational Adaptation

The primary implication of the culture concept in this chapter is a call for a revised version of the anthropological tradition of cultural ecology to be used in the analysis and description of organizing. Organizational cultural ecology focuses on examination of cultural mediation of environmental enactment in the organizing processes of selection and retention. Thus, the cultural ecology of organizing explores how the organization's culture informs and constrains environmental enactment, and, by extension, organizational adaptation. The primary implication of culture acting as a strong selective subsystem within the selection process is that adaptation to enacted environments will be affected by the selective subsystem — the organizational culture.

Within Weick's model, adaptation is held to be the adjustments made to enacted environments. This is an important difference between Weick's version of sociocultural evolution and conceptions of sociocultural evolution in anthropology. In the latter, adaptation results from the interaction of system and environment through the differential selection of biological and cultural traits. In Weick's model, organizational adaptation is the means by which the organizational sociocultural system adjusts to changes in enacted environments. According to Weick (1969), adjustments are best understood as emanating primarily from organizing (specifically, internal selection criteria in the selection process), rather than from agents of change from outside the system.

Weick's formulation of adaptation carries important implications for the organizational literature on adaptation and the use of a reworked cultural ecology in organizational communication studies. First, a debate central to much organizational literature concerns whether and to what extent adaptation actually characterizes organizations (e.g., Hannan & Freeman, 1977). Weick's conceptualization of adaptation suggests that the debate exists due to a focus on the wrong source for adaptation. In terms of Weick's model, claims that adaptation rarely characterizes organizations result from looking to agents of selection outside the organization (e.g., markets and customers in the management literature, and interorganizational effects in the literature of organizational sociology), rather than the cognitive processes within the organization as primary to understanding adaptation. The significance of this proposition is that cultural ecology is immediately relevant to the discovery and description of the salient features of adaptation. Since enactment entails understanding and response to ecological change, and since the organization's culture is essential to the processes by which organizational and environmental change become known to organizational members, the study of organizational cultural ecology is a key to unfolding these relationships.

Application of the perspective of cultural ecology argued in this chapter within organizational contexts is derived from the anthropological tradition of Steward (e.g., 1973, 1977). However, there are important diagnostic differences. The analytical level of organizations sharply distinguishes the focus of this approach from that of anthropology. An important implication of this difference in the level of analysis is how the concept of time appears in the two uses of cultural ecology. When one adopts the perspective of cultural ecology in order to examine the evolution of organizational sociocultural systems (as in Weick's model), the diachronic dimension (i.e., time depth) of evolutionary processes of variation, selection, and retention is significantly shorter than what is found in anthropological studies of evolving sociocultural systems. While Weick's model posits the same components of sociocultural evolution to organizations as for larger sociocultural systems, the problem of the dimension of time when using evolutionary concepts to discuss organizations is a central one, and needs to be addressed in future research.

Orlove (1980) argues that the integration of actor-based models within cultural ecology follows from the assumption that "the ecosystem and decisions made by individuals affect each other reciprocally" (p. 248). Orlove's contention is a direct (although unintended) response to strong criticism of cognitive models and explanations in organizational theory. Pfeffer (1982) presents the case for this criticism. He argues:

> The literature on organizations appears to be fascinated with cognitive processes. Such processes take the form [of the] . . . social construction of reality, in which accounts are produced that come to be shared and condition actor's perceptions of, and actions in, the world. In each of these approaches there is reliance on unobservable hypothetical processes that occur inside people's heads and that, furthermore, make most sense when discussed and described at the individual level of analysis. Consequently, what might begin as a study of organizational behavior comes, in many instances, to look like a study of individual attitudes. The two are not the same thing. Organizations need to be studied on their own terms as relational, demographic, and physical entities. Whether or how the analysis of individual cognition and affect can help in this analysis remains to be demonstrated. (p. 257)

The demonstration that Pfeffer seeks is one of the long-term goals of organizational cultural ecology. The significance of work in ecological anthropology to this goal is quite clear. It provides an imperative for similar work to begin in studies of organizations, and suggests important directions for this work to take.

REFERENCES

Bantz, C. R., & Smith, D. H. (1977). A critique and experimental test of Weick's model of organizing. *Communication Monographs, 44,* 171–184.

Bee, B. L. (1974). *Patterns and processes.* New York: The Free Press.

Bougon, M., Weick, K., & Binkhorst, D. (1977). Cognition in organizations: An analysis of the Utrecht Jazz Orchestra. *Administrative Science Quarterly, 22,* 606–639.

Campbell, D. T. (1965). Variation and selective retention in socio-cultural evolution. In H. R. Barringer, G. J. Blanksten, & R. W. Mack (Eds.), *Social change in developing areas* (pp. 19–49). Cambridge, MA: Schenkman.

Duncan, R., & Weiss, A. (1979). Organizational learning: Implications for organizational design. *Research in Organizational Behavior, 1,* 75–123.

Durham, W. H. (1976). The adaptive significance of cultural behavior. *Human Ecology, 4,* 89–121.

Durham, W. H. (1982). Interactions of genetic and cultural evolution: Models and examples. *Human Ecology, 10,* 289–323.

Ellen, R. (1982). *Environment, subsistence and system.* Cambridge: Cambridge University Press.

Fowler, C. S. (1977). Ethnoecology. In D. L. Hardesty (Ed.), *Ecological Anthropology* (pp. 215–243). New York: John Wiley and Sons.

Gregory, K. L. (1983). Native-view paradigms: Multiple cultures and culture conflicts in organizations. *Administrative Science Quarterly, 28,* 359–376.

Hannan, M. T., & Freeman, J. (1977). The population ecology of organizations. *American Journal of Sociology, 82,* 929–964.

Harris, M. (1980). *Cultural materialism: The struggle for a science of culture.* New York: Vintage Books.

Harris, L., & Cronen, V. E. (1979). A rules-based model for the analysis and evaluation of organizational communication. *Communication Monographs, 27,* 12–28.

Hawley, A. H. (1986). *Human ecology.* Chicago: University of Chicago Press.

Holland, D., & Quinn, N. (Eds.). (1980). *Cultural models in language and thought.* Cambridge: Cambridge University Press.

Hutchins, E. (180). *Culture and inference.* Cambridge: Harvard University Press.

Jochim, M. A. (1981). *Strategies for survival: Cultural behavior in an ecological context.* New York: Academic Press.

Johnson, A. (1974). Ethnoecology and planting practices in a swidden agricultural system. *American Ethnologist, 1,* 87–101.

Keesing, R. (1974). Theories of culture. *Annual Review of Anthropology, 3,* 73–97.

Keesing, R. (1976). *Cultural anthropology: A contemporary perspective.* New York: Holt, Rinehart and Winston.

Kreps, G. L. (1980). A field experimental test and revaluation of Weick's model of organizing. *Communication Yearbook, 4,* 389–398.

McKelevy, B., & Aldrich, H. (1983). Populations, natural selection, and applied organizational science. *Administrative Science Quarterly, 28,* 101–128.

Morey, N. C., & Luthans, F. (1984). An emic perspective and ethnoscience methods for organizational research. *Academy of Management Review, 9,* 27–36.

O'Donnell-Trujillo, N., & Pacanowsky, M. E. (1982). The interpretation of organizational cultures. Manuscript submitted for publication.

Orlove, B. S. (1980). Ecological anthropology. *Annual Review of Anthropology, 9,* 235–273.

Pacanowsky, M. E., & O'Donnell-Trujillo, N. (1982). Communication and organizational cultures. *Western Journal of Speech Communication, 46,* 115–130.

Pfeffer, J. (1982). *Organizations and organization theory.* Boston: Pitman.

Pondy, L. R., & Mitroff, I. I. (1979). Beyond open system models of organization. *Research in Organizational Behavior, 1,* 3–39.

Sahlins, M., & Service, E. (Eds.). (1960). *Evolution and culture.* Ann Arbor: University of Michigan Press.

Schein, E. H. (1985). Coming to a new awareness of organizational culture. *Sloan Management Review, 25,* 3–16.

Smircich, L. (1983). Implications for management theory. In L. L. Putnam & M. E. Packanowsky (Eds.), *Communication and organizations: An interpretive approach* (pp. 13–30). Beverly Hills: Sage.

Smith, E. A. (1981). Evolutionary ecology and the analysis of human behavior. In R. Dyson-Hudson & M. A. Little (Eds.), *Rethinking human adaptation: Biological and cultural models* (pp. 23–40). Boulder, CO: Westview Press.

Spiro, M. E. (1984). Some reflections on cultural determinism and relativism with special reference to emotion and reason. In R. A. Shewder & R. L. Levine (Eds.), *Culture theory: Essays on mind, self, and emotion* (pp. 323–346). New York: Cambridge University Press.

Steward, J. S. (1973). *Theory of culture change: The methodology of multilinear evolution.* Urbana: University of Illinois Press.

Steward, J. S. (1977). The concept and method of cultural ecology. In J. C. Steward & R. F. Murphy, (Eds.), *Ecology an evolution* (pp. 43–57). Urbana: University of Illinois Press.

Van Maanen, J., & Barley, S. R. (1985). Cultural organization: Fragments of a theory. In P. Frost, L. Moore, M. R. Louis, C. C. Lundberg, & J. Martin (Eds.), *Organizational culture* (pp. 31–53). Beverly Hills: Sage.

Vayda, A. P., & McCay, B. J. (1975). New directions in ecology and ecological anthropology. *Annual Review of Anthropology, 4,* 293–306.

Weick, K. E. (1969). *The social psychology of organizing.* Reading, MA: Addison-Wesley.

Weick, K. E. (1977). Enactment processes in organizations. In B. M. Staw & G. R. Salancik (Eds.), *New directions in organizational behavior* (pp. 267–299). Chicago: St. Claire Press.

Weick, K. E. (1979a). *The social psychology of organizing* (2nd ed.). New York: Random House.

Weick, K. E. (1979b). Cognitive processes in organizations. *Research in Organizational Behavior, 1,* 41–74.

Weick, K. E. (1985). The significance of corporate culture. In P. Frost, L. Moore, M. R. Louis, C. C. Lundberg, & J. Martin (Eds.), *Organizational culture* (pp. 381–391). Beverly Hills: Sage.

8

Culture and Effectiveness: Perspectives on the Relationship

Pamela Shockley-Zalabak

INTRODUCTION

Scholars from a variety of disciplines engage in lively debate about how organizations construct the social realities that constitute organizational life and what role socially constructed realities play in organizational effectiveness. Proponents of the "strong culture" perspective view the construction of social realities that contribute to shared values as the very core of culture and central to high organizational performance (Deal & Kennedy, 1982). Others suggest that this relationship between high performance and the clan or "strong culture" holds true only when organizational conditions exhibit ambiguity, complexity, and interdependence of transactions. The clan may, in fact, require too much time and agreement to be efficient and effective when conditions of high certainty exist (Wilkins & Ouchi, 1983). Eisenberg and Riley (1988), representing a more contemporary perspective, contended a careful review of research suggests that sharing can never be complete and varies from organization to organization; that shared realities are not always positive; that understanding of rules or contexts is not equated with agreement or consensus about issues; that organizations frequently have multiple subcultures; and that cultures can be characterized as serving both cohesive and divisive function.

Regardless of the position taken in the "strong culture" debate, central to the notion of organizational culture and performance are the communication processes in which organizational members engage. Berger and Luckmann (1967) underscore the centrality of communication for organizations when they suggest "logic does not reside in the institutions and their external functionalities, but in the way they are treated in reflection about them . . . . Language provides the fundamental superimposition of logic on the objectivated social world. The edifice of legitimations is built upon language as its principal instrumentality" (p. 64). As early as 1938, Barnard described communication as the principal function of the executive, while Drucker (1954, 1986) has consistently suggested the importance of communication for organizational success.

Numerous scholars have defined organizations as essentially communication phenomena (Farace, Monge, & Russell, 1977; Schall, 1983; Wiio, Goldhaber, & Yates, 1980). Putnam (1983) supports this view when she describes the ongoing meaning process in organizations. Distinguished from simple movement or transmission of messages, she sees the meaning process as "the ongoing, everchanging sets of interlocked behaviors that create as well as change organizational events" (p. 40). This meaning process, the construction of social reality, can be described as organizational culture.

The interrelatedness of communication and culture has been attested to in a variety of ways but rarely more directly than when Hall (1959) stated, "Culture is communication and communication is culture" (p. 191). Indeed consistent throughout the work of numerous researchers (Bormann, 1983; Cushman, 1977; Fine, 1979; Gregory, 1983; Pacanowsky & O'Donnell-Trujillo, 1983; Spradley, 1979) is a concept of culture as a subjective construct to describe complex communication processes.

Given the complexity of simultaneously understanding organizational communication processes, culture, and performance, the purpose of this chapter is to examine two dominant views of communication and culture relationships, describe frequently proposed dimensions of the construct of organizational effectiveness, and detail current research relating culture to effectiveness. Finally, the chapter discusses implications and limitations of current research while suggesting directions for future inquiry.

ORGANIZATIONAL CULTURES AND COMMUNICATION

Descriptions of organizational culture abound in both popular media and academic journals. Researchers seek to understand the processes and influences of culture while practitioners make attempts to gain control of culture in order to ensure organizational survival and effectiveness. Although their assumptions, goals, and methodologies differ, they share what Deal and Kennedy (1983) have described as "a long standing agreement. . . that something elusive and powerful governs the behavior of social collectives" (p. 503). These attempts to understand the informal, ongoing meaning processes in organziations are the basis of the current intense interest in applying the culture metaphor to the values, symbols, heroes, rituals, and stories that powerfully influence organizational life.

Deetz (1988) suggested culture studies can be organized around two essential goals:

The first goal is to generate insight into basic cultural processes, to understand how human beings at this particular historical juncture organize sense and meaning in their lives, and to demonstrate how the organization of work life articulates more basic cultural processes. The second goal is to work toward the continued development and reformation of organizational practices focusing primarily on decision making within a complex changing environment with a number of "stakeholders" with competing interests. (p. 336)

The current emphasis on the importance of the symbolic in providing meaning, purpose, and influence for organizational life reflects an important tradition of concern for the bounded rationality and informal dynamics of human behavior. As early as 1935, Arnold wrote about words, ceremonies, and symbols as the basis for belief in reality while Barnard (1938) proposed that "feeling organizations" contributed to our understanding of society. Deal and Kennedy (1983) argue that our renewed interest in the symbolic results from the failure of more rational models of organziation to either provide an understanding of organizational life or bring about desired change. Specifically, they argue that evidence continues to accumulate that expected relationships among structural elements and goals or technology cannot be empirically demonstrated, that current theories about organizations provide little guidance for innovation, that recognition is growing that views of organizations are relative, and that new awareness of the importance of the symbolic fosters interest in alternative views of organizational life.

Deal and Kennedy (1983) suggest that "culture by definition is elusive, intangible, implicit, and taken for granted. But every organization develops a core set of assumptions, understandings, and implicit rules that govern day-to-day behavior in the work place" (p. 501). Stonich (1982) describes culture as "a pattern of beliefs and expectations shared by members of an organization. These beliefs and expectations produce rules for behavior— norms—that powerfully shape the behavior of individuals and groups in the organization" (p. 35).

Schein (1984), in response to efforts to relate organizational cultures to organizational excellence, calls for a definition of culture that goes beyond shared meanings that facilitate interpretation and action to an understanding of how culture comes to be and how it can be altered. Schein proposes that "organizational culture is the pattern of basic assumptions that a given group has invented, discovered, or developed in learning to cope with its problems of external adaptation and internal integration, and that have worked well enough to be considered valid and, therefore, to be taught to new members as the correct way to perceive, think, and feel in relation to those problems" (p. 3). Schein contends that organizational cultures reflect taken-for-granted, invisible, and preconscious basic assumptions about relationships to environment, the nature of reality and truth, the nature of human nature, the nature of human activity, and the nature of human relationships. These assumptions, in turn, influence the development of values that are at a greater level of awareness than basic assumptions. Values contribute to the visible but not always decipherable artifacts and creations (technology, art, visible and audible behavior patterns) of organizational life.

Schall (1983), in suggesting that organizations, cultures, and cultural rules can be understood as communication phenomena, proposes a description of culture that emphasizes common characteristics from cultural anthropology and sociology. Schall defines culture as "a relatively enduring, interdependent symbolic system of values, beliefs, and assumptions evolving from and imperfectly shared by interacting organizational members that allows them to explain, coordinate, and evaluate behavior and to ascribe common meanings to stimuli encountered in the organizational context" (p. 557). Schall further contends that communication rules can be discovered that operationalize values and, therefore, directly reflect an organization's culture.

Disagreements exist about the aspects of organizational culture and how culture can be meaningfully studied (Deetz, 1988; DeWine, 1988; Pilotta, Widman, & Jasko, 1988). Morey and Luthans (1985), while acknowledging definitional and conceptual difficulties as the concept of culture is displaced through metaphor and analogy from anthropology to the disciplines of organizational study, suggested that certain attributes of culture are particularly relevant for organizational research:

> First, culture is learned. It is not genetic or biological. . . . Culture is shared by people as members of social groups. . . . Culture is transgenerational and cumulative in its development. . . . It is symbolic in that it is based on the human capacity to symbol. Culture is adaptive; it is the basic human adaptive mechanism. . . . Of particular relevance for organizational studies are its patterned, shared, learned, and symbolic characteristics.

In describing the expansiveness of communication and culture interrelatedness, Smircich (1981) articulates both the functionalist view of culture as a variable of the organization and culture-as-a-metaphor view, making it synonymous with the organization and reflective of an interpretist paradigm.

Smircich (1983) concludes that "a variety of research agendas flow out of the linkage of different conceptions of culture and organization. . . Some researchers give high priority to the principles of prediction, generalizability, causality, and control, while others are concerned by what appear to them to be more fundamental issues of meaning and the processes by which organizational life is possible . . . Despite the very real differences in research interest and purpose represented here, whether one treats culture as a background factor, an organizational variable, or as metaphor for conceptualizing organization, the idea of culture focuses attention on the expressive, nonrational qualities of the experience of organization. It legitimates attention to the subjective, interpretive aspects of organizational life" (pp.

354–355). The distinctions between culture as a backdrop or organizational variable and culture as a metaphor have become the dominant paradigms for understanding organizational culture. The culture as a variable approach is embodied in the functionalist tradition while the culture-as-metaphor view is reflective of an interpretivist perspective.

The Functional Tradition

The functionalist tradition dominates inquiry for organizational analysis. The functionalist paradigm is based on an objective view of reality that emphasizes the discovery and regulation of social order. As the dominant norm for social scientific research, the functionalist tradition emphasizes definitions, operationalization, measurement, causality, and generalizability. Putnam (1982) describes this paradigm thus: "Functionalists view society as objective and orderly; behavior is concrete and tangible, and society has a real and systematic existence. Research aims, through scientific rigor and objectivity, to discover empirical knowledge which has pragmatic and regulatory value" (p. 194).

The functionalist paradigm describes organizational communication as a concrete substance operating within and without the organizational structure. The functional approach helps us understand organizational communication by describing what messages do and how they move through organizations. This perspective describes communication as a complex organizational process that serves organizing, relationship, and change functions—what messages do. The way messages move through organizations is described by examining communication networks, channels, message directions, communication load, and distortion. The functionalist approach suggests that communication transmits rules, regulations, and information throughout the organization. Communication establishes and defines human relationships, helps individuals identify with goals and opportunities, and is the process by which the organization generates and manages change. These functions occur during the repetitive patterns of communication interactions in which organizational members engage (Pacanowsky & O'Donnell-Trujillo, 1983; Putnam, 1982; and Shockley-Zalabak, 1988). As Pacanowsky & O'Donnell-Trujillo (1982) suggest, research approaches related to the functionalist tradition "presuppose that the purpose of organizational communication theory is to provide a causal understanding of how organizations work and thus render the ultimate task of the communication researcher to be the linking of communication variables to organizational outcome variables, such as productivity, survival, or effectiveness" (p. 116).

The functionalist paradigm and related views such as comparative management and corporate culture (Burrell & Morgan, 1979; Putnam, 1982, 1983; Smircich, 1983) treat culture as a variable of the organization.

Comparative management approaches, for example, depict culture as a background, an explanatory variable, to facilitate understanding of organizations across countries. Research from a comparative management perspective focuses on differences and similarities across cultures from which implications for organizational effectiveness can be drawn (Smircich, 1983). The related corporate culture view suggests that organizations are culture-producing phenomena (Deal & Kennedy, 1982; Smircich, 1983). Smircich (1983) concludes that "the implication is that the symbolic or cultural dimension in some way contributes to the overall systemic balance and effectiveness of an organization" (p. 344).

Research generally attributed to the functionalist tradition suggests that the variable of culture serves to develop shared values and beliefs which, in turn, function in several important ways. Smircich (1983) summarizes these functions: "First, it (culture) conveys a sense of identity for organization members (Deal & Kennedy, 1982; Peters & Waterman, 1982). Second, it facilitates the generation of commitment to something larger than the self (Peters & Waterman, 1982; Schall, 1981; Siehl & Martin, 1981). Third, culture enhances social system stability (Louis, 1980; Kreps, 1981). And fourth, culture serves as a sense-making device that can guide and shape behavior (Louis, 1980; Meyer, 1981; Pfeffer, 1981; Siehl & Martin, 1981)" (pp. 345–346).

In sum, the culture-as-a-variable approach embodied in the functionalist tradition assumes culture to operate as an element that interacts with other elements or variables in the social world. As such, the variable of culture can be measured, managed, and evaluated. It is this evaluative dimension where culture can be studied for its contribution to organizational effectiveness.

The Interpretive Approach

Putnam (1982) describes the interpretive approach as a paradigm where "organizational reality is socially constructed through the words, symbols, and actions that members use. It is language use and the meanings enacted from verbal and nonverbal messages that create and sustain social reality" (p. 200). As an alternative to positivist thinking and the centrality of objective reality, the interpretive approach focuses on the centrality of meaning in all social interaction. Research based on the interpretive perspective "focuses on how organizational reality is constituted. It seeks understanding of symbol systems, rules, and norms that account for everyday routines and organizational practices. The researcher learns the language of the actors, assembles their texts, and then derives a sense of unity from interpreting the whole in light of its parts . . . In critical research, however, evaluation governs the processes of describing, explaining, and understanding" (Putnam, 1983, pp. 47–48).

The interpretivist perspective is concerned with how organizational reality is generated through human interaction. As such, message functions and message movement are secondary to understanding communication as the construction of shared realities (human interaction). The interpretivist approach helps us understand organizational communication by describing all ongoing human interaction as communication in one form or another. The interpretivist approach suggests that organizations exist through human interaction; structures and technologies result from the information to which individuals react. Shared organizational realities reflect the collective interpretations by organizational members of all organizational activities.

Interpretivists describe organizing and decision making as essentially communication phenomena while identification, socialization, communication rules, and power all are communication processes that reflect how organizational influence occurs. Culture, as a metaphor for organizational communication, is the unique sense of a place that reflects the way things are done and how people talk about the way things are done (Shockley-Zalabak, 1988). Pacanowsky & O'Donnell-Trujillo (1982) suggest that research using the culture approach of the interpretivist view "ought to be a non-managerially oriented account of sense-making in a particular organization. This account should not be a compendium of problems and solutions; rather, it should be a story of organizational life in all its fullness. . . .In short, organizational culture research has theory-generative, theory-contextualizing, and even theory-testing possibilities" (pp. 128–129). Pacanowsky and O'Donnell-Trujillo support a variety of utilities for the interpretivist approach, namely: (a) ". . . an organizational culture study can serve as necessary, prequantitative description for those researchers interested in devising quantitative measures for further research in the same organization . . . (b) . . . each organizational culture study can provide any member (manager, worker, volunteer) with an overall picture of the organization . . . (c) . . . each organizational culture study reaffirms the centrality of communicative behaviors in organizational inquiry . . . (d) . . . each organizational culture study stands as a critique of the assumptions of traditional organizational communication research, and . . . (e) . . . each organizational culture study serves, in Geertz's terms, to 'expand the universe of discourse' " (pp. 128–130).

Culture as a root metaphor for organization is reflected in cognitive, symbolic, structural, and psychodynamic organizational perspectives. Smircich (1983) summarizes the underlying assumptions of these perspectives when she states, "The mode of thought that underlies cultures as a root metaphor gives the social world much less concrete status. The social world is not assumed to have an objective, independent existence that imposes itself on human beings. Instead, the social or organizational worlds exist only as a pattern of symbolic relationships and meanings sustained through the continued processes of human interaction. . . . When culture is a root metaphor, the researcher's attention shifts from concerns about what do organizations accomplish and how may they accomplish it more efficiently, to how is organization accomplished and what does it mean to be organized" (p. 353)?

The culture as root metaphor approach assumes that understanding and usefulness are the primary criteria for research as opposed to the replicability, generalizability, and reliability tenets of the functionalist tradition (Deal & Kennedy, 1983). Usefulness, in the Deal & Kennedy perspective, "means that concepts must be penetrable, parsimonious, and powerful" (p. 504). In their view, interpretivist approaches provide a framework and language for understanding experience; establish a consensus about the identities of heroes, priests, and storytellers of a particular culture; provide an approach for initiating creative ameliorative strategies; and promote the means for understanding conflicts. Smircich and Stubbart (1985) suggest that an interpretive approach places emphasis on an examination of the processes and rules that people follow, their reasoning for behavior, and assignment of meaning as opposed to emphasis on cause–effect logic. As such, interpretive research is done from the point of view of the participants, embraces multiple perspectives, and is historical–contextual.

THE CONSTRUCT OF ORGANIZATIONAL EFFECTIVENESS

Although scholars and practitioners generally agree that organizational effectiveness is desirable, less certainty surrounds the way to define or understand this important yet ambiguous dimension of organizational life. Variously referred to as productivity, adaptation, creativity, or performance, most approaches to describing organizational effectiveness represent a macro view of organization-wide events and processes. Effectiveness is generally conceptualized to represent the degree to which an organization realizes an established goal or goals within a particular set of environmental conditions. Individual behavior is less often an important level of analysis even though a vast body of organizational literature seeks to understand the individual in relation to a variety of organizational environments, processes, and events.

Attempts to measure or describe organizational effectiveness frequently have used an "ultimate" or "significant" criterion such as productivity, growth, or profit. Campbell (1973), in surveying univariate models of effectiveness, identified overall performance, productivity, employee satisfaction, and financial return as the most frequent univariate measures of effectiveness.

Although univariate measures of effectiveness have appeal, their usefulness is challenged by those who believe single measures to be an oversimplification not reflecting the complexity of organizational life (Campbell, 1973; Steers, 1975). Downs and Hain (1982) illustrate the definitional difficulty for

TABLE 8.1.   Functionalist and Interpretive Approaches to Culture Research

Functionalist Paradigm	Interpretivist Paradigm
Research Values	*Research Values*
Definition	Symbol Systems
Operationalization	Rules
Measurement	Norms
Causality	Interpreting the whole
Generalizability	Centrality of meaning
Empirical relationships	Organizational reality
	Understanding & usefulness
Organizational Descriptions	*Organizational Descriptions*
Objective and orderly social systems	Patterns of symbolic relationships and meanings
Composed of interacting variables	Based on subjective human interactions
Culture Assumptions	*Culture Assumptions*
Variable of the organization	Root metaphor for organization
Pragmatic & regulatory value	Understanding & usefulness value
Functions to establish identity, generate commitment, supports system stability, & guides & shapes behavior	Nonmanagerially oriented
Contributes to effectiveness	Centrality of communication
Managerially controlled	Explains experience

the single measure when they describe issues affecting measures of productivity. They point out that, although the traditional definition of productivity is a ratio between input and output as a measure of the efficient use of resources, there is merit in the argument that productivity should also include measures of adaptation to the organization's specific environment and financial profitability. Downs and Hain conclude that productivity is better represented as a multivariate concept.

Multivariate organizational effectiveness models are rapidly replacing univariate analysis. Based on a view of organizations as complex systems, multivariate models describe effectiveness as a function of specific factors found in organizations. Steers (1975) contends that multivariate models are of two general types: "(a) normative, or prescriptive, models, which attempt to specify those things an organization must do to become effective; and (b) descriptive models, which attempt to summarize the characteristics found in successful organizations" (p. 550). Normative models generally have been developed with deductive methods while descriptive models reflect an inductive approach. Normative models as reflections of the functionalist perspective seek generalizability while descriptive models are more organization-specific in concert with interpretivist methods.

Normative models of organizational effectiveness have been proposed by Georgopoulos and Tannenbaum (1957), Bennis (1962), Blake and Mouton (1964), Caplow (1964), Katz and Kahn (1966), Friedlander and Pickle (1968), Schein (1970), Mott (1972), Gibson, Ivancevich, and Donnelly (1973), Negandhi and Reimann (1973), and Cunningham (1978). Descriptive models of organizational effectiveness are provided by Lawrence and Lorsch (1967), Price (1968), Mahoney and Weitzel (1969), Webb (1974), Steers (1975), Ouchi (1980), and Peters and Waterman (1982).

Evaluation criteria represented in both normative and descriptive models of organizational effectiveness include adaptability–flexibility, innovation, resource utilization, return on investment, profit, productivity, satisfaction, resource acquisition, absence of strain, control over environment, development, efficiency, employee retention, growth, integration, open communications, and survival. A review of both normative and descriptive models reveals that adaptability–flexibility, productivity, and satisfaction are the most frequently mentioned criteria for effectiveness. Steers (1975) concludes that "the effectiveness construct is so complex as to defy simple attempts at model development" (p. 549).

Despite the diversity and breath of organizational effectiveness models, only recently has attention been focused on relationships between individual experiences and organizational functioning and effectiveness. Keeley (1984) analyzes how the concept of organizational effectiveness might be conceptualized to include organizational participants or constituents. He contrasts emerging participant-interest theories such as the relativistic approach, thedevelopmental approach, the power approach, and the social-justice approach, and proposes a harm minimization principle for evaluating organizational effectiveness. These theories generally reject an overall assessment of effectiveness in favor of multiple determinations of effectiveness based on the multiple groups or individuals who supply the criteria for evaluation. These approaches recognize the changing preferences of constituencies over time and the limitations of static or time-bound measures of effectiveness. Additionally, these theories raise questions about justice and effectiveness as parallel concepts rather than separate evaluations of organizational processes and outcomes. Finally, Keeley argues that effectiveness can best be evaluated as the minimization of harm or what an organization should *not* do rather than the attainment of multiple and often conflicting goals.

Generally, neither traditional goal operationalization or participant-interest theories of organizational effectiveness address the process nature of effectiveness with temporal dimensions. In response to the inadequacies of existing models, Steers (1975) rejects the notion that effectiveness can be measured as a set of static variables and proposes an operative goal approach capable of accounting for multiple and conflicting evaluation criteria. Indeed, it is the inadequacies to which Steers refers and the complexity of understanding the diverse and somewhat subjective construct of organizational effectiveness that has given rise to interest in the impact of culture on this evaluative dimension of organizational life.

Quinn and Rohrbaugh (1983) propose a framework which combines four previously developed models or approaches to performance: the rational goal, open systems, internal process, and participant satisfaction, or human resource models. As described in the work of Ostroff and Schmitt (1993):

> The four approaches to performance are defined along three bi-polar dimensions, two of which focus on organizational characteristics. In the first, organizational focus, an internal, person-oriented focus is opposed to an external, organization-oriented emphasis. The second structure, contrasts stability and control with flexibility and change. The third dimension, organizational means and ends, contrasts the processes of means (e.g., goal setting) to organizational outcomes and the outcomes or ends (e.g., productivity) themselves. . . . Relationships among organizational performance and the organizational characteristics associated with each model are likely to differ across organizations as a function of the importance of different domains (Cameron, 1981). (p. 1346)

Milliken (1990), in describing organizational responses to environmental change to organizational effectiveness, noted that most of the work in organizational change and its associated relationship to organizational effectiveness has described effectiveness as an outcome or result of change. He suggested an important counter perspective to treating effectiveness as an organizational outcome when he argued, "effectiveness is generally studied as an outcome variable, yet managers' perceptions of an organization's past or current effectiveness may also influence how they will interpret and respond to changes in their organization's environment" (p. 48). Along with understanding effectiveness as an outcome of complex organizational processes, the Milliken perspective of effectiveness as influence has potential to expand our understanding of a variety of organizational interpretation processes; that is, cultural processes.

THE IMPACT OF CULTURE

Communication, whether described as organizational culture or a variable of the organization, has long been related to a variety of measures of organizational effectiveness. For example, communication processes have been linked to managerial effectiveness (Barnard, 1938; Boyatzsis, 1982; Kotter, 1982); the intergration of work units across organizational levels (Likert, 1967);

TABLE 8.2   The Construct of Organizational Effectiveness

Effectiveness Definitions	*Effectivness Models*
Productivity	Univariate approaches
Adaptation	Evaluation Criterion:
Creativity	Performance
Performance	Productivity
Employee Outcomes	Employee satisfaction
Growth	Financial return
Profit	Multivariate approaches
Survival	Normative, deductive
Various combinations	Descriptive, inductive
	Participant-Interest approaches
Evaluation criteria:	Relativistic
Adaptability–flexibility	Developmental
Innovation	Power
Resource utilization	Social Justice
Return on investment	Harm minimization
Profit	
Productivity	
Satisfaction	
Resource acquisition	
Absence of strain	
Control over environment	
Development	
Efficiency	
Employee retention	
Growth	
Integration	
Open communication	
Survival	
Harm minimization	
Justice	
Equity	

Effectiveness Research
Based on Functionalist paradigm assumptions
Utilizes multiple research methodologies
Strengths
  Macroview of organization-wide events and processes
  Relates diverse organizational variables
  Provides models for prediction and control
Weaknesses
  Minimizes individual behavior
  Measures static variables
  Cannot account for conflicting evaluation criteria
  Lacks temporal dimension

characteristics of effective supervision (Redding, 1972); job and communication satisfaction (Goldhaber, Yates, Porter, & Lesniak, 1978); and overall
organizational effectiveness (Clampitt & Downs, 1983; Lewis, Cummings, &
Long, 1981; Pincus, 1986; Roberts, O'Reilly, Bretton, & Porter, 1974). In
summarizing eight field studies, Tubbs and Hain (1979) conclude that the
findings "provide consistent and strong support for the assumption that
management communication behaviors do play a significant part in contributing to or detracting from total organizational effectiveness" (p. 1).

Strong claims are made that the complex communication processes
frequently referred to as organizational culture directly influence organizational effectiveness (Peters & Waterman, 1982). Although these claims are
inherently reflective of a functionalist perspective, both functionalist and
interpretivist research strategies have been utilized in their support.

Kilmann, Saxton, and Serpa (1985) answer the question of culture impact
when they state, "There is not much point in attempting to study or change a
thing called culture if it does not affect what goes on in organizations. An
important assumption guiding all our discussions on this topic, therefore, is
that culture does affect organizational behavior and performance" (p. 3). They
further contend that there are three important aspects of impact: direction,
pervasiveness, and strength. Direction of impact relates to the influence of
culture on the course of organizational action. Does cultural communication
direct action toward goal attainment and innovation, or does it encourage
resistance and maintenance of the status quo? Is the culture widely understood and shared? To what degree is the culture pervasive and, therefore,
capable of broad influence? Strength refers to the level of pressure that
cultural communication has on organizational members. If culture is pervasive, it then can be assessed for its strength in influencing behavior and
subsequently all organizational events.

Schein (1984) argues that cultural strength may or may not be related to
effectiveness. He acknowledges that cultural strength has been broadly
described as desirable but challenges the direct relationship as overly simplis-
tic. He hypothesizes that "young groups strive for culture strength as a way of
creating an identity for themselves, but older groups may be more effective
with a weak total culture and diverse subcultures to enable them to be
responsive to rapid environmental change" (p. 7). Schein (1985) proposes that
the functions of culture differ by growth stages of organizations. During the
birth and early growth of organizations, for example, the founder or family
dominates the organization and culture functions to hold the organization
together, emphasize socialization, and develop commitment. Subcultures are
spawned during organizational midlife and loss of key goals, values, and
assumptions occurs. Organizational maturity is characterized by cultural
constraint on innovation with an emphasis on preservation of the past. Schein

proposes additional organizational options and cultural functions as he presents his description of how culture forms, develops, and changes.

Deal and Kennedy (1982) assert that culture has "a major effect on the success of the business" (p. 4). In their study of nearly 80 companies, those that had clearly articulated qualitative beliefs were uniformly outstanding performers. From their research, Deal and Kennedy identify the elements of culture they believe contribute to the strength or weakness of culture in a particular organization. They describe the business environment as the most powerful of all influences on shaping a culture. They argue that the type of culture developed relates to the type of business, resources, and constraints encountered by the organization. Values emerge as the basis of the culture and help organizational members determine success criteria.

Heroes are the role models espousing cultural values while rites and rituals signify the daily routines of organizational life. The cultural network — envisioned as a variety of informal communication exchanges — "carries" the culture throughout the organization. Deal and Kennedy underscore the importance of cultural communication by claiming that "working the network effectively is the only way to get things done or to understand what's really going on" (1982, p. 15).

The question of who works the cultural network is answered at least in part by a level of analysis focusing on how powerful organizational actors influence culture and organizational effectiveness. Hambrick and Mason (1984) argue for a new emphasis in macro-organizational research, namely an increased understanding of how the values and cognitive bases of powerful actors influence organizational strategies and effectiveness. They posit a model of strategic choice under conditions of bounded rationality, which is influenced both directly and indirectly by the values decision makers hold. These values are described as individually developed and influenced by the ingrained character present in the organization. In support of this perspective, Sapienza (1985) used case study methodology to assess whether organizational culture as shared beliefs influenced the decisions top managers made. Sapienza concludes that organizational culture as shared beliefs influenced the decisions of management by shaping how managers perceived certain aspects of events, by influencing the language used to discuss perceptions, and by the development of strategy designed to adapt the organization to an accepted metaphorical reality. Lorsch (1985) supports the importance of top management or powerful actors as cultural leaders. He relates their significance not only to cultural beliefs but to the development of organizational strategy and ultimate effectiveness. Lorsch contends that "it is important to recognize that culture affects not only what managers believe within the organization but also the decisions they make about the organization's relationships with its environment — in other words, its strategy" (p. 84).

Peters and Waterman (1982), utilizing descriptive methodologies, and Denison (1984), using an empirical approach, make powerful arguments for the relationships of strong cultures to organizational effectiveness. Both Peters and Waterman and Denison use basically functionalist outcome measures of business performance as operationalizations of organizational effectiveness. However, Peters and Waterman use qualitative analysis to describe cultural themes present in excellent companies, while Denison quantitatively assesses cultural dimensions within organizations and makes performance comparisons over time based on these dimensions. Peters and Waterman and Denison both conclude that strong cultures influence or are related to organizational effectiveness.

Specifically, Peters and Waterman (1982) used financial performance measures and the capacity for innovativeness over time to identify successful American companies. Following a variety of interpretive analyses, they conclude that eight attributes characterized excellent, innovative companies. Those attributes are: (a) A bias for action, (b) close to the customer, (c) autonomy and entrepreneurship, (d) productivity through people, (e) hands-on, value-driven, (f) stick to the knitting, (g) simple form, lean staff, and (h) simultaneous loose–tight properties. Peters and Waterman suggest that these attributes are reflected in the intensity that marks the excellent companies, an intensity "stemming from strongly held beliefs" (p. 16).

Denison (1984) used survey data as a measure of cultural managerial style and Standard and Poor's financial ratios as indicators of performance and effectiveness. Cultural managerial style was profiled in an organization-of-work index that characterized the degree to which work is sensibly organized, work methods are adapted to changing conditions, the appropriateness of decision levels, and the reasonability and clarity of organizational goals. Decision-making practices were characterized by degree of involvement and the extensiveness of information sharing across organizational levels. Organization-of-work characteristics and decision-making practices were compared to organizational return on investment and return on sales. Companies described as having a well-organized work environment reported significantly higher returns on investment over a five-year period. Denison concludes: "a culture that encourages the development of adaptable work methods linking individuals to the goals of an organization has a clear competitive advantage. This advantage appears to be substantial when expressed in terms of return on investment, and seems to have an even stronger impact when presented in terms of the efficiency measure, return on sales" (p. 13). Organizations engaging in participative decision-making practices outperformed their competitors with increasing advantage over a five-year period. Denison suggests that "these results may come as a surprise to those who think of corporate culture or participatory decision making as being too soft or too amorphous to have practical implications" (p. 17).

Although Denison argues the relationship of culture to performance, his definition of corporate culture equates culture with key processes such as participative decision making rather than the broader concept of shared beliefs, assumptions, and values.

Wilkins and Ouchi (1983) and Gordon (1985) modify the strong culture claims of Peters and Waterman and Denison. Wilkins and Ouchi suggest that culture is at times irrelevant to performance, at times promotes efficiency, and at times inhibits effectiveness. Gordon, in a study relating corporate culture to industry sector, concludes that the influence of culture is measurable and important but that there is no one "winning" culture. In contrast to the participative culture of the Denison study, Gordon's findings suggest that "factors such as the characteristics of the industry and the marketplace and the diversity, size, and market position of the organization define the broad outlines of an appropriate culture" (p. 121). Gordon's observations further support the notion that culture can be managed and changed with planned activities.

Hedbert, Nystrom, and Starbuck (1976) argue that the longer organizational success appears to continue, the greater the confidence in myths and programs (culture). This embedding in organizational ideologies may inhibit motivation for innovation because achievement criteria become maintenance and preservation activities rather than entrepreneurial criteria. Weick (1985) contends that strategy and culture promote organizational coherence and meaning, which potentially contribute to retarding change. Weick suggests, "Strong cultures are tenacious cultures. Because a tenacious culture can be a rigid culture that is slow to detect changes in opportunities and slow to change once opportunities are sensed, strong cultures can be backward, conservative instruments of adaptation" (p. 383). He concludes, however, that strong cultures, due to their coherence, may be forceful actors capable of creating the environments they envision.

Despite differing assumptions, definitions, methodologies, levels of analysis, environmental contingencies, and research goals, the aforegoing body of evidence attests to the impact and importance of culture for organizational effectiveness. Whether culture is depicted as causally influencing effectiveness, or whether culture is described as synonymous with effectiveness, research from both functionalist and interpretivist paradigms underscores and affirms the importance of the bounded rationality and informal dynamics of organizational life.

ISSUES AND IMPLICATIONS FOR FUTURE RESEARCH

Organizational culture research, as most organizational analysis, continues to be dominated by functionalist assumptions of measurement and generalizability. Indeed the very attempt to relate culture and effectiveness reflects tenets of the functionalist paradigm. Interestingly enough, however, much of the research relating culture and effectiveness is conducted with descriptive methodologies and incorporates many of the assumptions of knowledge generation based in interpretivist thinking. Those favoring the objective rigor of the functionalist approach criticize the application of interpretivist assumptions to establish relationships between culture and effectiveness. Proponents of the interpretivist view reject the need to establish empirical relationships, while those favoring the melding of approaches argue that the coupling of the subjective, informal side of organizational research with the quantitative and evaluative dimensions of organizational life yields a more comprehensive understanding, whether for the sake of knowledge or for prediction and control. This latter view is the one most frequently expressed in the culture and effectiveness literature.

Most attempts to relate culture and effectiveness suggest that strong cultures are positively related to organizational excellence. Taken as a whole, these attempts challenge the basic tenets of contingency theory while retaining a systems view of organizational and environmental relationships. This strong culture perspective also incorporates a view of managers as being keepers of culture and responsible for change and control. As with criticisms of other areas of organizational analysis, the strong culture view generally fails to incorporate the influence of diverse organizational members or recognize the existence of subcultures within organizations and multiple cultural environments. Deetz (1992), in a potent criticism of cultural research, suggested:

> In general, cultural studies can be seen to (a) emphasize the managers' picture of successful integration and corporate goals, (b) treat top management's culture as the organizational culture, (c) treat socialization and legitimation practices as positively affecting culture (when they work right) and as needed where cultures fail rather than as processes securing advancing domination, (d) judge cultural phenomena (e.g., stories, perceptions, and images) based on their functional value rather than truth value, and (e) downplay conflict and contradictions in the discovery and presentation of culture. (pp. 326–327)

Knowledge about culture and effectiveness is influenced by the difficulty and complexity of establishing a meaningful understanding of organizational effectiveness. Variously defined in the literature, diverse assumptions underlying the construct contribute to the difficulty of relating cultural processes to the evaluative dimension of effectiveness. In particular, the historical–contextual perspective that culture studies bring to organizations has not been well related to static- or time-bound quantified measures of effectiveness such as profit and return on investment. Additionally, almost no work to date has examined the construct of effectiveness as an influence for organizational behavior and as part of the rich interpretative processes of organizational life.

The challenges are numerous, yet two primary areas for future investigation seem particularly relevant. First, when organizatioinal communication is viewed as a cultural process, the opportunity exists for understanding not only the cohesive and shared realities of organizational members but the diversity and complexity of multicultures as they relate to continuing streams of organizational evaluations. In other words, culture and effectiveness research should move beyond rational or causal modeling to a view not only of culture as shared realities but effectiveness as shaping realities. This view potentially frees researchers to ask both qualitative and quantitative questions suited to understand the dynamic processes of the formal and informal in organizational life. Secondly, culture and effectiveness research should adopt a multiple-cultures perspective. This perspective incorporates the notion of organizational culture as numerous subcultures and extends beyond that view to studies across occupational, industrial, and societal cultures with broad effectiveness dimensions. Finally, as in all areas of inquiry, an examination of fundamental assumptions about research, organizations, and communication should guide the goals and methodologies of culture researchers. Our current thinking about culture and effectiveness both suffers from insufficient delineation of our assumptions and is strengthened by the willingness of some to use the culture metaphor to think about organizations in new and meaningful ways. In summary, the research on culture and effectiveness demonstrates the importance for examining illusive and complex constructs as we expand our understanding of all aspects of organized behavior.

REFERENCES

Arnold, T. (1935). *The symbols of government*. New Haven, CT: Yale University Press.

Barnard, C. (1938). *The functions of the executive*. Cambridge, MA: Harvard University Press.

Bennis, W. (1962). Toward a "truly" scientific management: The concept of organizational health. *General Systems Yearbook, 7*, 269–282.

Berger, P., & Luckmann, T. (1967). *The social construction of reality*. Garden City, NY: Anchor Books.

Blake, R., & Mouton, J. (1964). *The managerial grid*. Houston: Gulf Publishing Company.

Bormann, E. (1983). Symbolic convergence: Organizational communication and culture. In L. Putnam & M. Pacanowsky (Eds.), *Communication and organizations: An interpretive approach*. Beverly Hills: Sage.

Boyatzsis, R. (1982). *The competent manager: A model for effective performance*. New York: John Wiley and Sons.

Burrell, G., & Morgan, G. (1979). *Sociological paradigms and organizational analysis*. London: Heinemann Press.

Campbell, J. (1973). *Research into the nature of organizational effectiveness: An endangered species?* Unpublished manuscript, University of Minnesota, Minneapolis–St. Paul.

Caplow, T. (1964). *Principles of organization*. New York: Harcourt, Brace and World.

Child, J. (1974). Managerial and organizational factors associated with company performance — Part I. *Journal of Management Studies, 11,* 175–189.

Clampitt, P., & Downs, C. (1983). *Communication and productivity*. Paper presented at the Speech Communication Association Convention, Washington, D.C.

Cunningham, J. (1978). A systems-resource approach for evaluating organizational effectiveness. *Human Relations, 31,* 631–656.

Cushman, D. (1977). The rules perspective as a theoretical basis for the study of human communication. *Communication Quarterly, 25,* 30–45.

Deal, T., & Kennedy, A. (1982). *Corporate cultures: The rites and rituals of corporate life*. Reading, MA: Addison–Wesley.

Deal, T., & Kennedy, A. (1983). Culture: A new look through old lenses. *The Journal of Applied Behavioral Science, 19,* 498–505.

Deetz, S. (1988). Cultural studies: Studying meaning and action in organizations. In J. A. Anderson (Ed.), *Communication yearbook 11* (pp. 335–345). Newbury Park, CA: Sage.

Deetz, S. (1992). *Democracy in an age of corporate colonization*. Albany: State University of New York Press.

Denison, D. (1984, Autumn). Bring corporate culture to the bottom line. *Organizational Dynamics,* 5–22.

DeWine, S. (1988). The cultural perspective: New wave, old problems. In J. A. Anderson (Ed.), *Communication yearbook 11* (pp. 346–355). Newbury Park, CA: Sage.

Downs, C., & Hain, T. (1982). Productivity and communication. In M. Burgoon (Ed.), *Communication yearbook 5*. New Brunswick, NJ: Transaction Books.

Drucker, P. (1986). *The frontiers of management*. New York: Truman Talley Books.

Drucker, P. (1954). *The practice of management*. New York: Harper and Row.

Eisenberg, E. M., & Riley P. (1988). Organizational symbols and sense-making. In G. M. Goldhaber & G. A. Barnett (Eds.), *Handbook of organizational communication* (pp. 131–150). Norwood, NJ: Ablex.

Farace, R., Monge, P., & Russell, H. (1977). *Communicating and organizing*. Reading, MA: Addison–Wesley.

Fine, G. (1979). Smallg roups and culture creation: The idiocultures of little league baseball teams. *American Sociological Review, 44,* 733–745.

Friedlander, F., & Pickle, H. (1968). Components of effectiveness in small organizations. *Administrative Science Quarterly, 13,* 289–304.

Georgopoulos, B., & Tannenbaum, S. (1957). The study of organizational effectiveness. *American Sociological Review, 22,* 534–540.

Gibson, J., Ivancevich, J., & Donnelly, J. (1973). *Organizations: Structure, process, behavior*. Dallas: BPI.

Goldhaber, G., Yates, M., Porter, D., & Lesniak, R. (1978). *Organizational communication: 1978 state of the art*. *Human Communication Research, 5,* 76–96.

Gordon, G. (1985). The relationship of corporate culture to industry sector and corporate performance. In R. Kilmann, M. Saxton, & R. Serpa (Eds.), *Gaining control of the corporate culture* (pp. 103–125). San Francisco: Jossey–Bass.

Gregory, K. (1983). Native-view paradigms: Multiple cultures and culture conflicts in organizations. *Administrative Science Quarterly, 3,* 359–376.

Hall, E. (1959). *The silent language*. Garden City, NY: Anchor Books.

Hambrick, D., & Mason, P. (1984). Upper echelons: Organization as a reflection of its top managers. *Management Review, 9,* 193–206.

Hedberg, B., Nystrom, P., & Starbuck, W. (1976). Camping on seesaws prescriptions for a self-designing organization. *Administrative Science Quarterly, 21,* 41–65.

Katz, D., & Kahn, R. (1966). *The social psychology of organizations.* New York: John Wiley and Sons.

Keeley, M. (1984). Impartiality and participant-interest theories of organizational effectiveness. *Administrative Science Quarterly, 29,* 1–25.

Kilmann, R., Saxton, M., & Serpa, R. (1985). Five key issues in understanding and changing culture. In R. Kilmann, M. Saxton, & R. Serpa (Eds.), *Gaining control of the corporate culture.* San Francisco: Jossey–Bass.

Kotter, J. (1982). What effective general managers really do. *Harvard Business Review, 60*(6), 156–167.

Lawrence, P., & Lorsch, J. (1967). *Organization and environment:* Boston: Harvard University Press.

Lewis, M., Cummings, H., & Long, L. (1981). *Communication activity as a predictor of the fit between worker motoivation and worker productivity.* Paper presented at the International Communication Association convention, Minneapolis, MN.

Likert, R. (1967). *The human organization.* New York: McGraw–Hill.

Lorsch, J. (1985). Strategic myopia: Culture as an invisible barrier to change. In R. Kilmann, M. Saxton, & R. Serpa (eds.). *Gaining control of the corporate culture* (pp. 84–102). San Francisco: Jossey–Bass.

Mahoney, T., & Weitzel, W. (1969). Managerial models of organizational effectiveness. *Administrative Science Quarterly, 14,* 357–365.

Milliken, F. J. (1990). Perceiving and interpreting environmental change: An examination of college administrators' interpretation of changing demographics. *Academy of Management Journal, 33,* 42–63.

Mott, P. (1972). *The characteristics of effective organizations.* New York: Harper and Row.

Negandhi, A., & Reimann, B. (1973). Task environment, decentralization and organizational effectiveness. *Human Relations, 26,* 203–214.

Ostroff, C., & Schmitt, N. (1993). Configurations of organizational effectiveness and efficiency. *Academy of Management Journal, 36*(6), 1345–1361.

Ouchi, W. (1980). Markets, bureaucracies, and clan. *Administrative Science Quarterly, 25,* 129–141.

Pacanowsky, M., & O'Donnell-Trujillo, N. (1982). Communication and organizational culture. *Western Journal of Speech Communication, 46,* 115–130.

Pacanowsky, M., & O'Donnell-Trujillo, N. (1983). Organizational communication as cultural performance. *Communication Monographs, 50,* 126–147.

Peters, T., & Waterman, R. (1982). *In search of excellence.* New York: Harper & Row.

Pilotta, J. J., Widman, T., & Jasko, S. A. (1988). Meaning and action in the organizational setting: An interpretive approach. In J. A. Anderson (Ed.), *Communication yearbook 11* (pp. 310–334). Newbury Park, CA: Sage.

Pincus, J. (1986). Communication satisfaction, job satisfaction, and job performance. *Human Communication Research, 12,* 395–419.

Price, J. (1968). *Organizational effectiveness: An inventory of propositions.* Homewood, IL: Irwin.

Putnam, L. (1982). Paradigms for organizational communication research: An overview and synthesis. *Western Journal of Speech Communication, 46,* 192–206.

Putnam, L. (1983). The interpretive perspective: An alternative to functionalism. In L. Putnam & M. Pacanowsky (Eds.), *Communication and organizations: An interpretive approach.* Beverly Hills: Sage.

Quinn, R. E., & Rohrbaugh, J. (1983). A spatial model of effectiveness criteria: Towards a competing values approach to organizational analysis. *Management Science, 29,* 363–377.

Redding, W. (1972). *Communication within the organization: An interpretive review of theory and research.* New York: Industrial Communication Council.

Roberts, K., O'Reilly, Bretton, C., & Porter, L. (1974). Organizational theory and organizational communication: A communication failure? *Human Relations, 27,* 501–525.

Sapienza, A. (1985). Believing is seeing: How culture influences the decisions top managers make. In R. Kilmann, M. Saxton, & R. Serpa (Eds.), *Gaining control of the corporate culture* (pp. 66–83). San Francisco: Jossey–Bass.

Schall, M. (1983). A communication-rules approach to organizational culture. *Administrative Science Quarterly, 4,* 557–581.

Schein, E. (1970). *Organizational psychology.* Englewood Cliffs, NJ: Prentice-Hall.

Schein, E. (1984, Winter). Coming to a new awareness of organizational culture. *Sloan Management Review,* 3–16.

Schein, E. (1985). How culture forms, develops, and changes. In R. Kilmann, M. Saxton, & R. Serpa (Eds.), *Gaining control of the corporate culture* (pp. 17–43). San Francisco: Jossey–Bass.

Shockley-Zalabak, P. (1988). *Fundamentals of organizational communication.* New York: Longman.

Smircich, L. (1981). *The concept of culture and organizational analysis.* Paper presented at the Speech Communication Association/International Communication Association Conference on Interpretive Approaches to Organizational Communication, Alta, UT.

Smircich, L. (1983). Concepts of culture and organizational analysis. *Administrative Science Quarterly, 28,* 339–358.

Smircich, L., & Stubbart, C. (1985). Strategic management in an enacted world. *Academy of Management Review, 4,* 724–736.

Spradley, J. (1979). *The ethnographic interview.* New York: Holt, Rinehart and Winston.

Steers, R. (1975). Problems in the measurement of organizational effectiveness. *Administrative Science Quarterly, 20,* 546–558.

Stonich, P. (1982). *Implementing strategy: Making strategy happen.* Cambridge, MA: Ballinger.

Tubbs, S., & Hain, T. (1979). Managerial communication and its relationship to total organizational effectiveness. Cited in P. Clampitt & C. Downs, *Communication and productivity.* Paper presented at the Speech Communication Association Convention, Nov., 1983.

Webb, R. (1974). Organizational effectiveness and the voluntary organization. *Academy of Management Journal, 17,* 663–677.

Weick, K. (1985). The significance of corporate culture. In P. Frost, L. Moore, M. Louis, C. Lundberg, & J. Martin (Eds.), *Organizational culture.* Beverly Hills: Sage.

Wiio, O., Goldhaber, G., & Yates, M. (1980). Organizational communication: Time for reflection? In D. Nimmo (Ed.), *Communication yearbook 4.* New Brunswick, NJ: Transaction Books.

Wilkins, A., & Ouchi, W. (1983). Efficient cultures: Exploring the relationship between culture and organizational performance. *Administrative Science Quarterly, 28,* 468–481.

9

Performing Conflict in Organizations: The Role of Novel Metaphors

Lorin L. Blewett
Randall K. Stutman

With the development of interpretive approaches to organizational communication, the metaphorical structuring of organizational reality has become an increasingly popular topic. In this chapter we address the relationship between metaphors and organizational conflict. Specifically, we argue that, through an analysis of novel and conventional metaphors, one can "see" the expressed struggle of conflict even when conflict is not explicitly recognized by the organization. We define and analyze the linguistic device of metaphor, distinguish between novel and conventional metaphors, discuss the function of metaphor in organizations and organizational conflict, and describe a methodology that allows one to observe and analyze the expressed struggle of conflict. We critically examine and test our assumptions in a case study of a small, profit-oriented organization. This case study confirmed our prediction that organizational members who perceive conflict commonly express this struggle through the use of novel metaphors.

ON DEFINING METAPHOR

The word metaphor is derived from the Greek term *meta,* meaning "over," and *pherein,* meaning "to carry." Accordingly, Hawkes (1972) defines metaphor as referring to "a particular set of linguistic processes whereby aspects of one object are 'carried over' or transferred to another object, so that the second object is spoken of as if it were the first" (p. 1). In a more controversial analysis of metaphors, Black (1962) claims that metaphors are best understood as systems of beliefs, not individual "things." He describes metaphors as having two subjects: a principle subject and a secondary (or subsidiary) subject. In order to interpret a metaphor, one constructs a set of beliefs about the principle subject (the *man* in "man is a wolf") parallel to a set of beliefs about the secondary subject (the wolf). In interpretation, the two subjects "interact." The secondary subject highlights some features of the primary subject and suppresses others. Likewise, the primary subject can induce reciprocal changes in the secondary subject. Through this interaction, a belief system isomorphic to that of the secondary subject is created to fit the principle subject, and/or vice versa. The subjects of a metaphor are thus "nodes in isomorphic networks, in which assertions about [one subject] are correlated one to one with corresponding statements about [the other]" (Black, 1962, p. 31). Theorists such as Ortony (1979) use Black's description of metaphor to argue for a cognitive explanation of metaphor: the two subjects of a metaphor are from domains of experience (and, therefore, cognitive categories) too dissimilar to allow our beliefs about one subject to characterize the other directly. When we recognize a metaphor it is generally because of a clash between separate domains (Tourangeau & Sternberg, 1981). This clash often makes itself known as a semantic or pragmatic anomaly.

Customarily, a metaphor is described as a figure of speech differing from simile only in that it does not employ the term "like" or "as" and, therefore, involves a less direct comparison than does simile. However, several theorists have rejected this notion (Black, 1962; Garfield, 1986; Hawkes, 1972). Black and others claim that similes do not have the same rhetorical impact as metaphors, nor do they have the rich and complex interactive meanings of metaphors. They also argue that metaphors perform roles similes can not by virtue of their grammatical form. For example, metaphors can be used in catachresis (to fill in lexical gaps), whereas similes are not easily used for this purpose. With simile one can say "He is just like Cicero used to be," but with metaphor one can use the catachretical form "He is a cicerone."

The distinction between metaphor and analogy is even less clear than that between metaphor and simile. Aristotle (332 B.C./1924) defined analogy as one form of metaphor. "Metaphor," he said, "consists in giving the thing a name that belongs to something else; the transference being either from genus to species, or from species to genus, or from species to species, or on grounds of analogy" (c. 20, 1457[b]). Most researchers today use metaphor and analogy as equivalent terms. For the purposes of this chapter we will adopt Cooper's (1986) use of *metaphor* meaning "metaphor etc." which includes the concept of analogy, simile, metaphorical idioms, and metaphorical cliches—as long as the relationship between primary and secondary subject, as defined by Black (1962) and Hawkes (1972) is maintained.

NOVEL AND CONVENTIONAL METAPHORS

In addition to defining metaphor in relation to other figures of speech it is important to distinguish at least two subcategories of metaphors. Traditional scholars have described these categories using the terms *dead metaphors* and *live metaphors* and/or *literal metaphors* and *nonliteral metaphors,* with the referents of these two sets frequently overlapping. More recently the categories of "metaphor" and "metaphorical" have been suggested. In this section we describe and critique these divisions and suggest the categories "novel" and "conventional" as being useful in distinguishing types of metaphors.

The concept of dead metaphors has long been used to describe common metaphorical expressions that speakers do not consciously recognize as metaphors. "Dead" metaphors are distinguished from "live" metaphors by degree, not by structure or function. For example, one typology dissects metaphor into "stone dead," "three-quarters dead," "half-dead or dormant," "one-third dead," and so on, up through "live" metaphors (Fowler, 1983). Such typologies as well as more complex ones have been heavily criticized (see Davies, 1982–1983; Newmark, 1981). Some are criticized for using age as a distinguishing criteria, not recognizing that many "old" metaphors, which have dropped out of everyday use, appear more original today than "recent" commonly heard metaphors. Others are criticized for assuming that all metaphors are substitutes for literal expressions (see Cooper, 1984, 1986).

Sometimes contrasted with the terms *dead* and *live* are the terms *literal* and *nonliteral.* Defined in their simplest form, literal and nonliteral refer to the distinction between those expressions that are metaphors (or *metaphors, etc.*) and all other expressions that are not *metaphor, etc.* According to Cooper, the term literal metaphor is preferable to *dead* because *dead* misleadingly denies the systematization of everyday metaphorical talk. Lakoff and Johnson (1980a) and Lakoff (1987) claim our well-worn conventional expressions arise from a systematic way of thinking about one thing in terms of another. For example, we systematically talk about argument as war. We say our claims are "under attack," our arguments are "knocked down," we are "outflanked," and so forth. To talk about such everyday expressions as dead denies the generative power of the underlying metaphors. Underlying conceptual metaphors in everyday talk continually give rise to novel utterances. If these utterances appear "old" or "dead," it is because we are so familiar with the underlying conceptual frame in which they exist.

The distinction between literal and nonliteral, however, is made confusing by Lakoff's and Johnson's (1980) description of everyday metaphorical locutions as both literal *and* nonliteral. They claim that while such phrases are "metaphorically structured," the language is not "poetic, fanciful, or rhetorical: it is literal" (p. 5). This position is criticized by Cooper (1986), who responds: "If expressions are really metaphorical then they are not literal — however familiar and mundane they may be" (p. 22). Terms like "poetic" and "fanciful" do not, he says, contrast with literal but rather with "prosaic," "mundane," or "sober"; someone can speak poetically or fancifully without speaking nonliterally.

Cooper (1986) argues that everyday metaphors are "literal," but he makes a distinction between "metaphors" and "speaking metaphorically" (p. 137). He parallels this categorization with the distinction between such word pairs as poem/poetic and symbol/symbolic. Doing someting X-ically, he says, does not necessarily mean that one is producing an X. The stated intention of Cooper's categorization system is to register distance between established metaphorical talk and the use of fresh unconventional metaphors. According to Cooper, "stock expressions like 'invest time' have no meaning beyond their (derived) literal one" (p. 138). This claim appears unjustified, however, if one acknowledges the ability of conventional metaphors to frame and influence behavior.

Lakoff and Johnson's analysis of the meaning and function of everyday metaphorical talk shows that the metaphorical concept "time is money" does underlie the phrase "invest time." Furthermore, the entailments of this underlying structural metaphor (e.g., "time is valuable," "time is a commodity," "time should be saved," etc.) not only make sense and have meaning but have a meaning that structures our very conception of time. Therefore, to define common, everyday metaphors as literal, without a "true" underlying metaphor, seems unfounded and less than useful.

In analyzing the various categorization systems scholars use to talk about metaphors it is interesting that almost all, including Cooper's, are defined using terms such as "common," "everyday," "conventional," and "mundane," for one category, and "new," "original," and "creative" for its opposite. These adjectives seem to characterize a basic distinction between types of metaphors: metaphors are either novel or conventional. Within the metaphor typologies of Cooper, Lakoff and Johnson, and other scholars, distinctions are made based on the relative consciousness with which a speaker uses a metaphor or metaphorical expression. In this chapter we use the term *conventional* when we speak of a commonly heard metaphor used unconsciously in everyday talk. Such a metaphor may be so ingrained in a speaker's way of thinking about a subject that he or she does not even recognize it as a metaphor. A speaker may be unconscious of the underlying secondary subjects referred to by the entailments of a conventional metaphor. We use the term *novel* when we speak of an uncommon or original metaphor used consciously and deliberately. The speaker of such a metaphor is aware that she or he has suggested correlations between the primary and secondary subjects which, she or he believes, are not part of the listener's usual way of thinking about the primary subject.[1]

---

[1] By virtue of the necessarily subjective interpretation of what is novel and what conventional, these two categories are contextually specific and nonabsolute. Within a given cultural unit, however, it should be apparent to members whether or not a metaphor is novel or conventional:

FUNCTIONS OF NOVEL AND CONVENTIONAL METAPHORS

The functions of metaphors in organizations are related to the cognitive processes involved in metaphor interpretation. Expanding Black's description of metaphor, Osborn and Ehninger (1962) suggest that metaphors are comprehended and interpreted in a three-step, sequential process: error, puzzlement–recoil, and resolution. At first, the listener–reader makes the mistake of interpreting a metaphor as a literal statement. The puzzlement–recoil step occurs when the listener–reader recognizes that the word or phrase is not being employed in its usual sense and that a reinterpretation is called for. During this step, Osborn and Ehninger claim that the listener–reader suffers the agitation of uncertainty, an agitation she or he is motivated to resolve by solving the metaphor puzzle. Resolution occurs when the listener–reader indeed resolves the metaphor puzzle and the message of the metaphor becomes apparent. In a related description of this process, Ortony (1979) talks about "tension" related to the perception of the nonliteralness of a metaphor. Tension elimination, says Ortony, is achieved by the listener–reader ignoring those aspects or attributes of one subject that are perceived as being incompatible with the other. When the nonsalient attributes have been eliminated, the remaining salient attributes of the vehicle are attributed as a whole; that is, an entire cognitive substructure is mapped onto the topic.

Descriptions of "tension and tension elimination," or "error, puzzlement–recoil, and resolution," generally refer to novel metaphors. People do not recoil or experience tension when presented with a conventional metaphor. Conventional metaphorical expressions are not interpreted in the same manner as novel metaphors because they are ingrained in our very way of thinking about a subject. For example, because our conception of argument is structured in terms of war, "the normal way for us to talk about attacking a position is to use the words *attack a position*" (Lakoff & Johnson, 1980a, p. 5). This difference between the interpretive processes of novel and conventional metaphors is important for understanding how these metaphors function in organizations.

Theorists have described metaphors as having a number of functions. The functions of conventional and novel metaphors, however, are seldom separated. Here we discuss several descriptions of the functions of metaphors, putting special emphasis on modern perspectives. References to novel or conventional metaphors are included when theorists have made an obvious distinction. The traditional views can be summarized as follows: (a) metaphors are primarily employed to help people understand abstract and difficult notions, and (b) metaphors are primarily used to save the language from

---

whether they have often heard reality spoken of in terms of that metaphor or if the metaphor is new to their ears.

seeming mean and prosaic. Expanding on these, Ortony (1980) suggests that metaphors can be a means of expressing things that do not have a literal equivalent in the language in question. They may also, he adds, offer more compact ways of uttering otherwise very prolix literal statements and thus create more vivid images that even their best literal equivalents (if there are any) can not match.

In addition to traditional notions of metaphor's function, there are two modern trends in metaphor research, the social interaction perspective and the social construct perspective. The social interaction perspective is described most thoroughly in articles by Cohen (1979), MacCormac (1985), and Cooper (1986). These authors describe metaphors as functioning to "cultivate an intimacy" among speakers, similar to the way in which jokes can serve to draw people together. This view assumes that there are ties of interest, background, sensibility, and so on, which a metaphor presupposes for its interpretation. It also assumes there is an intimacy of attitude or viewpoint that is presupposed if the utterance of the metaphor, in place of something explicit (literal), is justified. MacCormac suggests that there are three illocutionary forces of metaphor: stimulating emotion, producing perplexity, and creating a sense of intimacy in shared language. Cooper bases his assessment of metaphor's function on Grice's (1975) notion that, in computing implicature, a listener–reader is sometimes required to reflect on why a speaker used the particular words she did rather than using others that on the surface seem more appropriate. Cooper suggests that a speaker of a metaphor, like one of an implicature, makes certain assumptions about a listener's attitude. Thus the use of metaphor, in this view, arises from a desire to maintain or to create intimacy on the part of the speaker.

The social construct perspective of metaphor is most thoroughly developed by Lakoff and Johnson (1980b) in *The Metaphors We Live By,* and Lakoff (1987) in *Women, Fire, and Dangerous Things.* These authors claim that metaphors are a pervasive part of everyday life and that they are not only a matter of labels, but a matter of thought. Accordingly, the "function" of metaphors is to influence our conceptual systems and, therefore, influence how we see and make sense of the world. They argue that one can discover the nature of our conceptual system by analyzing language: "Since communication is based on the same conceptual system, in terms of which we think and act, language is an important source of evidence for what that system is like" (Lakoff & Johnson, 1980, p. 454). They and others have analyzed the language people use when talking about such salient concepts as time, life, emotion, wealth, language, understanding, ideas, anger, spirituality, truth, conflict, and so on (Black, 1962; Lakoff, 1987; Lakoff & Johnson, 1980; Ortony, 1979). They discovered that these concepts are usually talked about metaphorically and, they claim, thus understood metaphorically. If our concepts of reality are metaphorical, then the underlying metaphors influence not only what we understand as reality, but also our behavior: what we create as knowledge, what we experience, and what we do. According to this perspective the primary function of metaphor in everyday language is to structure our reality and, consequently, our behavior.

This structuring function, however, is not necessarily arbitrary or innocent. Lakoff and Johnson point out that "a metaphor in a political or economic system, by virtue of what it hides, can lead to human degradation" (1980b, p. 236). They suggest, for example, that when human labor is metaphorically talked about as a "natural resource" to be "tapped," "invested," and "measured," the distinction between meaningful and meaningless work is erased (see also Stutman & Putman, 1994, on the legalization of organizations). Barthes (1972) speaks of myth (in his description a term very much related to *metaphor, etc.*) as used by speakers in order to avoid responsibility. He claims, "The very principle of myth is [to] transform history into nature" (p. 198). In other words, myth and metaphor put the *cultural,* for example, nation states, national economies, corporations, and so on, in terms of the *natural,* for example, families and organisms. The effect or function of such conventional metaphors is that people accept and support the status quo by treating as fixed and natural things that are historically contingent and for which human agents are responsible.

It is, however, yet unclear what function *novel* metaphors have in relation to the reality constructed by conventional metaphors. Lakoff and Johnson's social construct analysis refers primarily to conventional metaphors, and references made by social interaction theorists are ambiguous as to conventional or novel metaphors. The function of novel metaphors is important if we are to understand the consequences of introducing a novel metaphor into an organization and why an organizational member might do so. Following the reasoning of the social interaction perspective, a novel metaphor would be introduced in order to increase the intimacy or unity between the speaker and hearer. This explanation, however, is insufficient in light of field research on increased tension related to the introduction of novel metaphors under conditions of escalating conflict (Smith & Eisenberg, 1983). Furthermore, if an organization's conventional metaphors frame members' shared reality, use of a novel metaphor appears more likely to distance the speaker from the listener precisely because it does not, as Cooper and MacCormac suggests it should, draw directly on the members' shared attitudes or viewpoints. Rather, it introduces a foreign viewpoint relative to shared views expressed through conventional metaphors. A better explanation of the use of novel metaphor in an organization is seen by looking at the ability of metaphors to transform or reframe reality. The use of novel metaphors can be seen as a move to persuade a listener–reader to adopt an alternative view. Once a novel metaphor is accepted as a conventional metaphor, the shift in reality can benefit one part more than another (as described by Barthes above).

Novel metaphors are effective tools for persuasion for three apparent reasons: (a) They involve a relatively high degree of active participation, (b) they are highly vivid, and (c) they aid recall. Novel metaphors may influence persuasiveness by inducing cognitive elaboration through the procedures involved in interpreting them. They require the listener to generate information about characteristics of the primary and secondary subject in order to "eliminate tension" or "solve the metaphorical puzzle"; they require active participation. As described by Petty and Cacioppo (1981), active participation can increase persuasiveness because, "When we think about something, we may generate information that we did not consider when our initial attitudes were formed" (p. 220; see also Tesser, 1976; Tesser & Leone, 1977).

Novel metaphors may also increase persuasiveness because of their inherent vividness. According to Nisbett and Ross (1980), information may be described as vivid (that is, as likely to attract and hold our attention and to excite the imagination) to the extent that it is emotionally interesting, concrete, imagery-provoking, and proximate in a sensory, temporal, or spatial way. While research attempting to show vivid information as more impactful on judgments than pallid and abstract propositions has had mixed results, there is at least some evidence to indicate that the concrete, image-provoking nature of metaphors can have persuasive impact on a listener (Bell & Loftus, 1985; Taylor & Thompson, 1982).

According to some vividness researchers, information presented in vivid or concrete form leads to heightened cognitive elaboration and therefore affects recall ability and judgment (Bradshaw & Anderson, 1982; Carroll, 1978; Kisielius & Sternhal, 1984, 1986). This hypothesis is supported by empirical research on memory and metaphor. Marschark and Hunt (1985), in an experimental investigation of how metaphors are represented in memory, found that free recall across a variety of orienting tasks was positively correlated with ratings of the "imageability" of metaphor subjects. This research suggests that the degrees of vividness of metaphors influences people's ability to remember complex constructs. Ease of recall is no doubt an important factor in the effectiveness of persuasive messages. Thus, while *conventional* metaphors frame status quo reality, a function of *novel* metaphors is to persuade a listener to *change* their existing conceptual framework.

THE ROLE OF METAPHOR IN ORGANIZATIONAL CONFLICT

The function of metaphors in framing and reframing reality, as described in the previous sections, has at least two implications for the role of metaphors in conflict. First, when people have grossly different metaphorical concepts of reality they may be more likely to perceive themselves in conflict. Second, the use of novel metaphors in an organization may be an attempt to persuade or influence another party; thus, the introduction of novel metaphors in an organization may signal expressed struggle.

Conflict, as defined by Hocker and Wilmot (1985), is "an expressed struggle between at least two interdependent parties who perceive incompatible goals, scarce resources, and interference from the other party in achieving their goals" (p. 12). If metaphors frame organizational reality, they also influence perceptions of context-appropriate goals and means for reaching those goals. Thus, when interdependent people have differing conceptualizations of reality, it is possible that they will perceive disparate goals and interference from each other in reaching their goal. For example, if group leader X describes leaders using the metaphorical language of motherhood (e.g., family, safety, nurturing, etc.) and group leader Y describes leaders with the entailments of military command (e.g., troops, enemies, attacking, etc.), X and Y may perceive themselves in conflict, inhibiting each other by attempting to achieve mutually exclusive goals, even though both subscribe to what might be the equivalent organizational objectives of unity, security, and effectiveness. Likewise, metaphors may encourage conflict through their framing of the allocation of scarce resources. For example, if A perceives time as "money," and B perceives time as "love," it is possible that each party will perceive the other to be "allocating" time in ways that inhibit the achievement of their respective financial or relational goals.

The existence of difference within group members' metaphorical constructs (as expressed through differing metaphors) not only heightens the possibility for conflict, it can also indicate the expresson of conflict. While it is entirely possible, and often essential, for people to work together despite or because of the fact they have different conceptualizations of their work, the introduction of a *novel* metaphor for that work is perhaps always a sign that a conflict is perceived by the introducing party.

If novel metaphors are persuasive in changing people's attitudes and perceptions of reality, then the use of novel metaphors in organizations may be a clear signal of one party's attempt to persuade or influence another party. This persuasion is most likely to occur when one party perceives itself in a conflict. Presumably, by persuading another party to adopt a novel metaphor, the first party gains an "upper hand" because the organizational reality has been redefined in ways favorable to the realization of the persuader's goals.

While many organizational researchers have looked at metaphors, few have looked at the relationship between metaphor and organizational conflict (Ilkka, 1977; Koch & Deetz, 1981; Pondy, 1983; Tracy, 1978. For exceptions, see Kellett, 1987; Smith & Eisenberg, 1987). Smith and Eisenberg present one of the few comprehensive studies on this topic in their paper *Conflict at*

Disneyland: a Root-Metaphor Analysis. The authors argue that conflict at Disneyland (including a labor strike) can be better understood through an examination of the structural metaphors used by management and employees in the 30 years prior to the strike. They claim that conflict at Disneyland was exacerbated by conflict between interpretive frameworks (i.e., differing metaphors) and by conflict between differing interpretations of the same metaphors.

According to Smith and Eisenberg (1987), the metaphor "Disneyland in drama" was the earliest metaphoric conceptualization of the organization. It emphasized the "business of show business"; employees put on a show of "the happiest place on earth" for audiences, but behind the curtain everything was business. Later, Disneyland's primary structural metaphor changed from "drama" to "family." The family metaphor, fostered by employees and adapted by some managers, emphasized goals of internal harmony, sharing, and friendly familial relations. As financial problems grew, management began to emphasize the business aspects of the organization more, laying off longtime workers and hiring younger part-time employees. In order to minimize resistance to these changes, management presented employees with a reinterpretation of the family metaphor: "Truly close families learn to make sacrifices in order to survive" (p. 375). Employees, feeling betrayed by management, resented the shift in interpretation.

In their analysis, Smith and Eisenberg make the assumption that the "root-metaphors" they found were, in our terms, conventional metaphors. These metaphors are described as guiding members' ways of thinking about the organization, although members were largely unconscious of their presence. However, the authors also describe a conscious, persuasive use of novel metaphor, stating, for example, that "management tried in vain to counteract the growing discontent with their own interpretation of 'family'" (p. 375). Because of the research methods adopted for the study, one cannot be sure whether the family metaphor was truly conventional or management's interpretation of the family metaphor was truly novel.

Smith and Eisenberg based their study primarily on: (a) responses to interview questions, such as "What is it like working at Disneyland?"; (b) participants' identification of relevant metaphors when given a list of metaphors elicited from management in previous interviews; and (c) participants' completion of the sentence, "Life at Disney is like. . . ." Using these questions, they found frequent use of the "drama" and "family" metaphors. However, the questions required that members consciously abstract from their experiences and conceptualize the organization in metaphorical terms. This method lends itself to the uncovering of novel and conventional metaphors alike. It does not allow us to distinguish the novel metaphors of expressed struggle from conventional metaphors used unconsciously as part of everyday organizational life. Thus it is *possible* that "drama" was the conventional metaphor both Disney management and employees used in everyday working situations, while "family" was a novel metaphor used strategically by both in order to influence the conflict outcome.[2]

CASE STUDY

As a means of critically examining our assumptions, we arranged to study a small profit-oriented organization consisting of 37 members involved in the food-processing business. The organization, which is family-owned, produces and markets specialty food products nationwide and is hierarchically structured in three layers. The top layer includes the company's principal owner and executive as well as 3 senior executives who oversee the various operations and departments in the firm. The second layer consists of a sales and marketing force with 12 members, 3 production managers, and 2 engineers. Each individual in this layer reports directly to one or more of the four executives. The third organizational layer consists of 13 laborers and a three-person clerical staff, all of whom report to designated members of the second tier. A generous profit-sharing schedule for all members was designed as an incentive to promote efficiency, productivity, and commitment to the organization. Because of this feature, we believed increased interdependence and conflict intensity would also be manifest in this organization, and thereby intensify the elements under study.

The study centered on extensive interviews with organizational members and was designed to assess and evaluate three factors: perceived conflict within the organization, organizational commitment, and the use of conventional and novel metaphors. The interviews were structured around the following set of questions specifically designed to elicit conventional and novel metaphors: (a) Describe the organization as you would to a friend; (b) Describe the organization as you would to a prospective member; (c) Describe how people get along in the organization on a daily basis; (d) How would you describe the conflicts that occur in the organization?; and (e) Describe how conflicts are resolved in the organization. In addition, interviewees were asked to respond to a questionnaire designed to measure perceived conflict. A measure of organizational commitment was also administered (Mowday, Steers, & Porter, 1979). Once completed, the interviews were transcribed and analyzed for metaphor usage.[3]

---

[2]Smith and Eisenberg describe "drama" as a metaphor emphasized by management in training sessions and clearly adopted by employees in their descriptions of life at Disney. The researchers note that "there are special ways to look, talk, and behave that constitute the Disney 'role' and are part of the Disney 'script' ".

[3]The authors agreed that anonymity of the interviewees and the identity of the company would be protected.

Discerning Novel Metaphors

The ideal system for assessing and distinguishing novel and conventional metaphors is the use of historical judgment; that is, judgments based on the historical knowledge of events as they are perceived by ordinary actors over the course of years. By definition, when a metaphor does not enjoy commonplace usage, it may be classified as novel. The difficulty confronting an outside observer, however, is how to reliably make this judgment without prolonged immersion into the organizational culture. For example, given our definition of novel metaphors, a figurative and idiomatic expression known only to socialized members would appear novel, when it in fact held common status among language users. For this reason, we chose to discern novel metaphors on the basis of the persuasive function they serve. In contrast to conventional metaphors, novel metaphors promote change through the consistent and purposeful reframing of organizational reality. We reasoned, therefore, that to promote change, novel metaphors require intensive elaboration. Since any orginal reconception involves a metaphorical tension, this elaboration will resurface as a means of extending its conception.

For example, during an interview one member, in describing the organization, referred to the company as a sea vessel: "They run a tight ship here, and I'm proud to work for these people." Compare this with a similar, but elaborated, metaphor used by another member: "We're on a submarine. What these people don't realize is that you can't open the door just a little bit. Either you're dry or you inundate the entire crew." In a response to another question, this member also added: "Everyone may very well sink together if we don't clarify who's running the ship." While the latter member is clearly disgruntled whereas the former is not, the critical distinction here is one of metaphorical elaboration.

To promulgate a reconception of the organization, the second interviewee naturally extends the submarine metaphor, making its meaning more explicit. Although some novel metaphors may not require this clarity, conventional metaphors by definition do not. Because they are conventional and a part of the everyday conceptions of actors, conventional metaphors necessarily stand without explanation. Essentially, then, when actors elaborate their own metaphors, they are always novel. This elaboration, we contend, takes one of three forms. First, as in the submarine metaphor, actors may explicitly offer an analogy that is elaborated. Second, actors may elaborate through the repetition of figural terms. Third, actors may extend a metaphor by weaving its features into the narrative description of events or people.[4]

---

[4]We recognize that individual idiosyncrasies may account for the use of some novel metaphors. In other words, some actors may stylistically employ novel metaphors in the course of interaction. Although this may explain the frequency of usage in some cases, it is unlikely that

Findings

After interviewing 23 organizational members over a three-month period, two trained coders analyzed the descriptions for novel metaphors using the criteria outlined above. The transcripts were first divided into thought units and then coded. These coders achieved an acceptable level of reliability in discerning novel metaphors (inter-rater reliability $K = .79$; inter-rater reliability $K = .88$).

Interestingly, members did not share any single novel metaphor, although two conventional metaphors, the organization as a family and the organization as a team, were held by several members. By comparing the self-report measures of perceived conflict and organizational commitment to the employment of novel metaphors, we tested the strength of our foundational premise; namely, that members who perceived conflict and reported low organizational commitment would be more likely to express their struggle in the form of a novel reconception. Generally, we found that members who perceived conflict did use novel metaphors in their descriptions (9 of 12 members), while members who did not perceive incompatible goals or interference relied solely on conventional metaphors in their descriptions (11 of 11 members). The variable of organizational commitment proved insignificant in its relation both to conflict and metaphor usage. Members in this organization all maintained substantial commitment to the organization, even when they perceived themselves or others to be in conflict. Two narrative examples taken from the interview data best illustrate these findings.

Narrative Examples

Terry, as we will call him, has been with the company for seven years. His primary role during that time has been to oversee the quality testing for the sundry soups and sauces produced in the manufacturing plant. An average day for Terry involves a morning discussion with the vice-president to update him on the previous day's testing as well as to project any problems or ingredient shortages. He then manages three subordinates in the chemical testing of every product produced during the day, sometimes halting production to correct problems. Because Terry believes he is well paid and respected by management, he is highly committed to the organization and loyal to the CEO who hired him from a rival processor. In his perception, there is "no noticeable conflict" in the organization and when there is "it is quickly dealt with." In describing the organization, he relies on several conventional metaphors without apparent connection:

---

this tendency will result in a coherent set of metaphors that are elaborated or extended throughout interaction.

This is a fabulous environment to work in. Supportive. Professional. Other *shops* don't compare to this place. Mr. K runs things with quality first and that's just fine with everyone because we all profit from his *stand*. When *signals occasionally get crossed,* people don't get upset. They just help each other to *fly right* and get the line *back on track*.

While Terry is highly figurative in his organizational description, his metaphors remain unelaborated and disconnected, denoting their conventional nature. He continues with this style throughout the interview, even when he describes how members get along on a daily basis:

Responsibility is a *key* here and people *warm* up to you once you demonstrate your responsibility. Everyone I know gets along and honestly respects each other. Even several of the laborers come in here to chat and *shoot the breeze* when they have a minute. Take lunch. Can you imagine us all eating in that awful room if we didn't like each other? There are plenty of alternatives.

In contrast to Terry, a second organizational member — call him Tracy — sees matters as much more divisive. Tracy has been with the company for five years and serves a sales and marketing role. It is not unusual for Tracy to travel extensively throughout the United States or to be tied to the home office scouting and serving clients. Although highly committed to the organization, Tracy perceives members as holding incompatible goals and interfering with one another's progress. He reports directly to the vice-president in charge of sales and openly acknowledges that he holds different views from this executive.

In describing the organization as he would to a friend, Tracy elaborates a novel metaphor of a religious nature:

A salesman is treated with the same respect they offer to others. There aren't any high priests in this office like some I've seen but that doesn't stop the weak-hearted from bowing and kissing the CEO's ring.

Later he adds jokingly about the success of the company: "The man upstairs obviously watches out the for the man upstairs." When the question centers on how people resolve conflicts, Tracy continues this elaboration in more subtle ways:

I can't really speak for the entire staff, though I know and talk with everyone. For the sales team, we commonly walk straight *upstairs* and state things outright. They prefer that here. People here aren't worried about stepping on toes. They want things out in the open so they don't fester. The only trouble with this approach is what never gets stated for *sin* of not being seen as a player.

Whereas Tracy also uses conventional metaphors, he continues to elaborate a godlike conception of the company's management. (We should point out that the organization's physical plant does not have an "upstairs.") Through this novel metaphor, we contend, Tracy exerts his influence over organizational reality. This performance is manifest in the language used to describe and recount organizational experience. For this reason, the existence of differences in perception as expressed through differing metaphors also indicates the expression of conflict. While we agree that it is commonplace for people to work together despite the fact they have different conventionalized conceptualizations of their experience, the introduction of a novel metaphor for that reality is perhaps a flag that a conflict is perceived by the introducing party.

Another example will illustrate this point. Unlike Tracy and Terry, a third member — call her Kim — is split between satisfaction with the company and its policies and dissatisfaction with a specific problem with the executive staff. As a member of the clerical staff for only two years, Kim's role is to coordinate the activities of the sales force and provide them with updates of inventory and production projections. This assignment involves reporting directly to one of the three senior executives who oversees sales. Generally, Kim is both committed and pleased with her role in the organization with one minor exception: In her view, the senior executives expect too much from the clerical staff and are intolerant when they fail to live up to these expectations. Interestingly, Kim's use of metaphors parallels this minor conflict. In describing the organization and organizational conflicts, Kim relies exclusively on conventional metaphors. In Kim's words, the company is "a progressive place to work, not the mainstream. We form a strong team where everyone plays a significant role." Only when Kim is asked to describe how people get along in the organization on a daily basis does she rely on a novel metaphor to express her role conflict with the senior executives: "Everyone here works well together, and they genuinely seem to care about each other. Occasionally, people walk a tightwire with the [senior executives], but you learn how to balance yourself after a few months." Interestingly, only when Kim is clearly in conflict with others does she resort to an original conception of behavior in the organization. We believe that this novel metaphor represents Kim's struggle over organizational reality and provides a clear picture of her perceptions of incompatibility on this topic.

SUMMARY

While our case study does not establish a clear and exact relationship between organizational conflict and the usage of novel metaphors, it serves to verify and illustrate the utility of this distinction for understanding organizational conflict. Of central concern to conflict scholars are two functions metaphors serve in framing and reframing reality as displayed in the study. First, when people have largely different metaphorical concepts of reality they are more likely to perceive themselves in conflict. Second, the use of novel metaphors in an organization may be viewed as an attempt to persuade others or influence organizational reality; thus, the introduction of novel metaphors in an organization signals struggle.

In summarizing the significant claims of this chapter, it is important to reflect on the nature of conflict, power, and language. Scholars in the area of conflict generally concur that power forms a cornerstone of the conflict process (Rubin & Brown, 1975). Recent work also suggests that power, like conflict, is continually negotiated by social actors (Folger & Poole, 1984). In order for this negotiation to occur, however, a medium must exist in which struggle takes place and is thereby expressed. Language is a primary site for the negotiation of power and reifies an organization's reality, including the power structures of that reality. A conflict, which inevitably involves a struggle of power, must in some way challenge the continual reification or "creation" of the extant realities within the organization. Metaphors are important to the process of conflict and influence because they are an important part of the reification process. Conventional metaphors function to maintain current conceptualizations of the organization and do so largely without the conscious participation of organizational members. Generally, people speak metaphorically not by choice but by convention. When there are multiple conventions or conceptualizations of reality, members may find themselves in contention with one another over appropriate goals or means for reaching those goals. This is not to say that conventional metaphors create conflict; nor do novel metaphors create conflict. Rather, novel metaphors are a violation of the reality reified by conventional metaphors. Some violation of an organization's conventions and norms is necessary for change: the object of struggle. One reasonable vehicle for an organizational member to challenge the status quo is through the use of figurative language that alters the "constructive/reconstructive" descriptions of the organization. As a result, novel metaphors signal the expression of struggle. Essentially, novel metaphors are a sign that the emergent process of language is being exercised in pursuit of goals seen as not obtainable within the current description reality.

REFERENCES

Aristotle. (1924). De poetica. In W. D. Ross (Ed.), (I. Bywater, Trans.), *The works of Aristotle. Vol. II.* 1447^a-1462^b. Oxford, UK: Clarendon Press. (Original work produced in 322 B.C.)

Barthes, R. (1972). *Mythologies.* (Annette Lavers, Trans.). New York: Hill and Wang.

Bell, B., & Loftus, E. (1985). Vivid persuasion in the courtroom. *Journal of Personality Assessment, 49*, 660–664.

Black, M. (1962). *Models and metaphors.* New York: Cornell University Press.

Bradshaw, G., & Anderson, J. (1982). Elaborative encoding as an explanation of levels of processing. *Journal of Verbal Learning and Verbal Behavior, 21*, 165–174.

Carrol, J. S. (1978). The effect of imagining an event on expectation for the event: An interpretation in terms of the availability heuristic. *Journal of Experimental Social Psychology, 14*, 88–96.

Cohen, T. (1979). Metaphor and the cultivation of intimacy. In S. Sacks, (Ed.), *On Metaphor.* 1–10. Chicago: University of Chicago Press.

Cooper, D. (1986). *Metaphor.* Oxford: Basil Blackwell.

Cooper, D. (1984). Davies on recent theories of metaphor. *Mind, 93*, 433–439.

Davies, M. (1982–1983). Idiom and metaphor. *Proceedings of the Aristotelian Society.* New York: Pergamon Press.

Folger, J. P., Poole, M. S., & Stutman, R. K. (1993). *Working through conflict.* New York: HarperCollins.

Fowler, H. W. (1983). *A dictionary of modern English usage.* Oxford: Oxford University Press.

Garfield, E. (1986). The metaphor science connection. *Current Contents, 42*, 3–10.

Grice, H. (1975). Logic and conversation. In P. Cole and J. Morgan (Eds.), *Syntax and semiotics III: Speech acts* (pp. 41–58). New York: Academic Press.

Hawkes, D. F. (1972). *Metaphor.* London: Methuen.

Hocker, J., & Wilmot, W. (1985). *Interpersonal conflict.* (2nd ed.). Dubuque, IA: William C. Brown Publishers.

Ilkka, R. J. (1977). Rhetorical dramatization in the development of American Communism. *Quarterly Journal of Speech, 63*, 413–427.

Kellett, P. (1987). The development of an interpretive approach to conflict analysis and management: A case study of the function of metaphor in the dynamics and resolution of a management-labor conflict. Unpublished paper.

Kisielius, J., & Sternthal, B. (1984). Detecting and explaining vividness effects in attitudinal judgments. *Journal of Marketing Research, 21*, 54–64.

Kisielius, J., & Sternthal, B. (1986). Examining the vividness controversy: An availability-valence interpretation. *Journal of Consumer Research, 12*, 418–431.

Koch, S., & Deetz, S. (1981). Metaphor analysis of social reality in organizations. *Journal of Applied Communication Research, 9*, 1–15.

Lakoff, G. (1987). *Women, fire, and dangerous things: What categories reveal about the mind.* Chicago: University of Chicago Press.

Lakoff, G., & Johnson, M. (1980a). Conceptual metaphors in everyday language. *Journal of Philosophy, 8*, 433–486.

Lakoff, G., & Johnson, M. (1980b). *Metaphors we live by.* Chicago: University of Chicago Press.

MacCormac, E. (1985). *A cognitive theory of metaphor.* Cambridge: MIT Press.

Marschark, M., & Hunt, R. R. (1985). On memory for metaphor. *Memory and Cognition, 13*, 413–424.

Mowday, R. T., Steers, R. M., & Porter, L. W. (1979). The measurement of organizational commitment. *Journal of Vocational Behavior, 14*, 224–247.

Newmark. (1981). *Approaches to translation.* New York: Pergamon Press.

Nisbett, R. E., & Ross, L. (1980). *Human interference: Strategies and shortcomings of social judgment.* Englewood Cliffs, NJ: Prentice Hall.

Ortony, A. (Ed.). (1979). *Metaphor and thought.* Cambridge: Cambridge University Press.

Ortony, A. (1980). Some psycholinguistic aspects of metaphor. In R. P. Honeck & R. R. Hoffman (Eds.), *Cognition and Figurative Language* (pp. 78–102). Hillsdale, NJ: Erlbaum.

Osborn, M., & Ehninger, D. (1962). The metaphor in public address. *Speech Monographs, 29*, 223–234.

Petty, R., & Cacioppo, J. (1981). *Attitudes and persuasion: Classic and contemporary approaches.* Dubuque, IA: William C. Brown Publishers.

Pondy, L. R. (1983). The role of metaphors and myths in organizations and the facilitation of change. In L. R. Pondy, P. J. Frost, G. Morgan, & T. C. Dandridge (Eds.), *Organizational Symbolism* (pp. 157–166). Greenwich, CT: JAI Press.

Rubin, J. Z., & Brown, B. R. (1975). *The social psychology of bargaining and negotiation.* New York: Academic Press.

Smith, R., & Eisenberg, E. (1987). Conflict at Disneyland: A root-metaphor analysis. *Communication Monographs, 54,* 367–380.

Stutman, R. K., & Putman, L. L. (1994). The consequences of language: A metaphorical look at the legalization of organizations. In S. B. Sitkin & R. J. Bies (Eds.), *The Legalistic Organization* (pp. 281–302). Thousand Oaks, CA: Sage.

Taylor, S. E., & Thompson, S. C. (1982). Stalking the elusive vividness effect. *Psychological Review, 89,* 155–189.

Tesser, A. (1976). Thought and reality constraints as determinants of attitude polarization. *Journal of Experimental Psychology, 10,* 183–194.

Tesser, A., & Leone, C. (1977). Cognitive schemas and thought as determinants of attitude change. *Journal of Experimental Social Psychology, 13,* 262–270.

Tourangeau, R., & Sternberg, R. (1981). Aptness in metaphor. *Cognitive Psychology, 13,* 27–55.

Tracy, D. (1978). Metaphor and religion. *Critical Inquiry, 5*(1), 91–106.

10

Drama in Organizational Life

Iain L. Mangham

Morgan (1986) argues that one of the interesting aspects of metaphor rests in the fact that it always produces a "kind of one-sided insight." In highlighting a particular interpretation of reality, it blinds us to other possible ways of interpreting the phenomenon. His book sets out to explore the implications of key metaphors for "thinking about the nature of organizations." In pursuit of this laudable goal, he has chapters on organizations as machines, as organisms, as brains, as cultures, as political systems, as psychic prisons, as flux and transformation, and as instruments of domination. Surprisingly, he has no chapter specifically concerned with organizations as theatre. Odd, this, given his propensity throughout the book to use terms derived from the theater. He talks of *actors playing roles,* of *performances,* of *staging,* of *decor, sets and properties,* and of *scripts,* but aside from a few lines in which he claims that the notion of life as theater is subsumed under the broad heading of culture, he has nothing to say about the oldest metaphor of them all.

The neglect is even odder because life as drama and action as performance may be held to be an *essential* metaphor. The notion derives from Snell's (1960) book *The Discovery of the Mind* and my particular use of it from Wilshire's (1982) impressive *Role Playing and Identity.* The latter argues that "if a specific metaphor is unavoidable and if endless variations upon it are endlessly revealing, then the metaphor is an essential one" (p. 242). With inessential metaphors there is some other way to state the comparison expressed by the metaphor. Social and organizational life as a psychic prison, for example, appears to me to be an interesting, mildly startling, and perhaps even amusing metaphor, but it is far from essential. Its emphasis on the ways in which "repressed sexuality may shape day-to-day activity" and on organization as an "expression of patriarchy" can readily be encapsulated in the simple terms I have used. The metaphor adds nothing to the literal statement. It has no residue, few valuable entailments, no sense that the literal does not do it justice. It offers no sense of discovery, no feeling that prior to its utilization we were failing to see some important feature of organizational/social life. For an essential metaphor, on the other hand, there is no acceptable literal way to express the comparison other than the chosen metaphor. In Wilshire's felicitous phrasing, it becomes a pivot "allowing us to turn knowingly towards the world." Essential metaphors "ramify in every direction in the most coplex and far reaching manner. They are the coordinating tissue of our experience" (p. 243).

I am not opposed to all or even most of the metaphors adduced by Professor Morgan. I am saying that one must pick one's metaphor carefully. For my own part, I would rather hold to a metaphor that resonated with my experience of life in organizations than to one plucked out of the air simply because it provides a different perspective. I have spent many years both as a participant and an observer of behavior in enterprises of all shapes and sizes; that experience has convinced me of the provisional and processual nature of activity in such places and has emphasized for me that the relevant concept is *organizing* rather than *organization*. To use Morgan's terms, the flux and changefulness of the social scene is at least as apparent as its static or structural quality. I see people *interacting* and, as day follows day, I see the consequences and entailments of their interacting, consequences and entailments which, in turn, give rise to further interacting, further consequences. What form there is to this I see as essentially a dramatic form. Plays and social events contain persons acting on each other "and by such acting generating the reality that is relevant for them, and achieving all this while taking account of the passage of time, by recognizing the processual nature of the same reality" (Perinbanayagam, 1985, p. 128). Dramaturgical analysis focuses on the elements that are used by social actors to constitute a situation and how others construe or interpet them. My interest is the same as Goffman's (1967):

> I assume that the proper study of interaction is not the individual and his psychology, but rather the syntactical relations among the acts of different persons mutually present to one another. . . . Not then men and their moments. Rather *moments* and their men. (p. 5)

Elsewhere I have written about the broad sweep of the metaphor (Mangham, 1986; Mangham & Overington, 1987, 1990) and it is not my purpose to rehash that material here. In this chapter, my conscious and one-sided focus is on the way in which interactions within enterprises of great pitch and moment are put together. I am concerned with two issues of interactional eloquence (Trujillo, 1987). I begin by outlining the mindful, cognitive, or strategic playing of roles. The ideas are well known through the work of Erving Goffman, are often referred to as impression management, and are very well documented. I will go on to explore interactions that are characterized more strongly by emotion and where it is not always obvious that the actors are in strategic control of the action. In both sets of circumstances I make use of the theatrical metaphor.

NOW LET ME TRY IN MY ORATION

Goffman (1959, 1963, 1967, 1969, 1974), probably the most celebrated social scientist to use the theatrical analogy, conceives of social behavior as a matter of "performances among actors" who seek to "manage impressions" so that they are taken to be who they claim themselves to be. Using theatrical terminology, but otherwise showing very little familiarity either with actors or the theater, he describes how social actors "rehearse" and "prepare" their performances "backstage" before appearing to others, going "on," as he terms it, and how they seek to align "settings, appearance and manner" and avoid missed "cues," "unmeant gestures or faux pas" that would undermine their claims to a particular course of action. Social actors appear to create "strategic interaction scripts," improvising them as they interact with other social actors. The strategic intent is to persuade others that the claims each makes to a particular identity or course of action are valid and justified. What is more, Goffman argues, in this mode at least, the actors may be aware of what they are doing—they can monitor their rhetorical communications and make changes in the scripts as necessary. They appear, that is, to have a playwright's consciousness. I have characterized this elsewhere as the capacity to adopt a metatheatrical perspective on social life. The term is borrowed from the work of Abel (1963) and suggests that each of us is aware (or can become aware) of his- or herself as a performer, and each of us can, and, on occasion, does adopt an ironic stance, one from which each of us can observe and manipulate the way social life is constructed and how effects are brought about (Mangham, 1986).

Although the interest of social scientists in the notion of life as theater and behavior as strategic role playing has surfaced relatively recently, both notions were commonplace in the reign of the first Elizabeth. Its expression is to be found in letters of the time, in the poetry, and, of course, in the contemporary theater. The major characters of English Renaissance drama are obsessed with the metaphor, in particular with aspects of disguise and deceit, and often address the audience on matters of acting, of feigning and impersonation (Worthen, 1984). Shakespearean drama is positively stuffed with the imagery of the theatre, although he was certainly not alone in displaying a reflexive theatrical self-consciousness in his work. Fergusson (1949) has pointed out that *Hamlet,* for example, a play concerned with role playing like no other before or since, displays an "an extremely modern and skeptical, a Piran-dellesque, theatricality" (p. 49). In many passages of the play, both Hamlet the character and Shakespeare the writer invite us to stand back and watch how theatrical effects are achieved on the stage and, by inference, off. It is not to *Hamlet,* however, but to *Julius Caesar* that I turn for my illustration of the kind of manipulation that some adherents to the dramaturgical perspective hold to be at the center of social life. Shakespeare depicts the process clearly and unequivocally. I follow this passage by another drawn directly from behavior in an organization.

Here is part of the famous speech of Mark Antony, delivered to a hostile crowd immediately after the assassination of Caesar:

1st Pleb: Stay ho! and let us hear Mark Antony.

3rd Pleb: Let him go up into the public chair. We'll hear him. Noble Antony, go up.

Antony: For Brutus' sake I am beholding to you.

4th Pleb: What does he say of Brutus?

3rd Pleb: He says, for Brutus' sake, He finds himself beholding to us all.

4th Pleb: 'Twere best he speaks no harm of Brutus here.

1st Pleb: This Caesar was a tyrant.

3rd Pleb: Nay, that's certain, We are blest that Rome is rid of him.

2nd Pleb: Peace! Let us hear what Antony can say.

Antony: You gentle Romans—

All: Peace, ho! let us hear him.

Antony: Friends, Romans, countrymen, lend me your ears,
I come to bury Caesar, not to praise him.
The evil that men do lives after them;
The good is oft interred with their bones;
So let it be with Caesar. The noble Brutus
Hath told you Caesar was ambitious,
If it were so, it was a grievous fault;
And grievously hath Caesar answered it.
Here, under leave of Brutus and the rest—
For Brutus is an honourable man;
So are they all, all honourable men—
Come I to speak in Caesar's funeral.
He was my friend, faithful and just to me;
But Brutus says he was ambitious
And Brutus is an honourable man.
He hath brought many captives home to Rome,
Whose ransom did the general coffers fill;
Did this in Caesar seem ambitious?
When that the poor have cried, Caesar hath wept;
Ambition should be made of sterner stuff,
Yet Brutus says he was ambitious;
And Brutus is an honourable man.

You all did see that on the Lupercal
I thrice presented him a kingly crown,
Which he did thrice refuse. Was this ambition?
Yet Brutus says he was ambitious;
And sure he is an honourable man.
I speak not to disprove what Brutus spoke
But here I am to speak what I do know;
You all did love him once, not without cause.
What cause withhold you, then, to mourn for him;
In judgment, thou art fled to brutish beasts
And men have lost their reason! Bear with me
My heart is in the coffin there with Caesar,
And I must pause till it come back to me.

1st Pleb: Methinks there is much reason in his sayings.

2nd Pleb: If thou consider rightly of the matter,
Caesar has had great wrong. . . .

As we sit back and watch this scene, we can maintain sufficient distance from the scene to discern how Antony works on the crowd. We can, as it were, deconstruct the *moment,* hear the phrases that recur in subtly changing emphasis, witness the workings of Antony's mind, perceive his motive. Lest we miss it, he tells us what he is about before he goes into the market place to meet the crowd: "There shall I try /In my oration, how the people take /The cruel issue of these bloody men"; and, having subtly urged the crowd to rise and mutiny, he concludes the scene with the chilling lines: "Now let it work. Mischief, thou art afoot. Take what course tho wilt." The crowd, those worked upon, the plebeians, can achieve no such distance; they are swept up in Antony's rhetoric, believe his protestations: "I come not, friends, to steal away your hearts; I am no orator as Brutus is, /But as you know me all, a plain blunt man." A daring stroke indeed, followed up by another: "For I have neither wit, nor words, nor worth, /Action, nor utterance, nor the power of speech, /To stir men's blood; I only speak right on." The result is mischief indeed, the plebeians breaking into disorder with cries of: "Most noble Caesar, I will revenge his death!"

As on the stage, so in social life; we make manifest who we wish to be taken for in any given episode and what behavior we consider to be appropriate and in so doing, cue others into responding. We can all be seen as readers and wrighters (sic) of events, interpreting and shaping what goes on around and about us, expressing what we take to be important and, in so doing, seeking to persuade others that they should go along with our definitions and our presentations. Let me seek to consolidate this point with an example from an organization.

The scene is the main room of a company social club. At one end of the room is a bar—shutters down at the moment—at the other is a small stage which usually features, bands, singers, and coarse comedians. On the stage is the Chief Executive of the company, Tony Mitchard. In front are nearly a thousand people, employees of his firm waiting to confront him about a recently announced program of redundancies. Here is how he described what happened:

I remember having announced all these redundancies, being asked by the Union on the Friday before the Sunday when they were going to have a branch meeting if I would be prepared to go and address them and I said that of course I would, although some of the management were distinctly unhappy about it. So they said, "Well, we'll have to raise it at the meeting, so could you sit by the telephone?" I said "yes" and it was a typical February morning, it was pouring with rain, and I wasn't feeling exactly on top of the world, and the telephone rang and on the other end was Eric Bates, who was chairman of the Union branch and, incidentally, our branch in those days was the biggest single branch of the Transport and General Workers' Union in the West of England, which had been in existence for many years. Anyway, I got the telephone call, I got into my car and I drove over to the Assembly Hall at Melksham, which is a hall which, if quite a lot of people are prepared to stand up, holds about a thousand people. As I drew up, the leaders of the Union were there to meet me and asked me if I would get my message across in about 20 minutes. So I got up there on the stage, got the microphone and there was this mass of faces. I would think 90% male, 10% female, and many were standing. The meeting had already been going for about an hour, so I stood up with the microphone and basically said to them, "Look, I am convinced that we can secure the future of this company, but it does mean, I'm afraid, that we are going to have to do things that in our wildest nightmares we could never have imagined would be necessary and I'm going to have to ask for a reduction of about 600 jobs." Anyway, I spoke, I suppose, for about 20 minutes and then answered a number of questions of which only a couple were hostile, all the others were very pertinent questions. Anyway, I must have been on the stage for about 50 minutes altogether and Eric Bates, who chaired this large meeting extremely well, he said, "Well, that's it now, brothers and sisters. Mr. Mitchard has been good enough to answer your questions." So I said to them, "Thank you very much for listening to me in the way that you have. All I will say to you again is that if we can grasp these nettles together, I feel sure that we can pull through." Not that I was wholly convinced myself! Anyway, I handed the microphone back to Eric Bates and as I was going down the steps from the stage, to go out of the side door, I was suddenly aware of all this noise—applause, would you believe? (Mangham & Pye, 1990, p. 46)

The parallels with the quote from *Julius Caesar* must not be overdone; both of the protagonists face potentially hostile audiences; both are prepared "to try in my oration, how the people take the cruel issue"; both effect to be blunt and direct — as Tony Mitchard put it later: "I think that this was one of the most important experiences in my life, because not only did it put some steel into my spine, it certainly indicated that if you are prepared in the most direct way to tell people the facts of life, you will not only get a fair hearing, but the majority will support you." Both succeed in turning the crowd around by simple, direct appeals: in the first instance, "Caesar was a pretty decent cove really," in the second, "the world out there is hostile and I am very sorry about it, but we are going to have to ask for a reduction of about 600 jobs. We, working together, accepting that this is the way that it has to be, can pull through. Thank you very much for listening." Although clearly lacking the eloquence of his namesake, Tony Mitchard pulls it off. He persuades his audience, or at least a large part of it, that his reading of the situation is not only correct, but it is the only one and that his shaping of events — sacking 600 — equally is correct and the only possible course of action.

Mark Antony differs from Tony Mitchard in that he appears aware of what he is doing. His speech is carefully crafted, his appeal to emotion has about it a sense of calculation. The phrase "Brutus is an honourable man" echoes throughout the passage, a rhetorical device which by the end of the speech succeeds in signaling the very opposite: "Brutus is a very dishonourable man." Mitchard, however, appears to employ no such rhetorical devices (or none to which we have access). It would be wrong to conclude, however, that he does not craft his performance. Were he not to do so, he would be unable to communicate with his audience. The dramaturgical perspective holds that we are all actors, life is irremediably histrionic. I cannot know what is on your mind unless you display it to me; you cannot know what is on mine unless I display it to you. What Perinbanayagam (1985), closely following Wittgenstein, terms the *mental states* of an actor are manifest in his or her acts of utterances; indeed he argues that these very utterances and acts "are the mental states and are taken by a respondent as sufficient basis on which to proceed." Theatricality or dramaturgy itself is a "language" — what Perinbanayagam calls "an artifice for the mind to create and express itself and a device or a method to achieve communicative goals." The stage mirrors everyday life in that the primal issue to overcome is the achievement of communication: as one expresses oneself, one reveals whatever is necessary to enter a relationship with an other. It is very likely that once having been invited to address the workforce, Tony Mitchard sat down and worked through what he was going to say. Sitting by the telephone awaiting the summons to the Drill Hall, he may well have practiced a few phrases, tried out the odd gesture. He is a smart enough manager to know that it is not simply a matter of what one says but how one says it, a matter not of integrity but of conveying the impression of integrity. Unfortunately, writers like Sarbin pick up the legacy of Erving Goffman when they emphasize masks, deceit and deception as elements of strategic impression management. The fact that it is possible to dissemble should not blind us to the circumstances in which impression management is not a matter of duplicity. The arts of impression management are as important to honest souls as to dishonest ones; Mark Antony may be dishonest and manipulative, Tony Mitchard honest and manipulative. Both need to monitor and control their performances.

Goffman notes that in normal circumstances it is not difficult to bring off a performance. It does, he argues, take "deep skill, long training and a psychological capacity to become a good stage actor," but, he claims, it is clear that "almost anyone can quickly learn a script well enough to give a *charitable audience* some sense of realness in what is being contrived before them" (italics are mine). In many circumstances the audience is likely to be charitable. Much of the time we collude to protect each others performances; we exercise tact and discretion in order to support the situation. Our intent, our motivation made manifest in our words and actions as both performers and audience, is to accept the profferred definitions, thereby creating a smooth interaction. As in the theater, we offer each other the willing suspension of disbelief in order that the interaction can proceed. Nonetheless, interaction can be put in jeopardy by ourselves or by others. As Erving Goffman reminds us, the problem of interaction is the problem of situational control over the "giving" and "giving off" of impressions. A hesitation in Tony Mitchard's voice, a stumbling in his syntax could have put him at risk: nervously fiddling with his spectacles, failing to meet the eyes of his audience, bumping into the furniture, realizing halfway through his monologue that his fly is undone, could all have threatened his performance.

From Kenneth Burke's (1962a, 1962b) perspective, moments, episodes, performances, acts, situations, like other texts, are assembled according to definite rules: Certain types of act are related to certain types of places, occasions, and participants and any violation of these rules is taken as an offense. Situations—moments and their men—are assemblages of place, props, and participants who serve to present an occasion and enact the appropriate acts. Burke's grammar of situations claims that the generating principles—act, scene, agent, agency, purpose—and their interrelationships with each other are constrained by a ratio. Burke observed: "Comic and grotesque works may deliberately set these elements at odds with one another, [and] audiences make allowance for such liberty, which reaffirms the same principle of consistency in its very violation" (p. 121). In Mark Antony's case, each element ties in with each other to produce a credible performance: There is no inconsistency of setting, agent, agency, act or purpose. The mood is set by the presence of Caesar's body, by the demeanor of Antony and, for that matter, by that of Brutus. In a similar fashion, the mood is set for Tony Mitchard's speech by those party to it and by, in this case, the high seriousness of the issue (the body, as it were, of the company over which he stands) which overcomes the problem of the setting.

Interaction can, of course, be put at risk by the responses of others, those who refuse to go along with our performances. For all his eloquence, Mark Antony could have been stopped in his tracks by the Elizabethan equivalent of: "Mark Antony, you are all mouth." Similarly, a cry of "Mr. Mitchard, your analysis is a load of horsefeathers" may have brought him up short. Perhaps a challenge along the lines of the following may even have made him reconsider his entire performance: "As a representative of the vicious Thatcherite tendency which is destroying the working classes of this country, what right have you to turn up here on a Sunday morning and threaten us?" The mood of the interaction can change very quickly indeed. Such considerations remind us that it takes rare and virtuosic skill to pull off a performance before a hostile audience.

IS IT NOT MONSTROUS?

The use of the term *mood* alerts us to a further key aspect of the comparison of social life with the theater: the importance of the display of emotion both on the stage and in everyday interaction. It is difficult to imagine Mark Antony's speech being delivered without emotion, just as it is difficult to imagine the scene in the Drill Hall occurring without the display of affect. Emotions are brought into play in a whole range of circumstances; as Perinbanayagam (1985) notes, the presence of emotions in the gestures and expressions of social actors (and stage actors, for that matter) are read by all involved, thereby creating "an interactional resonance." Mark Antony does not need to declare his grief in words, although later in the scene he does talk of weeping, because his grief is present in his every inflexion, gesture and act. Tony Mitchard does not have to articulate his sadness, regret and determination to fight on in words (although, again, he probably did so), because his demeanor casts others into the appropriate response.

The notion of *mood,* as I have used it above, derives from the work of Denzin (1984), who claims that "moods always accompany states of mind." He goes on to observe that "prior to the mood or the feeling is the person's state of mind which reflects their cognitive, moral and emotional attachment to themselves and their situations" (p. 16). In terms of the present discussion I take it that the mood Mark Antony conveys is a consequence of determining that Caesar's death is a matter of consequence to himself and that it is a matter for at least giving the appearance of grief rather than the appearance of justified regret that Brutus and his fellow conspirators seek to convey. Similarly, Tony Mitchard determines that the potential demise of the company is a matter for him of sadness and regret rather than joy and celebration. The determination to fight on, to appeal to a sense of "we'll show them that we will not be defeated," comes after his conclusion that the failure of the company is to be regretted. It is important to remember that it does not matter whether or not either of these two performers subjectively feel grief, regret or whatever. What is important is what others party to the interaction take to be the protagonist's subjective feelings. In Perinbanayagam's telling words: "Emotion, like other attitudes, become semiotic achievements rather than acts of intersubjective clairvoyance" (p. 145).

Emotion displays from this perspective are not simply just physiologically caused bodily reactions to stimuli. Folk psychology (and, until recently, academic psychology) appears to hold that emotions are universal biological phenomena — phenomena which are likely to well up and, indeed, overwhelm us if once we allow them to surface. More recent work suggests that they are meaningful displays and like other forms of communication they follow particular rules. (See Clark, 1992; Harré & Gillett, 1994; Oatley, 1992.) There are right and wrong ways of doing "grief" or doing "anger," acceptable and unacceptable ways of showing "pride" and showing "joy." These ways are subject to local standards of correctness. In another culture, Tony Mitchard may be required to display sadness and regret in a much higher profile manner than he is expected to do in the United Kingdom. What he is expected to show in the circumstances that he finds himself in is that he has strong feelings about the situation, but he is in control of those feelings and is determined to battle on and win. Clearly this is the message that he succeeds in conveying; so well that he is applauded by his audience.

Sarbin (1986) distinguishes between strategic interaction, lacking in emotion, where he takes the social actor to be the author of his or her performances and that which, somewhat confusingly, he terms dramatistic interaction: the presentation of emotion, which he finds less easy to attribute to particular authorship. It seems to me that emotioni can be as readily conceived of as strategic and within the control of the social actor as any other element of his or her performance. Shakespeare shows us an Antony in control of his emotions and deploying them to great effect. Tony Mitchard also appears to be in control of his feelings and to display them appropriately and strategically. Some feel uncomfortable at the notion of the strategic deployment of emotion. Some may well regard it as monstrously deceptive. Shakespeare again, Hamlet on actors:

> Is it not monstrous that this player here,
> But in a fiction, in a dream of passion,
> Could force his soul so to his own conceit
> That from her working all his visage wanned,
> Tears in his eyes, distraction in his aspect

A broken voice, and his whole function suiting
With forms to his conceit? And all for nothing!

Yes, it is monstrous and it occurs everyday. But not for nothing. Here is an example of another managing director who, but his own commentary after the event, claims to have been deliberately provoking one of his subordinates in order to have him take a particular action. We join as the group has been discussing cost cutting for some time in an atmosphere of belligerence, accusation, and acrimony:

Bill: Cross it out, Bob. Not doing very well, are we? Cars no change. Travel no change. So where does the money come from? You tell me! What about the Forest Road Site, Nigel? Savings to be had there, I've no doubt.

Nigel: We won't know that for some time. We are just doing a study on what our overall needs will be.

Bill: When will that be ready?

Nigel: End of September.

Bill: (*with mock astonishment*) End of September? Three bloody months. Not good enough. It's only a matter of walking around and deciding whether or not we want it. You can do that tomorrow, can't you?

Nigel: It's not simply a matter of walking around. And Forest Road will save us nothing. Our estimate for staying at Tadcaster is in the restructuring budget and is wrong, as you know. We put in something like a million, million two, and latest figures are looking at nearly three and a half. Forest Road may save on that but they are not going to get us near the original million, million two.

Bill: (*adopting a peremptory tone*) What are you doing tomorrow? You can get round there tomorrow. Take Tony with you. I need a report by Thursday afternoon.

Nigel: Thursday afternoon. It's not possible, Bill. Not possible. It's not a matter a simply pacing the floor. We don't know what we need, we haven't got a fix on the space required, nor do we know precisely what we currently have, some stuff is counted under different headings.

Bill: (*dismissively*) Cigarette packet stuff. Do it on a cigarette packet. You've been at this for what—3, 4 months. Need to know by Thursday.

Nigel: (*with mounting exasperation*) I am not around Thursday. I'm in London.

And as I keep saying, Bill, even if I were to be around, I could not give you any better answer.

Bill: I don't accept that.

Nigel: Look, Bill, this is daft. I've got some slides here — the Forest Road site is on the agenda, I was going to take you through it this morning. . .

Bill: How many slides have you got?

Nigel: (puzzled by the turn of events) How many?

Bill: Yes, how many? As in "How many?"

Nigel: About 20.

Bill: (with anger) Twenty! I haven't got time to sit through 20 slides. Cigarette packet stuff! Give me an answer by Thursday.

Nigel: (with anger) O.K. If you want an answer, I'll give you one! We will keep Forest Road! Tell Group not to sell it! We will have it. Then, if it doesn't work out when we know the correct figures, if we can't get in it, we can give it back to them. They can sell it in September rather than now.

Bill: That's not acceptable. I'm not going in with one message one day and the complete opposite a couple of months later. Get round it, give me the figures, see me on Thursday.

I have indicated elsewhere (Mangham, 1986) that contrary to the traditional view that emotional acts are irrational and lacking in intent, in some, perhaps many, circumstances they do follow a logic and may be strategic. They may be displayed and pursued in the interest of securing or maintaining power and influence. Here Bill displays anger and provokes Nigel into responding with anger. Bill claimed that he deliberately set out to "wind Nigel up"; indeed, "they all need winding up, they would sit around forever if I did not get after them every other week." Nigel's response is also strategic. He probably reads Bill's behavior as personally insulting and offensive, as declaring that he, Nigel, is not competent. As Pierce wrote, "If a man is angry, he is saying to himself that this or that is rude and outrageous. If he is in joy, he is saying 'This is delicious.' If he is wondering, he is saying, 'This is strange.' In short, whenever a man feels, he is thinking of something." (Pierce, quoted in Perinbanayagam, 1985, p. 147). It is a sentiment echoed by Solomon (1976) who in his book The Passions argues that "we intend to revenge ourselves in anger, to redeem ourselves in shame, to restore our dignity in embarrassment, to help another person in pity" (p. 190). Burke (1962a, 1962b) takes this a little further and claims that displays of emotion are not only acts in and of themselves they are also "first steps towards" other acts. They are as he terms them incipient acts. A display of anger (contrived or otherwise) is a verbal sign that another act is likely to follow; anger demands further congruent acts (p. 236). Nigel responds in kind because failure to respond in kind may lead Bill to follow up his display in ways which Nigel would not find attractive. Nigel's response declares "get off my back or you may find that you will get more than you have bargained for." In this sense, both his and Bill's behavior can be seen as strategic and subject to rules and conventions.

Tony Mitchard's display of emotion is not so overtly strategic. One has little sense that he constructed it, that he deliberately set out to metaphorically rent his clothes and shred his garments to signify his grief *in order* to have his audience go along with his intentions. Nonetheless, like each one of us if he is to achieve his aims he must fashion and shape his performance. Striding into the Drill Hall with a large cigar and a big smile on his face, doing an impromptu dance, would not have furthered his cause. Nor, of course, would renting his clothes and shredding his garments. His display of sadness and regret played out according to local convention both met and created expectations which enabled him to propose a course of action which others could follow.

THAT WHICH PASSES SHOW

Sarbin's point about the authorship of the scripts that we play out in organizations and elsewhere, however, is an important one. Clearly the conventions that we observe in displaying emotion are the product of multiple authorship; they have been elaborated over the years in the groups and societies of which we are a part. They are passed down in both formal and informal ways and are underpinned by myths, legends, stories, poems, proverbs, and songs. Our characters are formed in such settings and it is as characters that we respond emotionally. Occasionally we respond in ways that others will not anticipate and with a force that transcends the rules, and may bring about a change in our sense of self (Mangham, in press). Difficult though it may be to recognize when someone is "putting on" an emotion, we can sometimes recognize when they are not. To quote Shakespeare again, here is Hamlet talking to his mother, Getrude, about emotion:

> Seems, madam? Nay, it is, I know not "seems"
> 'Tis not alone my inky cloak, good mother,
> Nor customary suits of solemn black,
> Nor windy suspiration of forced breath,
> No, nor the fruitful river in the eye
> Nor the dejected haviour of the visage,
> Together with all forms, moods, shapes of grief,
> That can denote me truly. Those indeed seem,

> For they are actions that a man might play,
> But I have within which passes show:
> These but the trappings and the suits of woe.

In this passage we are reminded that although it may be difficult to tell the difference, there may be at least two ways of experiencing and displaying emotion; the strategic and that "which passes show," that which is intensely felt and much less well controlled and less purposively deployed. As in the next example I offer, in which a group of executives are meeting over dinner. One of them, Graham, less drunk than the rest of them, is complaining about the removal of one of his key men to another division. The rest of the group including the Chief Executive, Eric, appear to be more interested in banter and in homing in on what they take to be the lack of commitment displayed by Graham's subordinates.

Eric: *(to the waiter)* And we'll need some more brandy. Bring another bottle. Right. Where were we before we were so rudely interrupted? Ah yes. The question of commitment, Graham?

Graham: I was not talking about commitment, I was talking about Personnel's right to shift people around without consultation.

Eric: But the rest of us *were* talking about commitment, Graham.

Colin: My people are committed to plan, Graham, are yours?

Graham: You might have been happy to join in, Colin, for reasons best known to yourself, but *I* was not talking about commitment. *I* was talking about poaching my people.

Roger: But your people are not committed, I've heard them say it themselves.

Graham: Roger, I do not give a toss what you claim to have heard. I am not talking about plans or commitment! I am talking about poaching!

Tony: *(drunkenly)* He's right! He's right! That's what we started talking about. That's what the boy started on about. I distinctly remember.

Roger: You're too pissed to remember anything. . .

Eric: Get it off your chest. Tell us what the issue is and then we'll talk about commitment.

Graham: Eric, I've told you what I think the issue is and I don't want to talk about commitment, as you keep calling it, now or later. Either I am running my unit or I am not. I deeply resent Steve telling me that he is moving one of my better — no, my best man — and giving him to Roger.

Steve: It wasn't like that, Graham and you know it. I talked to you about it. . .

Graham: You talked to me about it AFTER . . . AFTER you had decided with Eric, no doubt, and probably Roger—what you were going to do. He is my man, in my unit, working for me.

Eric: And for the good of the team as a whole, we decided that we needed his contribution elsewhere.

Graham: Cant! Sheer bloody unadulterated cant! "For the good the team." What bloody team? This lot? Us? Look at us! Senior managers in a public company, pissed as newts, debating nonsense, *commitment, the good of the team, working together, contributing to the company!* It's all wind! Bloody hypocrisy. Tripe. We make bloody biscuits and crisps, and snacks and pizzas. What's all this talk of commitment? It's not life or death, is it? It's no big deal. Biscuits, crisps, toffee bars, stuff everyone can do without. What is all this crap about *commitment* and *team spirit.* We are not a bloody religious order. We are not on some crusade to save the world! *Commitment,* for God's sake. Who cares if we make a few more Nut Surprises? Sell a few more Dream Delights? A handful of shareholders, that's who cares? We have to ask ourselves what all this is about. What is the point of pouring huge amounts of energy into making more and more things that are of no use to anyone? Dream Delights, for God's sake! What's it all come down to? What's it all about? We throw ourselves into this nonsense as if it mattered. As if we were working to free the world from cholera or something. We are riding a monster. Production, profit, grind it out. Push it on. Where is it all leading? I'll tell you where—bloody nowhere! It is not progress, making more and more biscuits, more and more crisps, the biggest pizza in the world. We go on about being *committed* as though a few thousand quid either way will make a difference.

    Right, if you want to know, I am not *committed,* as you put it. I do not spend every waking hour thinking about Nut Surprises or Dream Delights. I do not *want* to spend my life thinking about Nut Surprises or Dream Delights. I question the sanity of anyone who does! I don't want to be in the office at 7 in the morning and leave 9 or 10 at night. I do not want to spend time here. Now. Listening to this twaddle about *commitment.* Arguing about who works for whom. You are welcome to my staff Roger—all of them. I'd rather be at home. What do you want from me? Blood? I work to live, not the other way round. And so do most of the rest of you—if you don't, you are mad! I work hard not because I am *committed.* I work to support my wife and family. There is life beyond this company, and I am sick of pretending otherwise. You can have me from 9 to 5, beyond that I am my own man. . ."

Perinbanayagam (1991), as he does so often, offers some relevant thoughts on circumstances such as these. He proposes two forms of emotion: standard emotions and hyperemotions. The former are features of routine everyday interaction and are subject to the control of self and other. The kind of relatively mild displays of anger that are evident in the "winding up" of Nigel by Bill. Hyperemotions are more extreme and are usually disruptive. Graham's "outburst," as it came to be known, was seen as inimical to his self and "wholly uncalled for." It was seen as a sharp contrast to routine acts. "He should have seen we were only winding him up."

As Perinbanayagam points out, the definitional feature of hyperemotions is "that they do not lend themselves to reflection, analyses, or systematic verbal programming" (p. 150). He argues that they ignore convention, that they burst the bonds and "sweep aside the self in their wake." In short, they are not seen as subject to control and guidance and, in consequence, cannot be regarded as strategic. He goes on to point out that in Blumer's view, such acts and displays go beyond the normal vocabulary of emotions and are not capable of being subjected to customary interpretations. In other words, they render us—as the participants in this example—incapable of immediate response.

The response may well be delayed. The morning after Graham's outburst, a number of his fellow diners had ready explanations for his behavior. To be sure, some regarded it as strategic: "He wants to be given the push." Others thought that it reflected a turning point in Graham's life, a recognition that he was not happy in commerce, that he needed to "look at himself and sort out what he wanted to do." Just as with a strong emotional moment in a stage play, the outburst was thought to have provided Graham the opportunity to reflect *later* on what he had said and done; on who he was and who he might wish to be.

Here is Brutus reflecting on his behavior following a quarrel with Cassius:

O Cassius, you are yoked with a lamb
That carries anger as a flint bears fire,
Who, much enforced, shows a hasty spark
And straight is cold again.

SUMMARY

The oldest metaphor of them all can be used to remind us that the only way we can convey who we wish to be taken for in a particular encounter and what we wish to achieve in an interaction is by displaying ourselves and our intent. Both our cognitions and our emotions are conveyed by signs and, as minded creatures, we take such signs into account when constructing our responses. Social acts for the most part can be seen to be calculated efforts to steer others to conclusions that we desire. Emotions, no less than other perceptions, are used to delineate and to circumscribe action. Occasionally the force and intensity of a particular emotion breaks the conventions for its normal expression. The theater reminds us that all interaction is a matter of cognition, understanding, and emotion. Both sense and feeling are used to establish, sustain, and modify interactional relationships. In both the theater and everyday social activity, sense and emotions are intertwined and inseparable, notwithstanding the common injunction in organizations to "leave emotions out of it." Emotion, feeling, mood, call it what you will, is all pervasive and as subject to rule-governed behavior as language itself.

REFERENCES

Abel, L. (1963). *Metatheatre: A new view of dramatic form.* Hill & Wang.

Burke, K. (1962a). *A grammar of motives.* Chicago: World Books.

Burke, K. (1962b). *A rhetoric of motives.* Chicago: World Books.

Clark, M. S. (1992). *Emotion and social behavior.* Newbury Park, CA: Sage.

Denzin, N. (1984). The temporality of everyday moods. In S. Feinman (Ed.), *Social referencing, infancy and social psychological theory.* New York: Plenum.

Fergusson, F. (1949). *The idea of theater.* Princeton, NJ: Princeton University Press.

Goffman, E. (1959). *The presentation of self in everyday life.* London: Allen Lane.

Goffman, E. (1963). *Behavior in public places.* New York: The Free Press.

Goffman, E. (1967). *Interaction ritual.* New York: Anchor.

Goffman, E. (1969). *Strategic interaction.* Pittsburgh: University of Pennsylvania Press.

Goffman, E. (1974). *Frame analysis.* New York: Harper & Row.

Harré, R., & Gillett, J. (1994). *The discursive mind.* Newbury Park, CA: Sage.

Mangham, I. L. (1986). *Power and performance in organizations: An exploration of executive process.* London: Blackwell.

Mangham, I. L. (in press). Building a character. *Journal of Management Learning.*

Mangham, I. L., & Overington, M. A. (1987). *Organizations as theater: A social psychology of dramatic appearances.* New York: Wiley.

Mangham, I. L., & Overington, M. A. (1990). Dramatism and the theatrical metaphor. In D. Brissett & C. Edgley (Eds.), *Life as theater.* Berlin: Aldine de Gruyter.

Mangham, I. L., & Pye, A. J. (1990). *The doing of managing.* London: Blackwell.

Morgan, G. (1986). *Images of organization.* Newbury Park, CA: Sage.

Oatley, K. (1992). *Best laid schemes: The psychology of emotions.* New York: Cambridge University Press.

Perinbanayagam, R. S. (1985). *Signifying acts.* Chicago: University of Southern Illinois Press.

Perinbanayagam, R. S. (1991). *Discursive acts.* Berlin: Aldine de Gruyter.

Sarbin, T. (1986). Emotion and act. In R. Harré (Ed.), *The social construction of emotions.* London: Blackwell.

Snell, B. (1960). *The discovery of the mind.* New York: Harper & Row.

Solomon, R. (1976). *The passions*. New York: Anchor Doubleday.

Trujillo, N. (1987). Implications of interpretive approaches. In L. Thayer (Ed.), *Organization ↔ Communication: Emerging perspectives I*. Norwood, NJ: Ablex.

Wilshire, B. (1982). *Role playing and identity: The limits of theater as metaphor*. Bloomington: Indiana University Press.

Worthen, W. B. (1984). *The idea of the actor*. Princeton, NJ: Princeton University Press.

Author Index

Subject Index